e-Business Esse[ntials]

Frank Derfler
and the editors of
PC Magazine

Contents at a Glance

201 W. 103rd Street
Indianapolis, Indiana 46290

e-Business Essentials

International Standard Book Number: 0-7897-2474-x

Library of Congress Catalog Card Number: 00-107847

Printed in the United States of America

First Printing: October, 2000

02 01 00 4 3 2 1

Trademarks

All terms mentioned in this book that are known to be trademarks or service marks have been appropriately capitalized. Que cannot attest to the accuracy of this information. Use of a term in this book should not be regarded as affecting the validity of any trademark or service mark.

Warning and Disclaimer

Every effort has been made to make this book as complete and as accurate as possible, but no warranty or fitness is implied. The information provided is on an "as is" basis. The author and the publisher shall have neither liability nor responsibility to any person or entity with respect to any loss or damages arising from the information contained in this book.

Associate Publisher
Greg Wiegand

Acquisitions Editor
Angelina Ward

Development Editor
Gregory Harris

Managing Editor
Tom Hayes

Project Editor
Heather McNeill

Copy Editor
Cindy Fields

Indexer
Mary SeRine

Proofreader
Benjamin Berg

Illustrator
D&G Limited

Team Coordinator
Sharry Gregory

Interior Designer
Kevin Spear

Cover Designer
Gary Adair

Editorial Assistant
Angela Boley

Production
Darin Crone

Contents

About the Author

PC Magazine is the most successful business technology magazine in the industry. Today, its editorial mission is to analyze, evaluate, and review all the technology solutions that build a modern e-business. Its goal is to help business technology strategists, everyone from mom and pop to global CEOs, to make the right decisions for their businesses.

Frank J. Derfler is one of the most experienced editors at *PC Magazine* and an expert at explaining both the technology and the human side of the e-business equation. He has used the resources of the magazine to create a book that gives important advice and insight, but doesn't bury you in technobabble. After a career in computer system operation and acquisition in the federal government, Frank Derfler founded the *PC Magazine* LAN Labs in 1986. The LAN Labs developed the first widely distributed LAN benchmark tests and included both testing and editorial activities. As the senior networking editor he is directly involved with the editorial and testing activities for e-business and general computing infrastructure at *PC Magazine.* He is the author or co-author of more than a dozen published books on networking and data communications. His most popular titles include *Practical Networks* and, with co-author Les Freed, the award-winning *How Networks Work.*

Acknowledgments

Producing anything related to *PC Magazine* is a group process—a performance art. I've written many words for this book and stitched together many more words from a lot of people. This book enjoys the benefits of the talented work of many people.

Our *PC Magazine* contributing editors and outside writers are extremely valuable adjuncts to the staff. In the case of this book, Sarah Roberts Witt was a major contributor to the CRM chapter. Larry Seltzer gave us his insight on XML and all of those other development acronyms. Les Freed's thoughts and words contributed to the content of the infrastructure chapters and Gary Gunnerson's insight is in the chapter on directory services and authentication. Heath H. Herel's description of the basics formed the heart of the chapter on retail storefronts. Nate Lawson and John Garris provided an interesting security scenario.

Gail Shaffer's work on the *PC Magazine* Internet Business section and her careful review shows throughout this book.

I have the highest praise and thanks for two very talented people on the *PC Magazine* staff, Sebastian Rupley and Cade Metz. They each write about tough technical stuff with unmatched clarity, style, and insight. Their words are throughout this work, particularly in the case studies. They're spectacular.

Carol Venezia and Ben Gottesman have each taken turns steering the e-business coverage in *PC Magazine* and their influence is felt throughout this book. Michael Miller has taken us into these new waters while keeping us to high standards of testing, analysis, and reporting. Michael, thanks for the opportunity to put this together.

Tell Us What You Think!

As the reader of this book, *you* are our most important critic and commentator. We value your opinion and want to know what we're doing right, what we could do better, what areas you'd like to see us publish in, and any other words of wisdom you're willing to pass our way.

As a publisher for Que, I welcome your comments. You can fax, email, or write me directly to let me know what you did or didn't like about this book—as well as what we can do to make our books stronger.

Please note that I cannot help you with technical problems related to the topic of this book, and that due to the high volume of mail I receive, I might not be able to reply to every message.

When you write, please be sure to include this book's title and author as well as your name and phone or fax number. I will carefully review your comments and share them with the author and editors who worked on the book.

Fax: 317-581-4666

Email: `greg.wiegand@macmillanusa.com`

Mail: Greg Wiegand
Que
201 West 103rd Street
Indianapolis, IN 46290 USA

Introduction

This is a book written, edited, and researched by me and many other people associated with *PC Magazine*. It contains text that was published in various issues of the magazine and a great deal of text and illustrations never seen before. Certainly, this much work describing the who, what, why, and how of e-business has never been brought together in one place before.

I'm happy to say that *PC Magazine* doesn't look at e-business coverage as a series of personality profiles or even as a series of business reviews. We view it as a combination of technology, investment, and relationships. Indeed, in the end, e-business is more about relationships than anything else.

We take you through the relationships your company can have with other companies (B2B, e-purchasing, e-procurement, and vortals), with its customers (B2C, CRM, and e-tailing), and with its employees (B2E, corporate portals, access, and infrastructure). As we go through these topics you will learn about leading corporations and suppliers in each area and what their products can do for you. We illustrate important points with case studies and diagrams. We always talk about alternatives and decisions.

Because we understand the technical side of the systems, we understand that you can't build a house without a foundation. In Chapters 6, 9, and 10 we take you through the infrastructures you need to support e-business. In the software infrastructure we include authentication, directory services, and VPNs. Our guide to the hardware infrastructure describes load balancing, clustering, and other techniques for high availability.

The vocabulary of e-business is daunting, and we have taken special steps to guide you through the vocabulary while also using it in the context of regular business.

This book contains information, illustration, and insight. It also has a professional though personal attitude. I hope you enjoy it.

PART I

Why? And What? What Will e-Business Do for Me? What Problems Does It Solve and What Benefits Does It Provide?

CHAPTER 1

What Is e-Business?

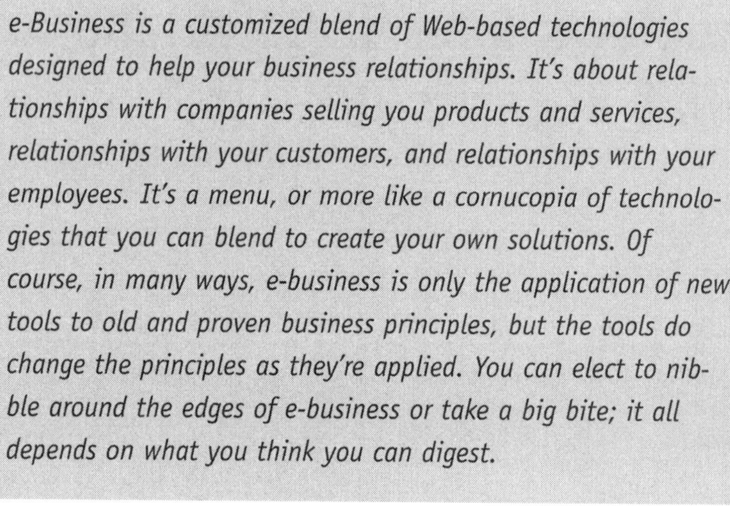

e-Business is a customized blend of Web-based technologies designed to help your business relationships. It's about relationships with companies selling you products and services, relationships with your customers, and relationships with your employees. It's a menu, or more like a cornucopia of technologies that you can blend to create your own solutions. Of course, in many ways, e-business is only the application of new tools to old and proven business principles, but the tools do change the principles as they're applied. You can elect to nibble around the edges of e-business or take a big bite; it all depends on what you think you can digest.

Want to see e-business explode on the Web? Want to see it again? When looking at the road ahead for commerce on the Web, the first observation to make is how fast we're all traveling down that road. In only five short years, bleary-eyed, cubicle-sleeping technologists, working side-by-side with a new breed of hyper-competitive entrepreneurs, have forever changed how business works. Harvard Business School, arguably the most venerable American business institution, recently overhauled its entire curriculum in one fell swoop to ensure that its MBAs emerge with the technology chops now needed to compete online. (If you got your MBA before this change, don't worry; this book is all about helping you keep up with the game.) That's a response to rate-of-change, and the pace of new e-business technology development is driving the changes.

Buzzwords

e-Commerce—A broad category encompassing all business done using Internet technologies.

Everybody seems to be doing e-business. (At least they *say* they are.) So your company now has email and a Web site, and maybe has even made some sales on the Web. But this doesn't necessarily mean that you're running an e-business. Becoming an e-business means rethinking your organization—large or small—to see where technology makes a difference. The managers and employees of a real e-business must have the willingness and desire to let technology improve every aspect of the business processes. This continual improvement and ability to adapt is part of what makes entering into the e-business world so powerful, so appealing, and yet so daunting.

Buzzwords

e-Tailing—Selling through a Web site or storefront.

We should make it clear right here that you don't embrace e-business all at once. You can move toward e-business in sweeping moves or in small steps, but each move comes with some disruption and adjustment. In practically every case you'll need outside help to implement highly integrated solutions. In many cases, you might elect to completely host processes outside your organization or to subscribe to specific services from outside organizations. Your e-business strategy doesn't come from just the information services (IS) staff or from just the CEO. Everybody from the members of the board of directors to the IS staff and to line managers in sales, marketing, support, manufacturing, and distribution must sign on, support, retrain for, and work toward e-business initiatives.

e-Business is not an end in itself, but an evolving process aimed at enabling better business processes. As Figure 1.1 shows, the e-business process has many elements and they fit into the business process in several ways.

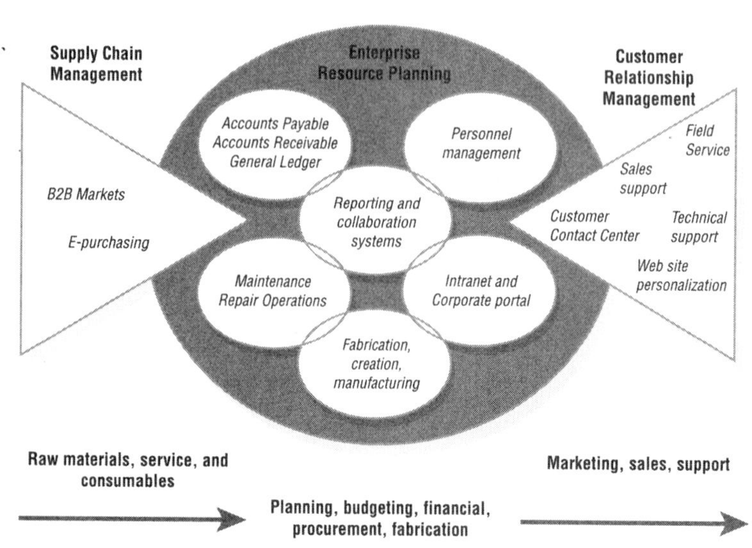

Figure 1.1

The many e-business elements fit into the business process in several ways.

The companies that are transforming the way business is done know this, which is why they are continually reexamining their strategies, techniques, and tools in the light of new technology. Because businesses come in all different shapes and sizes, no single set of e-business technologies is right for everyone. But in the end, almost all businesses come down to relationships. And that's what e-business is really about: e-Business uses technology, typically Web-based technology, to build better relationships with customers, suppliers, and employees.

The Internet Enables Business

It's easy to make comparisons between the steamboat, telephone, railroad, airplane, and the Internet. They each opened new markets, reduced the cost of interactions, and rearranged the value of certain goods and commodities. But the Internet has rearranged things faster and on a more international scale than anything since the asteroid that killed off the dinosaurs. Do you see the glow in the sky? The Internet looms larger all the time. Don't be a dinosaur.

Bezos on Customer-Centric Practices

Jeff Bezos, CEO of Amazon.com, pioneered many practices that any company embracing e-business can learn from. In Bezos's eyes, a series of separate goals is involved in doing business on the Web: "Amazon.com's over-arching mission is to become earth's most customer-centric company, and that means three things. Number one is listen to customers. Number two, invent on behalf of customers, because it is not their job to invent for themselves. And number three, personalize; if you have 20 million customers, you should have 20 million stores."

At Amazon's site, personalization software from NetPerceptions tracks data such as which books and CDs customers bought, and then, among other things, does database lookups to make ongoing recommendations for similar products whenever customers return to the Amazon site. In addition to NetPerceptions, Andromedia, Broadvision, and many other players offer cutting-edge personalization technology for Web commerce.

Successful e-business sites echo the customer-centric theme. The focus for the best site managers is not on ever-more glitzy technology, but on delivering better search results, avoiding site failure, organizing sites intuitively, facilitating intelligent product comparisons, making purchasing recommendations, and personalizing the customer experience. In many cases, efforts in these areas are leading to seismic improvements in both site traffic and bottom lines.

Dissecting a Living Organism

As we humans study any complex system, we try to take it apart and classify each piece by shape or function. We want to lay it out on the bench and look at its parts. Unfortunately, when we do this, the thing isn't alive or operating, so we get an artificial, although probably still useful, picture. As we go through this book, you will see the various pieces and parts of an e-business system. We look at each part as if it stands alone in isolation, but of course no part does. In the next chapter we talk about vertical portals, a special type of Web site, as if it is an isolated function. In the real world, it's much more difficult to classify an operation as a B2B Marketplace, a vertical portal, or e-procurement. Our pretty definitions can get pretty messy in the real world.

Buzzwords

B2B—Business-to-business (the greatest dollar volume in e-commerce).

Buzzwords

e-Procurement—Buying specialized products. Typically the raw materials and tools needed to produce manufactured goods or to provide specialized services. This typically involves browser-based purchase orders sent from behind a corporate firewall to electronic catalogs on the Internet. The orders are often logged and payment made through integration with other corporate programs.

Buzzwords

Marketplace—In e-commerce, a Web site where buyers and sellers of specialized products meet. Sellers can post catalogs, price sheets, and other information.

Buzzwords

Vertical portal—A Web site where people with common business interests meet.

The products don't stand still. As software companies, service companies, and value-added resellers enrich their products, they add more features and functions and they tend to blend together. So, although we might seem to describe vertical portals, e-procurement systems, or B2B Marketplaces as if they are static and isolated entities, we do this for the sake of study—the real world isn't like that. Each system can be part of a much larger system and can play several roles at the same time.

The Technology Changes Everything

From a bird's eye view, the landscape of e-business is undulating furiously as new technologies on the business-to-business side and on the business-to-consumer side promise to extend the reach of Web commerce, even as they extend the efficiency of it. In the end, one observation rings truest of all: e-Business sits squarely in its infancy. What we're building today, we won't recognize in three to five years, so we have to start now!

To help you think about e-business and your business, we've formulated some rules of e-business. Like the best guidelines, they're somewhat overlapping and subject to some interpretation, but we hope they'll give you some insight. So here you go:

What Matters in e-Business

Relationships matter—The most important e-business solutions help you improve your relationships with customers, suppliers, and employees.

Size matters—Many big companies are winners on the Web. Many small companies win in specific niches. But being in between is hard unless you have unusual vision or flexibility. The 500-person company often has a more difficult time embracing e-business than the 50-person company.

Velocity matters—Getting a quick solution is more important than finding the perfect solution. The key is to get a solution that works. The Internet technologies used in e-business allow you to fix things quickly as you go along.

Integration matters—The ideal e-business solution works for your whole business, not just one department. However, it's very difficult to maintain velocity while integrating across the company. If necessary, choose velocity over integration.

Partners matter—When choosing e-business solutions, you want partners that you can trust to stick around. Outsourcing is great, but will the outsourcing company be in your CEO's office the morning after the night of the Web server crash?

Uptime matters—No one cares how good your system would have been if it had been working. The key phrase is "high availability."

Privacy matters—You must make sure that private information about your customers, suppliers, and employees is kept private. This is a matter of administrative as well as technical practices.

Security matters—You must make sure that people are who they say they are. Then, you must make sure that they can easily access everything they need, but only what they need. The key technologies are strong authentication and directory services.

Flexibility matters—Listen carefully to your customers and suppliers so that you can be prepared for the changes that will come.

Training matters—You can't just tell employees to open a browser and go to work. Be prepared to train and be prepared for pain. Productivity could go down before it goes up.

Where your effort hits the bottom line matters—You can't do everything immediately, so prioritize e-business investment decisions based on the bottom line. Customer relationship management systems, customization, and electronic storefronts add to sales revenue. Adopting e-purchasing can cut the general cost of operating your business, whereas adopting e-procurement can cut the specific cost of producing a product. Various kinds of portals have specific beneficial effects. Each of these investments can make your balance sheet look a little different. Go for the maximum gain or the greatest reduction of pain—depending on your need.

Buzzwords

e-Purchasing—Buying common items online. See MRO.

Buzzwords

MRO—Maintenance, repair, and operation. The basic products needed to keep the doors open. Examples include floor wax, desks, office equipment and supplies, light bulbs, and services such as cleaning, snack bars, and travel. e-Purchasing is typically about buying MRO products.

Oh, Those Acronyms and Addresses

Sad, but true, the acronym junkies have outdone themselves in the e-business world. And the acronyms have "2B" so cutsie, too! New terms such as B2B and B2C combine with proven, but perhaps

Buzzwords

B2C—Business-to-customer—Includes storefront e-retailing and customer relationship management.

arcane business terms and techie Web and computer terms to create a rich acronym soup. We'll try to be very careful using acronyms and technical terms as we carry you through this e-biz world, but if we challenge you a little, remember that our goal is to help you master this information and your own e-business. To help, we'll provide a list of buzzwords in every chapter.

Similarly, in this book we won't bombard you with Internet addresses (URLs). Most companies have corralled a number of addresses that are close to their corporate name, so if you type `www.IBM.Com` or `www.internationalbusinessmachines.com` you'll wind up at the right place either way. We will, however, provide you with URLs when the correct address might not be intuitive.

Customer Relationships

Maintaining better relationships with customers is the most obvious advantage of implementing Internet technologies. After all, without customers your business would be doomed. Businesses reach customers across the Web in many ways, yet in many respects dealing with customers is the most complicated e-business issue that your business can face. At first it seems like a straightforward proposition: Put up a Web-based storefront and sell products. But even that apparently simple solution can be quite complicated. And remember that although Web-based storefronts are important for many retail businesses, retail operations account for only 18% of U.S. businesses, according to recent census data.

Customer relationship management (CRM) isn't a new idea or a new acronym. Taking orders, following through, providing support, and making sure your customers are happy are old business practices that take place face-to-face, over the telephone, and through the mail. But the ability to deliver CRM through the tools of e-business as e-CRM makes the ideal picture of customer relations come a lot closer to reality. Many businesses sell services or a combination of products and services. And increasingly, customers want complete solutions. For example, when businesses buy PCs nowadays, they aren't concerned only about the hardware. Purchasing PCs also involves the software and services that come along with it.

The bar where everybody knows your name is famous in song and story, specifically because personalization is so appealing. Now *that's* CRM! The best e-business sites make personalization an integral part of the buying experience. By remembering who you are and presenting a custom view of the storefront, a site can provide a better experience for repeat visitors. Depending on your business, the appropriate personalization technologies can range from simply tracking past accounts to setting up corporate buying pages to making recommendations based on past purchases.

Buzzwords

CRM—Customer relationship management—Automation of all of the best customer relationship practices.

Big Gains Right Now

"We're seeing costs of transactions declining tenfold by Web-enabling a process. We're seeing opportunities to reduce SG&A costs by twenty or thirty or forty percent in our business, and it's not five years out. It's in the short term."—Dennis Dammerman, CEO of GE Capital Services and Vice Chairman of General Electric on CNBC *Squawk Box* July 13, 2000.

Managing the entire customer experience is often the province of e-CRM software. e-CRM software keeps track of all aspects of your customers, including your interactions with them, what products they have bought, and any problems they report. At one time, this level of technology was limited to large companies with complex customer needs. Companies implemented automated call centers to take care of customer relations. The Internet, however, makes it easier for even the smallest companies to track all customer interactions. Call centers have become contact centers and they can be built within your company, outsourced, or highly automated.

B2C Versus B2B

In terms of dollar volume, business-to-customer e-business is projected to continue to be smaller than business-to-business traffic. However, B2C provides that critical element called revenue. In 2000, B2C already accounts for around 1% of U.S. retail sales, according to Gartner Group, and that promises to climb to 5–7% of all U.S. retail sales by 2004. Can you afford to miss that market?

An element of e-CRM called sales force automation tools tracks your customers or potential customers and alerts your sales staff when to contact them again. e-CRM tools perform many functions such as monitoring marketing promotions to determine which customers respond to a specific promotion so they can be targeted again in the future.

Also as a part of e-CRM, some solutions collect data specifically on customer support issues. It was once common for companies of all kinds to emphasize sales and to bury support, fearing that the costs would completely eat away any profits. But modern companies realize that good support will improve customer satisfaction and loyalty and ultimately increase the bottom line.

The ideal e-CRM solution combines sales force automation, customer support, Web-based storefronts, and integration with your internal systems. Unfortunately, the time and resources it can take to implement such a complex system can undervalue its benefits. Many businesses are finding it necessary to progress one step at a time, identifying the items that give their customers the most benefits and then moving forward. Even small steps can provide benefits and small steps typically come with the smallest disruption. As with most aspects of e-business, the technologies will change. The process of embracing, growing, and adapting e-business involves practically everyone in the business.

e-CRM Value

The users of e-CRM we've talked to say that they didn't anticipate the value of the reports they get from their systems. The e-CRM reporting tools can graphically present information such as who responded to marketing promotions and how the volume of contacts fluctuated during the month or by region. Managers use these reports as milestone summaries.

Fixing the Supply Chain

Communicating with customers can help you sell more, but it's equally important to use technology to improve the way your business buys materials. Improving supply-chain management can cut the prices you pay for components and supplies, making the buying process more efficient.

The Impact Of e-Business

According to Jamie Lewis, CEO and research chair of The Burton Group, "In the old economy, vertical integration provided efficiency and lowered procurement costs. In the new economy, connectivity replaces vertical integration. The new economy allows entrepreneurs to leverage core competencies among various e-business participants. The net effect is even greater efficiency and lower costs with less up front investment. Success in the new economy depends on a company's ability to build, maintain, and leverage business relationships using network technology."

Of course, how you deal with suppliers depends on your kind of business and the type of products you are buying. Most businesses need general products (such as office supplies) and special products tailored to their specific markets. For general products, everything from mops and floor wax to computers and travel services, companies can look to an e-business process called e-purchasing. Electronic marketplaces designed to implement e-purchasing can automate product ordering, order approval, delivery, tracking, and payment. All this is done using Internet browsers on relatively modest PCs or portable devices.

e-Purchasing or e-Procurement?

We'll say this many times: e-Purchasing is about buying the small stuff that keeps the business running. e-Procurement is about buying the pieces, parts, and services that go into the product. Many employees purchase, but few procure.

Buzzwords

Supply Chain Management—Controlling the procurement of high-cost raw materials, tools, and services that go directly into product cost. e-Procurement is an important part of supply chain management.

Coming: A Stronger Supply Chain

One of the hottest business-to-business commerce categories is supply chain management. Supply chain management technology such as Ariba's and CommerceOne's has allowed companies to procure products electronically by interacting from behind corporate firewalls with electronic product catalogs on the Internet.

A problem has arisen in the young supply-chain management category. Unlike non-electronic product procurement, electronic procurement solutions tend to ignore important parts of the procurement process such as order forecasting. Forecasting is when a company collaborates with a supplier to keep the supplier abreast of what orders might be coming soon. Other important parts of the procurement process that might be ignored by the electronic procurement solutions are order fulfillment (delivery) details, and direct electronic payment. A new category of collaborative filtering software dubbed

CPFR (Collaborative Planning Forecasting and Replenishment) is emerging, and it is expected to be incorporated as a software layer into many supply chain management products and exchanges. CPFR layers are rule-based software routines that can generate things such as system-generated forecasts of product needs based on historical purchasing patterns. Skyva International's Collaborative Commerce Platform (`www.skyva.com`) is one of the first standalone technologies in this category, and Lotus is also emerging as a player.

Vertical portals or vertical business-to-business (B2B) electronic marketplaces, on the other hand, are tailored to specific industries. For instance, marketplaces, actually special Web sites, are designed for everything from chemical supplies to apparel. Whether to join or create a B2B exchange or marketplace is an important decision. In other words, do you go alone and try to attract suppliers or do you combine with other similar consumers to attract suppliers?

B2B to Be Big

Business-to-business e-commerce is expected to account for a whopping 42% of such spending in the U.S. by 2005, or $6.3 trillion, according to Jupiter Communications. That's a 20-fold growth in online B2B from the year 2000. As much as 35% of such e-commerce takes place through "net markets" (consortia of buyers and sellers). Unsurprisingly, Jupiter cautions that "Net markets can completely disrupt current channels and alter how companies and industries conduct business."

Senior analyst Melissa Shore said, "Over the next several years, businesses will face an array of new opportunities to improve and expand their sales and procurement processes. They must invest now even though the payoff will take some time." That sounds like pretty good advice to us.

The answer, of course, depends on your market clout and what you're buying. If you're buying office supplies, you can do e-purchasing through special Web sites created by large and small office supply firms. That seems like an obvious choice. But when it comes to buying components for specialized products, you must balance the efficiencies of having your own private system against those of joining an industrywide consortium. If you set up your own special marketplace Web site, you protect your interests, you can integrate better with your other systems, and you can have more privacy and security. However, joining an industrywide buying system will certainly be less expensive, easier to implement quickly, and will probably bring in a wider range of potential suppliers.

Friend, Foe, or Partner?

Because e-business is all about relationships, those relationships can change quickly. Indeed a single company might be your customer, competitor, channel, and supplier at the same time. This means that your employees, your network, and your applications all need to understand the authorizations and limitations allowed within each interchange. This means you need smart people and smart directory services. Hey, we never promised that this would be easy!

The Challenge Inside

Let's move along our acronym string from B2B to B2E. Improving the technology and information your employees have can sound like a luxury. But it's not. In fact, helping your employees understand the business better can lead to better decision making. In turn, you can significantly improve the way you deal with customers and suppliers—not to mention improving the bottom line. Organizations typically try to improve internal communications through techniques such as company newsletters and magazines, songs, filmed reports, retreats, bulletin boards, and, the latest corporate talisman, the mission statement. In e-business we automate the process, make it live every day, and call it business-to-employee or B2E. But good B2E does more than just promote understanding and morale. It also provides a set of tools and information for improved productivity.

Buzzwords

B2E—Business-to-employee—This means of internal communications can include email, collaboration software, video conferencing, and corporate portals.

Relationships Inside and Outside Too

e-Business is about relationships: That's our theme and perhaps our best high-level insight. But you have to apply the relationship theme inside of any company starting on the road to e-business. About 30% of e-business is about technology and 70% is about people. Important human considerations inside the organization include administration, training, the roles of various managers, laws, and government regulations. e-Business systems must interact with and account for each of these human factors. When we talk to anyone who had really set up an e-business system, they always tell us that dealing with the people was a lot harder then dealing with the technology.

All sorts of internal systems lend themselves to being adapted to Internet technologies. These include traditional systems such as accounting, personnel systems, and more complex enterprise resource planning (ERP) systems that keep track of all the elements of your business.

Anyone who has managed a software project knows that the existing systems shape the new systems. As you develop ideas for improving employee communications and efficiency, you'll always come back to how those ideas work with existing systems. If you have a legacy ERP system, you'll have to start with an understanding of how that system fits into your new ideas.

Internet-based technologies also have a tremendous impact on how employees communicate. Employees are traveling more and working from remote offices, yet they still act as productive parts of the business through systems such as virtual private networks. New collaboration tools make it easier for people—both those inside your organization and colleagues from the outside—to work together.

Buzzwords

Corporate portal—A Web site containing information specific to the company and typically providing browser-based access to corporate applications such as ordering and inventory databases. Corporate portals now must also respond to demands for wireless entry.

Perhaps the biggest change is giving employees more access to information within the company. Every business has employees with specialized knowledge that could be useful to other workers. Knowledge management systems attempt to collect information and make it easier for employees to track down the material they need. Individually, any of these solutions can help make your business more efficient. But keeping track of the types of information and services that a business needs can be a challenge for your employees.

Many companies are trying to tie it all together in an internal Web site called a *corporate portal.* Corporate portals are the equivalent of My Yahoo!—a site that filters news and other information according to rules set by each individual user. But a corporate portal is designed specifically for your employees and perhaps for business partners. The ideal corporate portal system aggregates key data, resources, and applications (such as your e-mail and calendar information); links into your knowledge management systems and collaboration products; and provides alerts from CRM programs.

Almost no business can pull all of this together at once into an ideal portal, but the first steps can be the most important. To be a great e-business, you must choose the right technologies and solutions. This includes picking the right PCs, servers, peripherals, and components and creating a strong infrastructure. And as application service providers (ASPs) become more prevalent, it also means picking the right partners. Most importantly, it involves integrating all these products, services, and technologies in a way that allows your business to leverage e-business with the smallest amount of disruption and training.

The Digital Divide Is About More Than Retail

We've noticed that when news reporters comment on the digital divide, the difference between "have net and have not" countries or cultures, they somehow seem to make it a consumer matter. That's editorially appealing, but it misses the big picture. The digital divide is really much more about these countries or cultures either participating in a new global economy or staying behind in the economy of the last century. e-Business brings globalization of economies and the disintermediation of markets. The new economy is about providing speed of business and flexibility while maintaining or even improving the ability to deliver customized products and services.

Of course, personalizing the user experience at a commerce site, and boosting efficiency through things such as advanced search and intelligent shopping technologies can only take a site so far. At the end of the day, commerce sites need to deliver products on a timely basis, treat inventories efficiently, run stable sites, and leverage the Web in supporting customers. Much of that process is managed by technology on the back end of the B2C flow chart, where everything from order entry, database logging, and analysis tools comes into play. The back end is also where many of the big e-commerce sites are rushing to put in business-to-business supply chain management solutions, such as those offered by Ariba and CommerceOne.

Cisco on the Web

No long-standing business has had to adapt to faster growth in Web sales than Cisco Systems. Cisco now manages over 70% of its revenues through unassisted sales from its Web site, totaling tens of millions of dollar per day, and billions of dollars per year. Customers also have direct online access to technical support and order-status information at Cisco's Web site. As Cisco has moved all this product buying and support to the Web, it has saved hundreds of millions of dollars.

To facilitate this focus on selling and supporting on the Web, Cisco uses Oracle Database applications, Oracle Applications ERP software, Oracle e-Business Applications, and Oracle Financials on a back end powered by Sun servers (see the diagram in Figure 1.2). When these applications were implemented together, about 5,000 back-logged product orders were immediately converted in only one weekend. According to Cisco CIO Peter Solvik, the applications have had an enormous impact on getting products to customers efficiently and quickly. Speed in delivering products not only has an impact on customer satisfaction, but reduces inventory write-offs for Cisco.

An Integrated System

The completely integrated e-business probably doesn't exist, but if it did, it would look a lot like the business illustrated in Figure 1.2.

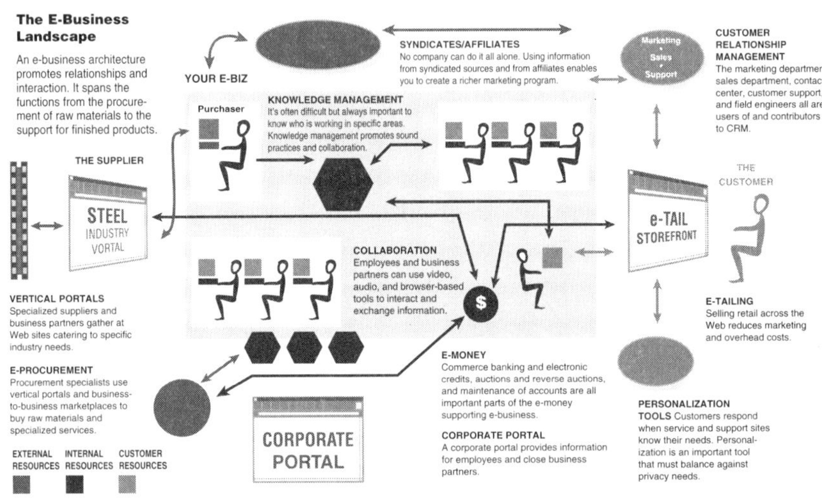

The E-Business Landscape
An e-business architecture promotes relationships and interaction. It spans the functions from the procurement of raw materials to the support for finished products.
YOUR E-BIZ
Purchaser
KNOWLEDGE MANAGEMENT
It's often difficult but always important to know who is working in specific areas. Knowledge management promotes sound practices and collaboration.
SYNDICATES/AFFILIATES
No company can do it all alone. Using information from syndicated sources and from affiliates enables you to create a richer marketing program.
Marketing
Sales
Support
CUSTOMER RELATIONSHIP MANAGEMENT
The marketing department, sales department, contact center, customer support, and field engineers all are users of and contributors to CRM.
THE SUPPLIER
STEEL
INDUSTRY
VORTAL
THE CUSTOMER
e-TAIL
STOREFRONT
COLLABORATION
Employees and business partners can use video, audio, and browser-based tools to interact and exchange information.
$
VERTICAL PORTALS
Specialized suppliers and business partners gather at Web sites catering to specific industry needs.
E-TAILING
Selling retail across the Web reduces marketing and overhead costs.
E-PROCUREMENT
Procurement specialists use vertical portals and business-to-business marketplaces to buy raw materials and specialized services.
E-MONEY
Commerce banking and electronic credits, auctions and reverse auctions, and maintenance of accounts are all important parts of the e-money supporting e-business.
CORPORATE
PORTAL
CORPORATE PORTAL
A corporate portal provides information for employees and close business partners.
PERSONALIZATION TOOLS Customers respond when service and support sites know their needs. Personalization is an important tool that must balance against privacy needs.
EXTERNAL RESOURCES
INTERNAL RESOURCES
CUSTOMER RESOURCES

Figure 1.2

If your business diagram looked like this, you probably wouldn't be reading this book.

Implement these technologies well and e-business can make a profound difference for your customers, suppliers, and employees. Ultimately, this will improve your entire business.

Big Losses

We've observed that those who have the most to lose, lose the most by inaction or slow response to changing conditions in e-business. However, some big companies—GE is a great example—can come late to the market but still capture a huge share through immense investment. There is, however, a steep correlation between how late you come in and how much it costs to catch up.

In the following chapters we take you through the specifics of B2-everything. Our goal is to help you find the right products and systems to build your Internet business environment. We talk about the top-end software, the servers in the basement, and the options in between. We hope you read and learn.

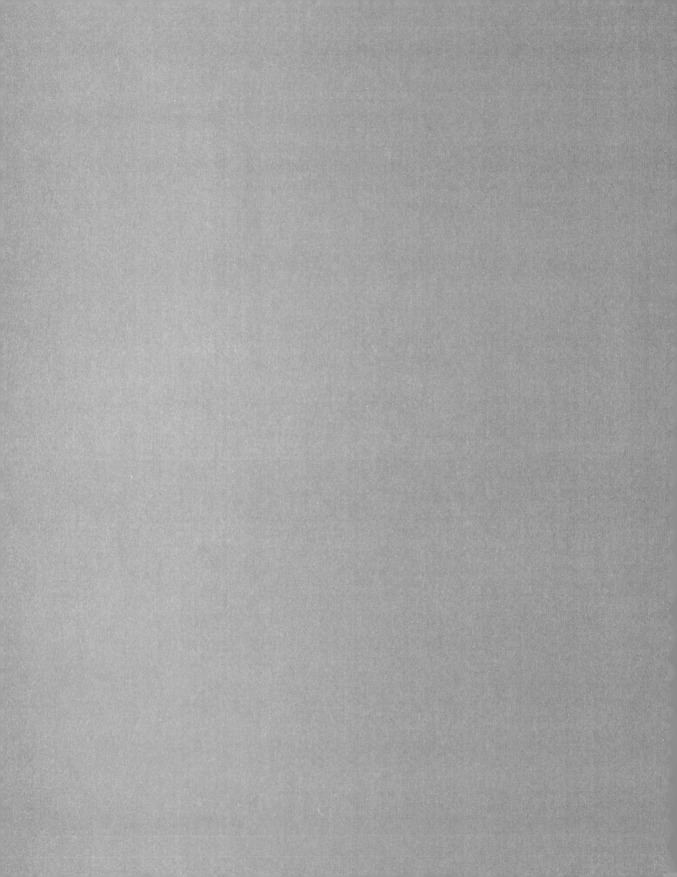

PART II

B2B: Business to Business—e-Marketplaces, Net Market Makers, B2B Exchanges, Vertical Portals, MRO

CHAPTER 2

Vertical Portals for B2B

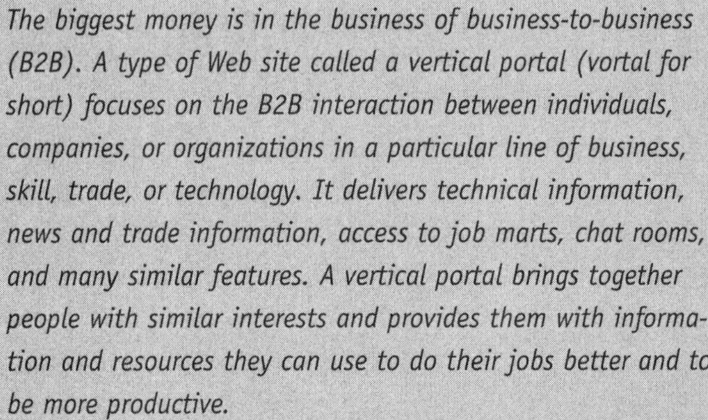

The biggest money is in the business of business-to-business (B2B). A type of Web site called a vertical portal (vortal for short) focuses on the B2B interaction between individuals, companies, or organizations in a particular line of business, skill, trade, or technology. It delivers technical information, news and trade information, access to job marts, chat rooms, and many similar features. A vertical portal brings together people with similar interests and provides them with information and resources they can use to do their jobs better and to be more productive.

But special content often isn't enough to keep visitors who want everything in one place. Portal operators can receive general-purpose and special-purpose content from various types of syndication operations. Syndicated information, together with specialized information and features, can create a powerful site that attracts and holds customers.

Seen Through a Vortal

We all enjoy being with people more or less like us. Common interests make birds of a feather. The idea of common business interests is behind a particular type of business-to-business (B2B) Web site called a *vertical portal* or *vortal.* A vortal's pages can include industry news, job finders, technical dictionaries and specifications, focused ads, specialized chat activities, and other industry information. Key to the vortal's definition is that the news and links are updated and that they come from more sources than just inside one company. Because vortals can lead to many links for people with specific interests, it's natural that many vortals lead to marketplace services described in the next chapter.

A Web site such as My Yahoo! is a good example of a general interest portal. At this site and others like MSN and Excite you can configure customized Web pages so they contain the information you typically want in the way you want it. A vertical portal is just like that, except the sources of information include specialized topics centered on a particular line of business, trade, or technology.

Buzzwords

Vortal—A vertical portal. The available information is specific to an industry, trade, technology, or special interest.

Buzzwords

Portal—A Web site that provides a variety of information presented the way you want it.

Buzzwords

Syndication—A way to get news stories, photos, and other specialized content from general-purpose sources.

Who Needs This?

Even a one-person business can find a lot of good value in a vertical portal. In fact, small businesses can get a lot of leverage from both using and running a vortal. Vortals are valuable for non-profit organizations focused on specific issues or technologies, and they're a great strategy for any business selling specialized services.

Buzzwords

Sticky—The attribute of having interesting content that can bring back customers.

Unfortunately, it's usually not enough to have only specialized information. If a site is going to be well used, it must be "sticky". It must keep its readers, but providing only vertical news and information is a poor way to stick to the fingers of your readers.

Consumer or Operator?

You can use a portal or you can create and operate a portal. You and others in your company might use a portal to access useful information and to become more productive. But you create a portal to market to and perhaps to even control an industry. Many companies that provide services to specialized interests create vertical portals to advertise to those interests. The advertising can be blatant, in the form of banner ads, or subtle, in the form of editorial content and logo. If you run a portal, it should act as a front door to your catalog, order forms, and services. You can use a vertical portal, an attractive spot to gather, as a major part of both your marketing and sales activities.

Cruise Some Good Vortals

Using a portal is a pretty nice experience—especially if you work in a particularly arcane or obscure field. Many examples of good vortals are only a few keystrokes away. Designed for the life sciences industry, `www.bio.com` brings together auctions and specialized services. MotorPlace.com, at `www2.motorplace.com`, is a vortal for automobile dealers leading to marketplaces for parts, cars, and services. PartMiner, `www.partminer.com`, provides news, software, and services for more than 100,000 electronic engineers and purchasing professionals worldwide.

If you want to establish a vortal, you should divide the project between equipment and content. From the perspective of equipment and connectivity, a portal isn't very difficult to set up. Because the size of the audience is limited, bandwidth to the server and server performance aren't big issues. For example, bio.com does well on a single T-1 line running at 1.5 megabits per second. Unlike corporate portals, described in Chapter 5, "Corporate Portals: Multiple Doorways to the Treasures," vortals don't integrate with general business or knowledge management systems, so designers use traditional Web site creation techniques such as Microsoft's Active Server Pages, XML, and cascading style sheets. In many cases it's smart to run a vertical portal on the equipment of a Web hosting service. Costs for the service typically run from $100–$600 per month depending on connectivity and server requirements. That's cheaper than hiring an IS staff for a 24-hour-a-day operation.

In-House or Outsource?

A vertical portal is a prime candidate for outsourcing. It doesn't have to tie into existing business applications, and a good Web hosting site can provide you with high reliability and fast connections for a reasonable monthly fee. Also, if you want to sell merchandise through your vortal, the hosting site can provide links to credit card services.

You can choose from among Web hosting companies with many different plans and capabilities. A local or regional ISP is a good choice if you think that most of your activity will be within a specific city or region. On the other hand, if you have an international business, a company such as Cable and Wireless (www.cwplc.com) can offer you service in professional facilities around the world. Other Web hosting companies we have reviewed include AT&T, bCentral, Concentric, DellHost, Exodus, IBM, Interland, Verio, and Web2010. These companies offer a variety of hosting and site operations plans at very competitive prices—typically not more than several hundred dollars a month and often less than a hundred dollars a month.

Buzzwords

XML—Extensible markup language. XML is the most popular and practical language for e-business, although it now has many extensions and special libraries. XML is the new generation of markup language for Web content designed to make it easier to efficiently search and automatically exchange data on the Web.

Maintaining the content of a vortal is much more difficult than maintaining its hardware or connections. A vortal attracts new users to the marketplace and provides added value for current users, but it's not easy to keep news fresh. You need strong content from a variety of sources.

Make It Sticky

"I built it, and they didn't come" is quickly becoming a cliché in the Web world, but the fact is, the competition for visitors is getting tougher. Even if customers do click into your vortal for special information, how do you convince them to stick around—and keep returning? The problem is twofold. Web businesses need to make their sites sticky, but often don't have the resources to produce enough fresh content to engage visitors. At the same time, many Web merchants and content producers need ways to give their merchandise and content more exposure and to draw in more potential customers. Without these visitors, sites will fall in the proverbial Web forest without making a sound.

VerticalNet Does Vortal

You can build a vertical portal using standard Web creation tools, but if you want rich content and quick deployment, you'll ask for help. VerticalNet, with a $100 million investment from Microsoft, develops storefronts and other e-business sites, but the company is very strong in vortals. VerticalNet powers more than 50 sites with names like adhesivesandsealants.com and pulpandpaperonline.com. Epicentric, a competitor, sells portal software and services, including options for content from more than 100 different sources. Value-added resellers of various types customize the software, and typical installations fall in the range of $175,000–$400,000.

You can also improve content and create symbiotic relationships through syndication and affiliate networking. Whereas syndication connects sites that need content-to-content providers, affiliate networking connects sites that need additional revenue to businesses that want to improve sales or increase online traffic. Think of the ubiquitous Amazon.com and barnesandnoble.com buttons found on other corporate Web sites for examples of affiliation. You can arrange either syndication or affiliate networking through hosted tools as well as through traditional licensed software.

There is a twist to all of this for healthy vertical portals. You'll probably begin operation as a vertical portal by taking content from a syndication service. But, there's also room for an operation with special insight and access to special information to become a contributor to a syndication service. If you know something special, you can sell it in many ways.

FringeGolf, an online golf magazine, has a small staff to write feature stories for the site and oversee its design, but has neither the time nor the resources to collect breaking news about the industry or to shoot photos. Instead, FringeGolf licenses such content through iSyndicate. By way of iSyndicate's Web-based service, FringeGolf augments its site with news feeds and photographs from the Associated Press, statistics and player profiles from SportsNetwork.com, and videos from Golf Span.com. "We do our own creative content," says Andrew Fritz, the company's founder and CEO, "but at the same time, we need to have standard golf content. Standard golf content is mainly news feeds and statistics. Through iSyndicate, we're able to provide that."

Each day, iSyndicate automatically streams content to the FringeGolf Web server, formatting that content according to the specifications of Fritz and his team. "Everything is hosted at iSyndicate," says Fritz, "but we give our own look and feel to the content. We can't create our own news or give our own tone or voice to the editorial [content], but we can at least control the presentation of it."

With syndication, as this process is called, everybody benefits. FringeGolf improves its Web site and with any luck attracts more users. Meanwhile, by syndicating its content, SportsNetwork extends the reach of its brand name and receives a fee from

FringeGolf. Certainly, vertical portals in almost every area from automobiles to biotechnology can find stories and information within their specific areas of interest from the world of daily news feeds. Just because a portal is vertical, it doesn't have to be closed. Figure 2.1 illustrates how syndication works with a special-purpose vertical Web site.

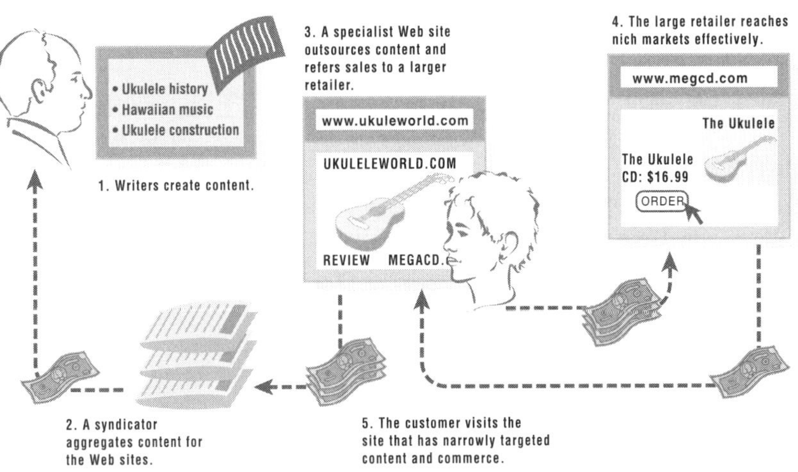

Figure 2.1
A vortal can integrate content from internal applications and Web sources.

Get the Domain Names!

One trick to running a successful vertical portal is to get every available domain name that is in any way associated with the topic—including all the misspellings! So, for example, if your portal aimed at veterinarians who specialize in pets is called `catsanddogs.com`, you also need to try to buy `catanddog.com`, `catsanddog.com`, `catsandogs.com`, and so on. (Yes, we know that `catsanddogs.com` is really a site for Internet technology—this is just an example!) You can then link all these alternative domain names to your site. You'll raise your initial investment, but you'll also increase the number of hits you get.

Although many Internet service providers and Web site hosting companies will offer to register your domain names for you, it's probably better that you do it yourself. You can work through any company that is an accredited registrar of The Internet Corporation for Assigned Names and Numbers (ICANN at `www.icann.org`). If you register the names yourself, there will never be a question of ownership should you decide to leave your present ISP or hosting service.

Syndication Sources

A company called ScreamingMedia offers syndication through a hosted service and a distributed software package. "We provide content to Web sites and wireless devices," says CEO Kevin Clark. "We aggregate, filter, and distribute real-time digital content, which would include text, photos, streaming video, and streaming audio."

The company offers select content from hundreds of content providers, including wire services such as Associated Press, New York Times Syndicate, and *USA Today*; magazines such as *National Geographic*; and Web sites such as Salon.com. Clark says, "Part of our secret is being able to aggregate a variety of content from a variety of different feeds. We take content in over satellites, FM signals, and leased lines. We even have a thread of operation in our technology called the Harvester. The Harvester goes out to Web sites and pulls down their content."

You can sign up to be a content provider, or you can purchase content from others and add it to your site, either through ScreamingMedia's Custom Content Service, which must be installed on your own Web server, or through its News!Stand service. The service can potentially provide more specialized content. You can have ScreamingMedia stream the content straight onto your site, or you can select the content you want before it's posted.

ScreamingMedia's News!Stand is cheap and easy to use, but it provides only news. "News!Stand provides content service offerings to more of a midprice-point customer," says Clark. "For $750 a month, you can get five stories twice a day out of 1 of 13 categories...You can go to News!Stand, become a subscriber, and have it turned on in 15 minutes." iSyndicate's primary-hosted service, used by FringeGolf, rivals ScreamingMedia's licensed tool. iSyndicate also offers a free service called iSyndicate Express, which offers users snippets of content, including small photos, news headlines, stock quotes, and search boxes.

Each of these services carries the news site's brand name and links back to that site. Though no money changes hands, you essentially become an affiliate in iSyndicate's affiliate network.

Let's Affiliate!

With help from a company such as Be Free (`www.befree.com`), you can develop an affiliate network—a group of partner sites that help attract new customers. Essentially, each affiliate site contains a promotion in the form of a piece of text or a graphic that links back to your site. You could arrange such a special interest network on your own by contacting individual companies and linking them to your site, but this would be inordinately expensive and time-consuming. Using Be Free, you can partner with affiliates that already have relationships with Be Free, easily attract additional affiliates using Be Free's Web-based tools, and quickly distribute promotions using those tools.

InfoSpace offers a similar service. For each click that leads to use of one of the company's premium services, you make money. You then pay affiliates for customers they send to your site and sales they generate, and Be Free takes a cut of each fee. "We're allowing e-businesses to place their promotions, or their goods and services, on tens of thousands of Web sites," explains Tricia Travaline, Be Free's vice president of marketing and communications. "Rather than just paying for the placements of promotions on these sites, they pay for performance. In other words, they pay only for those promotions that work—that either generate a sale or generate a lead."

"We're allowing e-businesses to place their promotions, or their goods and services, on tens of thousands of Web sites. Rather than just paying for the placements of promotions on these sites, they pay for performance."

Consequently, affiliates have an incentive to place promotions on pages where success is most likely. "For instance," says Travaline, "Baseball.com writes an article about the New York Yankees. Within that article, they can place either a text link or a graphic link selling a New York Yankees shirt that is sold by a merchant that they have a relationship with, such as Fogdog Sports.... The most effective type of advertising is placed right in context, so you can reach consumers when they're most likely to purchase." Participating companies are helping each other out, as they do with syndication. In helping other businesses, they're helping themselves.

Portals with Many Faces

A vertical portal can be many things, and the image often shifts. A vertical portal for a highly technical organization with little to sell is probably the purest example. But a vortal has a self-selecting specialized audience that forms a special high-quality market crying for sales. So a vortal is often both an entry point and a cross-link for a traditional Web storefront site. It might be difficult to tell when the editorial and news stop and the ads and catalogs begin.

Meta-Networks

Business-to-business exchanges and vortals have flourished recently, but some predict that new meta-networks will undermine the early-stage "network effect" that exchanges now enjoy. Meta-networks are networks of networks, and they allow Internet users to access many exchanges at the same time. Auction consolidators, such as Auction Watch and even Napster, are examples of how one piece of meta-network technology can allow users access to many exchanges.

A vortal can be a tool to build an industry or to support a charity. It can be a marketing tool or a service that is part of a larger package of services. Many reasons are evident to use, create, and support vortals in their many forms. A vortal builds relationships with people like you.

CHAPTER 3

Business-to-Business Markets

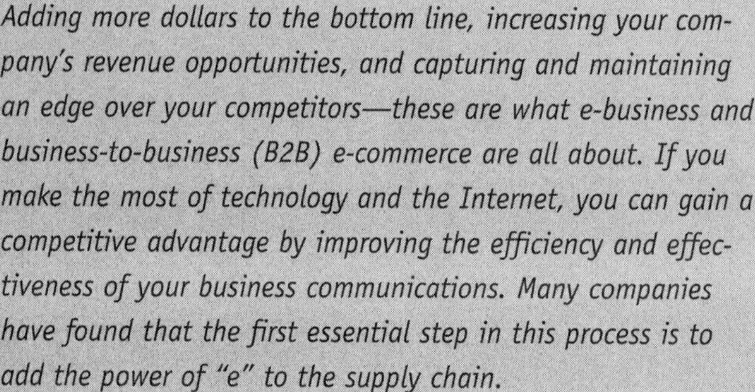

Adding more dollars to the bottom line, increasing your company's revenue opportunities, and capturing and maintaining an edge over your competitors—these are what e-business and business-to-business (B2B) e-commerce are all about. If you make the most of technology and the Internet, you can gain a competitive advantage by improving the efficiency and effectiveness of your business communications. Many companies have found that the first essential step in this process is to add the power of "e" to the supply chain.

Supply chain management is the process of optimizing a company's internal procurement practices, as well as the company's interaction with suppliers and customers, to bring products to market more efficiently. B2B e-commerce uses Internet technology to implement supply chain management in new and very efficient ways. An efficient supply chain reduces total cost of operations by reducing product cost. That can have a much bigger impact on the bottom line than even getting fresh sources of revenues and earnings.

Although sometimes it seems that net profit isn't important to new economy companies, in the long run it still determines management's success or failure. Many business plans show escalating net profit driven by gross sales, but in the real world it's often more effective to cut overhead. Reducing the cost of acquiring, handling, and warehousing raw materials is a great way to build the bottom line.

Buzzwords

B2B—Business-to-business

Any industry that consumes mass quantities of raw materials, such as chemical products, medical supplies, electronic parts, or automotive parts, must give a lot of management attention to its procurement process. These companies typically build a tight group of trusted suppliers. It takes sharp procurement professionals to keep updating and building relationships in what becomes a trading community.

The Internet brings these procurement professionals new tools for buying and bartering. At the same time, these tools open new markets and trading communities to suppliers.

Buyers and suppliers can meet in many places on the Web. Auctions are popular and bartering is growing. For example, a site named Ubarter.com automates the barter process. But sophisticated trading communities typically gather at specialized trading Web site systems called *B2B marketplaces.* A marketplace is an automated bazaar that cuts the number of middlemen and acquisition costs while maintaining quality. Companies can operate their own marketplace sites, join existing constellations of sites, or use online services. The models are still emerging, but any company can be a seller, a buyer, or a B2B market maker.

Buzzwords

Marketplace—A specialized Web site containing catalogs, order forms, and other useful information provided by product suppliers. Like a real market, it's a place to buy, haggle over, and exchange goods and services.

Who Needs This?

Small supply companies can benefit from joining a B2B marketplace because they can reach a wide world of potential buyers. Similarly, large companies can efficiently deal with many small companies through a marketplace. In a recent *PC Magazine* interview with Dave Clementz, the Chief Information Officer of Chevron Oil, Mr. Clementz reported that suppliers using Chevron's supply-chain experience cost-of-sale reductions ranging from 5–30%. So in addition to reaching a bigger market, a B2B marketplace can enable suppliers to more efficiently reach their traditional markets.

Any company that consumes raw materials and makes them into finished products can benefit from automated supply chain management techniques. Of course, the bigger the operation, the bigger the potential benefit and also the bigger the initial cost.

Buzzwords

Supply chain management—The supply chain feeds raw material into the manufacturing process. It's concerned with quality, quantity, delivery, timing, and payment of goods and services that go directly into a finished product.

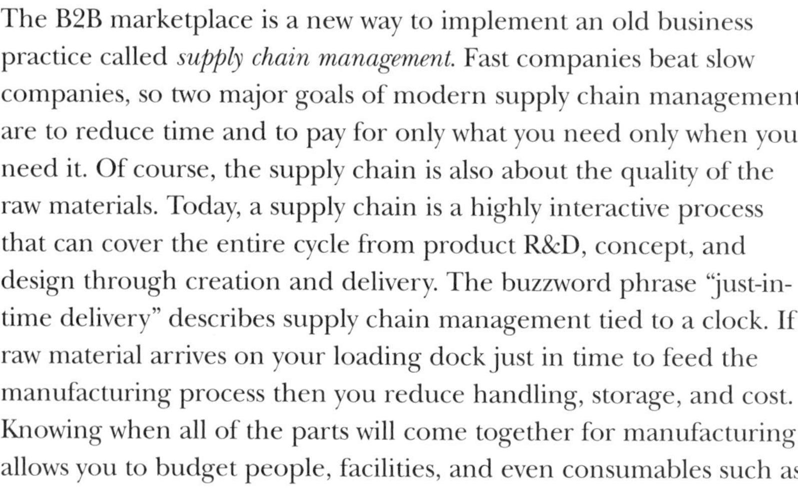

The B2B marketplace is a new way to implement an old business practice called *supply chain management.* Fast companies beat slow companies, so two major goals of modern supply chain management are to reduce time and to pay for only what you need only when you need it. Of course, the supply chain is also about the quality of the raw materials. Today, a supply chain is a highly interactive process that can cover the entire cycle from product R&D, concept, and design through creation and delivery. The buzzword phrase "just-in-time delivery" describes supply chain management tied to a clock. If raw material arrives on your loading dock just in time to feed the manufacturing process then you reduce handling, storage, and cost. Knowing when all of the parts will come together for manufacturing allows you to budget people, facilities, and even consumables such as electricity and gas while you beat the competition.

Buzzwords

Just-in-time delivery refers to the ability to deliver raw materials to the loading dock just before they're needed for production. This ability reduces the cost of inventory, warehouse space, and handling, so it significantly reduces production costs.

Supply chain management, depicted in Figure 3.1, focuses on the materials and goods that go directly into your product. Today, we often refer to it as *e-procurement.* It's usually done by a few procurement professionals. But companies need more than raw materials. The process of acquiring the supplies that you need to do business, from dust mops to office machines, is known as *indirect purchasing,* because the purchases don't go directly into the product. Today, we call it e-purchasing. We deal with e-purchasing in the next chapter, but the tools for e-procurement and e-purchasing are very similar. The major difference is that e-purchasing is done by many people throughout a company—often with a variety of job titles. e-Procurement and supply chain management are done by a few professionals.

Buzzwords

e-Purchasing—Buying common products and services that a company needs to do business. Examples are light bulbs, computers, coffee service, and travel tickets. Many employees with different job titles placed throughout the organization often do this.

The Elements of Supply Chain Management

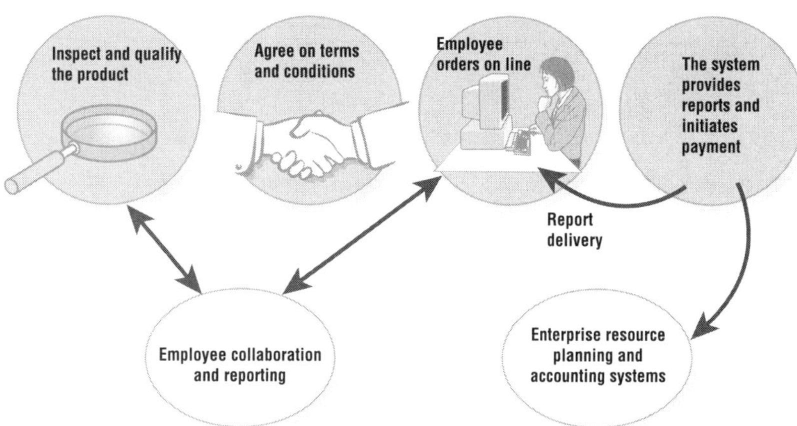

Figure 3.1
Supply chain management focuses on the materials and goods that go directly into your product.

Buzzwords

e-Procurement—Buying specialized goods, materials, and services that go directly into a finished product. Typically done by procurement professionals.

In Chapter 2, "Vertical Portals for B2B," we discussed vertical portals. Although a marketplace and a vertical portal have different content, they can serve the same audience and closely link to each other. Vertical portals often serve as a gateway to a marketplace. In some cases, particularly in areas such as auctions and technical reference libraries, the portal and marketplace become one.

As with vertical portals, you can decide to participate in a marketplace to benefit from the efficiency, or you can decide to set up a marketplace to better market your services or even to grow and influence an industry. Small companies particularly can benefit from the access to big markets they receive through a marketplace. If you're a bigger company and you want to influence an industry, you become what is called a *market maker.*

REALITY CHECK: B2B can improve efficiency and provide competitive advantages, but it must be the right kind of B2B for your organization.

- Many suppliers of equipment and consumable products—Cisco, Dell, and Grainger are good examples—have established customer relationship management systems. In many cases you're better off going to the suppliers rather than making the suppliers come to you.

- Adopting e-purchasing brings corporate cultural changes for both consumers and suppliers. When computers change people's jobs you need to give as much attention to the people as you do to the systems or the systems will fail.
- Small suppliers can benefit from joining trading groups, but they must keep listings up-to-date.
- A corporate supply chain management system has its greatest value when it's integrated with accounting and manufacturing applications, but custom integration isn't cheap. Budgets in six and seven figures are common.
- Money draws flies. You need both electronic safeguards, in terms of certificate servers and proper authentication, and strong administrative security practices.

The chemical industry, always big on bartering materials, provides good examples of the different roles available in a B2B market. CheMatch.com is an online marketplace dot-com company aimed specifically at the bulk chemical industry. Over 125 companies act as buyers, sellers, and traders on its marketplace. Eastman Chemical (`www.eastman.com`), an established chemical firm in Tennessee, is becoming a B2B market maker. Eastman is working with SESAMI.com to create a marketplace for the chemical industry in Asia and it's involved in a project called Shipchem.com that drills down into ordering specialized shipping services for chemical products.

Although a B2B marketplace can be as busy as a bazaar, each buyer sees the equivalent of a private library of catalogs and product brochures from different companies combined with a bulletin

CASE STUDY

E-CHEMICALS

Headquarters: Ann Arbor, Michigan

`www.e-chemicals.com`

Headquartered in Ann Arbor, Michigan, e-Chemicals provides end-to-end supply chain solutions for the chemical industry. Through machine-to-machine connectivity that links raw materials providers, chemical manufacturers, channel intermediaries, and chemical purchasers, e-Chemicals drives significant value by creating efficiencies and reducing costs. e-Chemicals is the first online company dedicated to meeting the comprehensive needs of the chemical industry including competitive pricing, methods of procurement, financial board for posting messages, an auction, ordering systems, and delivery systems. Figure 3.2 gives you the idea. Suppliers enter their catalogs and brochures into the marketplace as a series of files, but companies such as Ariba and Grainger are collaborating on specialized features written in the Commerce XML (CXML) scripting language to automate the handling of supplier content. Sellers receive orders by email, fax, or electroic document exchange and settle accounts by electronic links through banks, or maybe by paper mail. In the most elementary form, buyers only need an Internet connection, a browser, and a password to browse and search the combined material.

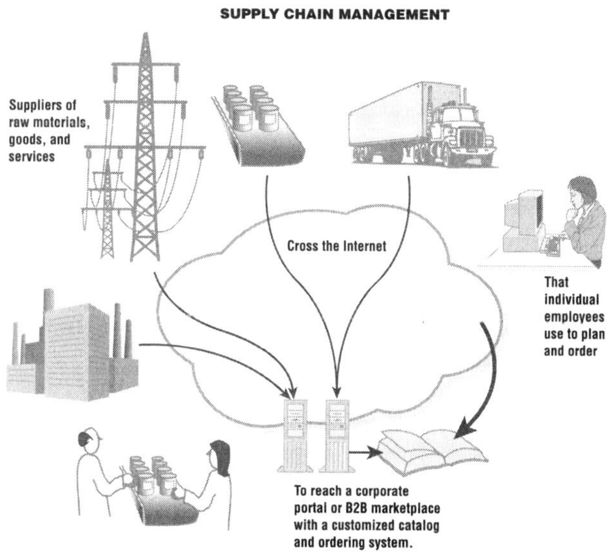

Figure 3.2

Each buyer in the B2B marketplace sees the equivalent of a private library of catalogs and product brochures from different companies, as well as ordering and delivery systems.

settlement, transportation, regulatory concerns, and inventory reduction.

e-Chemicals also provides a neutral online marketplace that enables its registered buyers to select a product, get a price, and order and track shipments online through its Web site, www.e-chemicals.com. The company's goal is to be the supply chain backbone of the chemical industry worldwide. e-Chemicals is a partner company of Internet Capital Group, an Internet company of more than 60 partner organizations committed to being the world leader in each of its industry segments.

Good examples of similar industry marketplaces include www.networkoil.com and www.e-steel.com.

CASE STUDY

CHEVRON

Headquarters: San Francisco, California

www.chevron.com

For a corporation with a multibillion-dollar supply chain, increasing operating efficiencies through the Internet will have a significant impact on the bottom line. At Chevron Corp., a global oil and gas company with more than $40 billion in annual sales, the costs of everything from paper clips to oil rigs can stack up quickly. With its cost of operations currently sitting at about $10 billion a year, Chevron spends money to make money. Until the Internet began to pick up steam, Chevron managed its supply chain largely on paper, through good old-fashioned purchase orders. But as we learned from Dave Clementz, president of Chevron Information Technology Co., that's changing.

"We had primarily paper-based purchase ordering in place around the time the Internet took off, five years ago," said Clementz. "But we saw the phenomenal growth going on out beyond our corporate firewall." Chevron did do some electronic procurement at the time, primarily through EDI systems accessing existing electronic catalogs, but on a relatively small scale. And various employees were using all kinds of different catalogs; most of them on paper, though a few were electronic.

"A couple of years ago, we stepped up our efforts in the product procurement area with an eye on centralizing on electronic catalogs and the Internet," Clementz said. Chevron partnered with a company called Requisite Technology, which uses a technology called e-Merge to turn paper product catalogs into Internet-based electronic catalogs quickly.

"Suppliers were eager to participate and give us lower unit prices for high-volume products bought electronically," Clementz added. "In the early going, we concentrated on bringing in the suppliers we spend the most money with."

Three SAP installations were sitting behind Chevron's firewall when the company started moving in earnest toward business-to-business commerce. As middleware to facilitate transactions, Chevron deployed Ariba's ORMS (Operating Resource Management System), because it integrated tightly with SAP and Chevron's back-office software.

How does a typical Chevron product transaction go? A Chevron procurement employee connects to the ORMS software through a browser. The software, sitting behind Chevron's corporate firewall and on top of the SAP systems, includes a customizable XML metadata layer and message synchronization services to talk with Internet-based catalogs, which offer office supplies and oil rigs alike. An employee fills an electronic shopping basket, and the software sends purchase orders out beyond the firewall to the catalogs. Chevron's suppliers then send filled purchase orders back to the software. The transactions are logged from those purchase orders in SAP.

According to Nick Solinger, Ariba's director of marketing, ORMS is scalable up to 200,000 seats and can process hundreds of thousands of purchase orders a day. For a big company like Chevron to put in place a solution like ORMS can take from 6–18 months, although according to Solinger, Dana Corp. completed a live installation in 11 days.

"Suppliers can really cut their costs of goods sold this way," Clementz said, "because they don't need 100 people in pickup trucks carrying briefcases to go do the selling. They can just log on." According to Clementz, Chevron's electronic catalog suppliers are reporting profit improvements ranging from 5–30% since moving their offerings online.

What's the bottom line for Chevron? Chevron's office in Bakersfield, California, where e-procurement is centralized, currently handles about $80 million of product procurement costs. By replicating the Internet procurement process in offices around the globe, Clementz said, "We plan to cut $200 million out of our $10 billion cost-of-operations spending by next year."

That can seem small percentage-wise—about 2% of the cost of operations—but in dollar terms, it's a significant savings. Beyond replicating the process in other global offices, where does Clementz see Chevron's Internet-centric supply chain trend going?

"About 40% of our cost of operations goes to supplies currently, and about 60% goes to services," he said, "so we think there is a big opportunity to do for our services procurement what we did with the Internet and product procurement. We think this is the next step. And the key for us in all of this was to look out beyond our firewall."

As we said in the introduction to this chapter, a B2B market doesn't exist in isolation. In its ultimate form, a marketplace becomes part of the supply chain management system of an enterprise. Companies using enterprise resource planning (ERP) systems such as those from Baan, J.D. Edwards, Oracle, PeopleSoft, or SAP to control production, inventory, and accounting can benefit from using special marketplace ordering programs tied to the ERP systems. Supply chain management, integrated with ERP, provides an automated way to order materials and settle accounts. It also supplies performance data on order fulfillment times, rejects, and other statistics that can give procurement professionals an objective way to measure vendors. This control allows managers to lower inventories and optimize production schedules.

Many companies also value the anonymity of ordering through a B2B marketplace. They can buy and sell raw materials without tipping off competitors to production plans. The automated system allows companies to give different prices or terms to different trading partners. Sellers like the capability of an automated B2B system to provide fast settlement.

Many ways exist to establish a marketplace and many interaction styles also exist. If you go to `http://b2b.yahoo.com`, you'll see dozens of vertical markets run by Yahoo. Ebay is in the act at `http://pages.ebay.com/business_exchange`. You can buy everything from shop lathes to bandages in these specialized auctions. The Ebay and Yahoo online auction services offer an open and easy way to start using a simple vertical marketplace.

Dovebid.com, a company known for six decades as Dove Brothers, LLC, is a brick-and-mortar auction house for industrial materials that has gone click-and-mortar. Dovebid.com maintains vertical auction sites and does Webcasts of real-world auctions. The company has an agreement to feed B2B Yahoo, but Dovebid.com offers a wider range of services including equipment valuations and logistics support.

Although auctions can be a part of a B2B marketplace, the marketplace concept depends on facilitating customized relationships between buyers and sellers. Ariba, CommerceOne, and Trilogy are the heavyweights in the marketplace industry and each one partners with a mind-boggling list of companies acting as market makers in vertical marketplaces.

There's power in togetherness. Ariba, CommerceOne, and Trilogy each offer a central service that can cross-feed into sites with similar software. The Ariba Network, the CommerceOne Marketsite, and Trilogy's Buying Chain Marketplace each provide central services that can include applications for special orders, taxation advice, distribution services, invoicing, payment, and customized reports. So, for example, a market maker with a CommerceOne site in the automotive parts industry might link to Marketsite to order shipping services or perhaps electrical parts common to other types of businesses.

It's important to note that these central markets have real advantages for smaller buyers and sellers. Even if a big business has a regular set of suppliers in its own marketplace, it can also tap into the pool of suppliers entered into the central marketplace. Smaller buyers can benefit from volume discounts often given to any company purchasing through the common systems. Smaller sellers compete shoulder-to-shoulder with the big companies. However, each company in the system has total privacy and can reach special terms with any other company.

CASE STUDY

GUESS? CORPORATION

Headquarters: Los Angeles, California

www.guess.com

In January, 1999 the management at the clothing manufacturer Guess? committed to taking a leadership position in the apparel industry by embracing e-commerce. The first area they attacked was the supply chain because of its payback and cost containment virtues. The design was to create a specialized vertical portal for the common use of employees, suppliers, and retail partners. In effect, Guess? acts as an application service provider for smaller manufacturing and retail companies in the apparel industry.

But big technical and operational changes don't come easily. Bryan Timm, the CIO, and Craig DeMerit, the director of technology of Guess? recognized that they would need help in many areas of hardware and software and they also knew that the initiative would need broad support within the company. Their strategy included sending senior management to Silicon Valley to visit the upper management at Cisco and get a commitment to the project. They developed similar partnerships with Microsoft for software and with AT&T and SurfNet for connectivity. After investigating both Ariba and CommerceOne, they decided to acquire the CommerceOne software through PeopleSoft, a channel partner of CommerceOne.

This system is strategic for Guess? and its ROI is difficult to measure. Sure, Guess? will have better control over the cost of indirect goods, everything from floor wax to computer paper, and direct goods, the fabric and zippers. There should be good savings in both areas. But the real benefit of the system is that the company can extend its chain of suppliers to manufacturers of finished goods used by Guess?. This allows Guess? to uphold standards of quality in the raw materials and to influence manufacturing processes. In the end, this system cuts the planning, manufacturing, delivery, cycle time.

Inside Guess? the supply chain management system particularly changes the job of purchasing agents. They move from administrative details to working with suppliers to develop strategic sources and to managing relationships with suppliers for better efficiency of delivery and pricing.

Suppliers interact with the Guess? portal through a browser. Special functions enable the suppliers to upload catalogs, price lists, and inventory lists. Old habits die hard with many small suppliers, so often they elect to receive purchase orders through a fax generated by the portal software. They can elect to receive purchase orders through electronic document interchange, CXML, or email.

Each user of the Guess? portal sees a customized set of Web pages. All users enter the system after a check of their rights with a VeriSign server. The system displays the pages within the user's rights. Because this is an integrated portal, the same screens can lead to corporate email, scheduling, messaging, and human resources applications. The company has many road warriors managing its worldwide retail operations and, according to Craig DeMerit, the mobile users have really bought into the value of the portal.

DeMerit feels that it will be easy to scale up the portal system. The Microsoft IIS Web server software runs on multiple Compaq Intel-based servers running NT with distributed load balancing running under Cisco's Local Director. Plans call for balancing Web servers across multiple locations for even better system availability. A suite of application servers runs the PeopleSoft software with Windows NT and Microsoft SQL Server on clustered hardware. The application servers use multiple Xeon CPUs and at least 2 gigs of RAM. An Enterprise Storage system from EMC Corporation provides high availability centralized data storage.

Overall, the IS staff as Guess? takes a large role in project management, tries to get by with as little customization as possible, and relies heavily on their experienced system suppliers. That formula has resulted in an automated system that controls costs while leading the old and established apparel industry into e-commerce.

Ventro Corporation is a blossoming B2B market maker conglomerate with five operating companies: Chemdex in life sciences, Promedix in specialty medical products, Broadlane in high volume hospital and medical supplies, Industria Solutions (`www.industria.com`) in process plant equipment, and Amphire in the food service industry. Ventro bills itself as a builder of vertical marketplace companies, so it competes with and cooperates with companies acting as market makers, buyers, and sellers.

A new entry in the marketplace software arena, Firmbuy, started its service in early 2000, but its backers include iPlanet E-Commerce Solutions, a Sun-Netscape Alliance (which includes AOL), and other deeply connected companies. Firmbuy focuses on what are termed *indirect purchases.* Indirect goods are those that don't go directly into a manufactured product such as the supplies consumed in the maintenance, repair, and operation (MRO) of a corporate infrastructure. Direct goods go directly into finished products. Ariba and CommerceOne have a strong presence in the indirect procurement business, but they also focus on buying direct goods.

Buzzwords

MRO—Maintenance, repair, and operations. The common materials acquired through e-purchasing. MRO costs are indirect costs. Typically, many employees can purchase MRO products.

Commerce One Services

When you sell products in a B2B marketplace, the marketplace service companies make tools available that help you list your goods and take orders. On a CommerceOne Marketsite, here are some of the hosted applications used by suppliers. These hosted applications require a Web browser for access and will enable suppliers to manage their orders and update their catalog content at the CommerceOne MarketSite:

- **Catalog Management**

  Catalog Management is a simple and quick process to update product and service catalog information in the CommerceOne MarketSite.

- **Order Management**

  Receive, view, and manage purchase orders securely through a standard Web browser. Sort and search existing purchase orders to match specific business processes. Update purchase orders in real-time, so customers can quickly check order status through their electronic procurement applications.

- **Price Management**

  Adjust pricing for your buyers in real time to ensure your customers of the best possible deals!

- **Inventory Management**

  Keep your customers current with your latest inventory of your products and services.

The Ariba ORMS and ORMX software packages enable system designers to establish e-purchasing applications. The Ariba Network platform is a Web-based B2B meeting place that includes value-added services such as supplier content management and access to all manner of dynamic pricing models. The online system ties into the Ariba Internet Business Exchange and Ariba Market Suite, which contain specialty business exchanges and auctions in business areas that include consumer products, energy, financial services, transportation, and many others.

Similarly, Market Web is a well-established cluster of trading communities linked through the use of Commerce One software modules. A professional organization or similar group using Commerce One services sponsors each open community. If, for example, your company is a hospital or a physician's office, it might be a buyer on the Market Web Healthcare trade zone. Membership in a trade zone allows your employees to search general and specialized product catalogs online and to place orders within limitations set by your management. Typically, all that any individual sees of an e-purchasing system is a few customized Web pages. Indeed, simplicity for both the supplier and consumer is the goal of e-procurement.

If you're a supplier, each of these trade zones lets you connect once to hit many markets. Your catalog and order forms are available across many trade zones. Buyers pay $0.25–$2 per order, depending on volume. Suppliers list for free, but they must contribute the resources to keep their price, catalog, and inventory information up-to-date. Yes, suppliers would be smart to be in Ariba, Commerce One, and other public trade zones, but fortunately maintaining the catalogs and price lists in each zone isn't a technically difficult job.

While trading communities can work for suppliers and buyers in companies of any size, if you're big enough, the suppliers will come to you. But be aware that there's not much sense in setting up your own system if it's not tightly integrated into your manufacturing and accounting systems and that integration doesn't come cheap. If you can't think about budgeting $300–500K for a customized supply chain system, stay with a vertical community.

Often, large enterprises, governments, or institutions can provide so much business that each one is its own market maker. California State University, Fullerton, for example, created a marketplace using CommerceOne to handle about $25 million worth of purchasing annually. Single enterprise marketplaces like the one at CSUF or the similar one at UCLA probably handle a broader selection of products than those targeted at the raw materials and equipment for a specific industry, so they're sometimes called a horizontal marketplace.

Behind The Marketplace

You can be a marketplace seller or buyer, or you can run the marketplace and be a market maker. The initial cost of participating in a marketplace as a buyer or a seller depends primarily on how much integration you want with your manufacturing, inventory, and accounting systems. Companies can start by ordering with a browser, mailing in product information on floppy disks, and accepting orders on a fax, but system integration allows companies to smoothly scale up their operations.

Integration isn't an easy job, but a lot of help is on call. For example, Ariba's Web site lists many system integrators and application service providers that will weave marketplace procurement with existing enterprise management systems. But customized integration projects can take months and run into tens or hundreds of thousands of dollars.

In contrast, these systems don't need much hardware. High availability is important, but the workload isn't heavy, so a couple of dual-CPU servers will do. As the size of the database grows a storage plan such as a storage area network becomes necessary.

Market makers have few if any system integration worries. Often they just outsource the entire operation through the software vendor. But they must know the industry and the important players.

CHAPTER 4

e-Purchasing: One Stop Shop

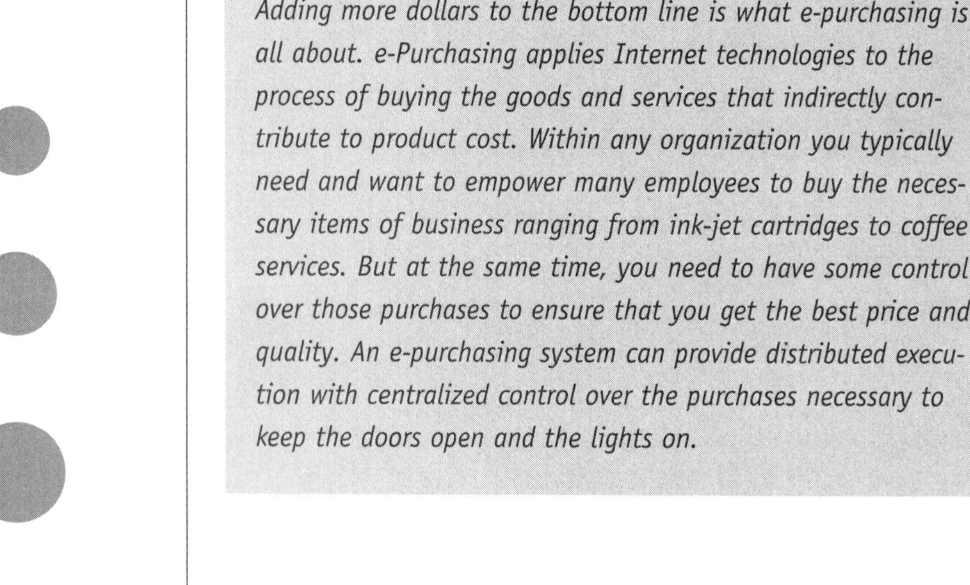

Adding more dollars to the bottom line is what e-purchasing is all about. e-Purchasing applies Internet technologies to the process of buying the goods and services that indirectly contribute to product cost. Within any organization you typically need and want to empower many employees to buy the necessary items of business ranging from ink-jet cartridges to coffee services. But at the same time, you need to have some control over those purchases to ensure that you get the best price and quality. An e-purchasing system can provide distributed execution with centralized control over the purchases necessary to keep the doors open and the lights on.

Crush your costs! Overhead costs can make even the most charismatic and financially savvy CEO look bad. Overhead does visible damage to a corporate balance sheet because it's subtracted as an indirect cost from the bottom line and highlights the difference between gross profit and net profit—a favorite measure of management effectiveness. A good portion of overhead costs, or what are called indirect costs, comes from MRO (maintenance, repair, and operations) services and supplies that include everything from floor wax, paperclips, light bulbs, and ladders to air travel and telephone services. As Table 4.1 shows, they're distinct from direct costs, which are the above-the-line costs of creating the goods or services your company provides. Table 4.2 spotlights differences between these costs.

Buzzword

e-Purchasing—Buying common products and services that a company needs in order to do business. Examples are light bulbs, computers, coffee service, and travel tickets. Many employees with different job titles who are placed throughout an organization often do this.

Who Needs This?

The bigger you are, the harder you'll fall for e-purchasing. Large and dispersed companies get the greatest benefit from controlling MRO purchases. However, even the smallest companies can take advantage of the catalog sales offered by outlets such as Grainger and Staples. Most companies that implement e-purchasing begin by using the online services of the suppliers they spend the most money with. This arrangement can provide immediate bang-for-the-buck and evidence of what a full e-purchasing system can do.

Buzzword

Direct costs are those costs paid for materials that go directly into the production of the product. They don't include the indirect costs of advertising, personnel, building space, and so on.

Table 4.1—Direct and Indirect Costs

Direct Costs:

- All purchases that go directly into the price of the goods or services
- Includes raw materials and manufacturing
- Above the gross margin line

Indirect Costs:

- All expenses that support keeping the business running
- Includes capital, travel, entertainment, marketing and sales, and MRO (maintenance, repair, and operations)
- Below the gross margin line

Table 4.2—Characteristics of Direct and Indirect Costs		
	Direct	**Indirect**
Immediately critical to the product?	Yes	No
Cost per purchase?	High	Low
Who buys?	Few	Many
What department?	Purchasing	Any
How approved?	Pre-purchase	Post-purchase
Control?	Tight	Light

Buzzword

Supply Chain Management—The supply chain feeds raw material into the manufacturing process. It's concerned with quality, quantity, delivery, timing, and payment.

Buzzword

MRO—Maintenance, repair, and operations. The common materials acquired through e-purchasing.

The merchandise marts and merchant districts of old economy cities provide a place for buyers and sellers with common interests to get the best prices and terms. The Internet fills the need with specialized Web sites called marketplaces (as discussed in Chapter 3, "Marketsites") and with vertical portals (see Chapter 2, "Vertical Portals for B2B") where people with similar business interests and needs can trade and talk B2B on a 24/7 basis. MRO suppliers have opened Internet stores with client services for good customers, and they post their catalogs on B2B marketplaces. But many ways are available to control your MRO purchasing costs on the Internet.

Buying a box of copy paper, airline tickets, and a ton of steel are each different processes involving different employees and different managerial controls, but Internet marketplaces can handle them all through the use of purchasing filters governed by buying rules. Within buying systems, managers can give specific individuals the rights to buy from specific categories of products, price limits, or product lists. Buying programs use workflow techniques to route actions

Workflow

A few years ago, software companies stirred up some excitement by introducing workflow software. The idea was that special programs would track the activity on specific files and alert workers and managers to the next step in a pre-defined process. Well, the work of setting up the process was hardly worth the effort, so these products disappeared as separate entities. The idea was turned on its head, and workflow control became a function built in to other special purpose programs such as e-purchasing.

Modern e-purchasing software knows who can make purchase requests of specific types and who must approve requests of specific types. Software can route actions appropriately and call for action as appropriate. These are the workflow elements of e-purchasing that provide convenience and control.

Buzzword

Marketplace—A specialized Web site containing catalogs, order forms, and other useful information provided by product suppliers.

e-Purchasing companies are still evolving their products. New developments include collaborative filtering software technologies that automate important parts of the purchasing process. For example, software using these technologies can analyze data and forecast product needs based on seasonal or regional data. This can help suppliers prepare for demand and help companies plan their purchasing more effectively.

Controlling MRO overhead is an important business practice, but it isn't easy. Employees resent what they see as unreasonable limitations placed on buying the supplies and tools they need to work, but management needs rules and an approval process. Management must somehow control what people buy and who does the buying to control both quality and cost.

Some organizations see centralized procurement and distribution schemes as the key to controlling costs. They run their own warehouses and have their own tricks. But these centralized systems generate their own overhead and are wide open to abuse. Most companies don't want to be in the business of warehousing and distributing their own supplies.

Progress can come around and bite you in another way. Some new B2B supply-chain management initiatives that reduce the cost of raw materials going directly into products can actually pinch your budget for MRO supplies. Accounting principles often cap the indirect budget as a percentage of the direct budget, so if you're successful in reducing the cost of the raw materials going into the product, you might find that you get less money for computers and printers! Strange but true! So, it's good to have a plan for controlling indirect costs as you enter into supply-chain management and other techniques for reducing direct costs.

Organizations from the U.S. government down to the corner grocery store struggle to control what they spend for the overhead items needed to keep the doors open. For example, the Government Services Administration (GSA) exists specifically to contain MRO costs. GSA was established in 1949 to avoid "senseless duplication, excess cost, and confusion in handling supplies." A message is here for all modern businesses. Today, the GSA has an online shopping mall that gives federal agencies access to 800,000 products and services, but businesses of any size can do the same thing on a more appropriate scale.

Easy to Start

Managers implementing some e-business services face the choice of building a system in-house or hosting in an outside service. This is particularly true, for example, of vertical portals. To get started in a portal requires a large minimum cost. But that's not true of e-purchasing.

You can start an e-purchasing system simply by asking all authorized employees to make purchases using a password and a browser and visit a specific supply Web site. (Office supply companies know this, which is why more and more of them are advertising their Web sites these days.) A company can test the e-purchasing waters by setting up an electronic purchasing system with only one large supplier to begin with. This can give a feel for the process and the possible effects of cost of operations both in-house and at the supplier's end. Or, if necessary, you can expand the system to include more checks, balances, and reports. But you have the opportunity to start e-purchasing activities quickly and with little or no cost. Figure 4.1 shows both e-procurement and e-purchasing. Table 4.3 lists some of the benefits of implementing an e-purchasing system.

Table 4.3—e-Purchasing Benefits

Startup costs:	Low
Installation time:	Small
Maintenance and operations costs:	One administrator
IT involvement:	Low
Administrative maintenance:	Low
Risk:	Low

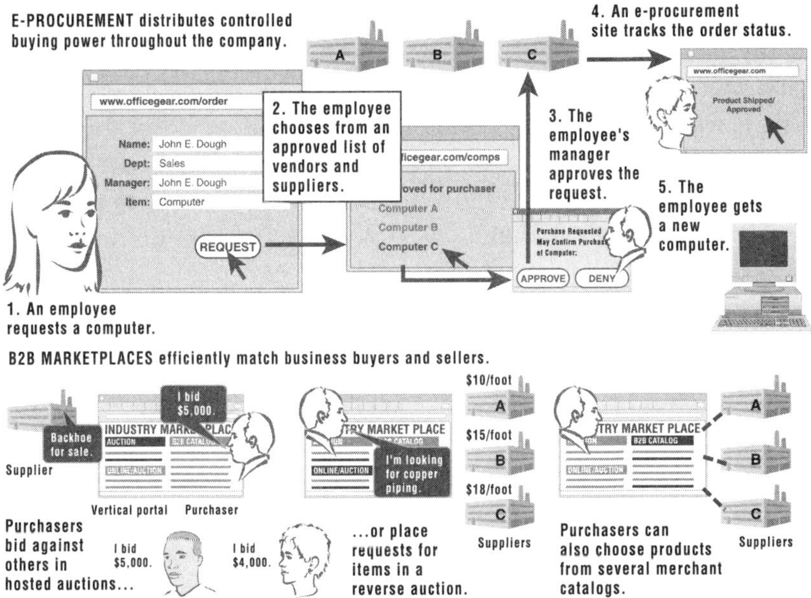
E-PROCUREMENT distributes controlled buying power throughout the company.
1. An employee requests a computer.
2. The employee chooses from an approved list of vendors and suppliers.
3. The employee's manager approves the request.
4. An e-procurement site tracks the order status.
5. The employee gets a new computer.
www.officegear.com/order
Name: John E. Dough
Dept: Sales
Manager: John E. Dough
Item: Computer
REQUEST
Computer A
Computer B
Computer C
APPROVE
DENY
www.officegear.com
Product Shipped/ Approved
B2B MARKETPLACES efficiently match business buyers and sellers.
I bid $5,000.
Backhoe for sale.
Supplier
Vertical portal
Purchaser
Purchasers bid against others in hosted auctions...
I bid $5,000.
I bid $4,000.
I'm looking for copper piping.
...or place requests for items in a reverse auction.
$10/foot
$15/foot
$18/foot
Suppliers
Purchasers can also choose products from several merchant catalogs.
Suppliers

Figure 4.1

e-Procurement and e-purchasing are each a component of B2B marketplaces.

Buying through the Internet enables managers to follow another good business practice: centralized guidance and decentralized execution. For example, by using the Grainger.com Web site, a company can establish a corporate account, authorize specific purchasing agents with specific capabilities, see the status of accounts and shipments at any time, and receive one consolidated bill. Grainger, Inc. is a 70-year-old distribution company that quickly took its 220,000 MRO products into the click-and-mortar era. Grainger's latest site, `OrderZone.com`, streamlines customers' purchasing processes across multiple suppliers.

Buzzwords

e-Procurement—Buying specialized goods, materials, and services that go directly into the finished product. Typically done by procurement professionals.

But ordering from just one company doesn't guarantee competition or lowest costs. Most managers would like to spread the competition and the risk by having several sources of supply. Competitive bidding is the policy in many organizations. You could, for example, increase competition by also opening a corporate account at the new `Stapleslink.com` Web site and receive consolidated discounts and billing on orders placed with Staples. Or, competing U.S. Office Products at `www.usop.com` will sell you everything from paper clips to coffee and vending machine services and consolidate your accounts.

"Wherever a need for a service exists, Web sites spring up to meet it."

Wherever a need for a service exists, Web sites spring up to meet it. Consolidated e-purchasing has spawned several online services offering routing of purchase requests for approval based on policies and rules, customized online catalogs, and reports to help you track spending and negotiate volume discounts. Trilogy Software's Buying Chain Internet Edition (`www.buyingchain.com`) carries goods and services, including travel services, from more than 150 suppliers.

Elcom.com, a "dot.com" startup that has become a leading global provider of remotely-hosted, Internet-based electronic procurement solutions for businesses, entered e-purchasing in several ways. `Starbuyer.com` is Elcom.com's digital marketplace, carrying office and computer products. Elcom.com also offers both online and in-house software approaches to e-purchasing. The PECOS Enterprise Procurement Manager is an application that creates an internal shopping mall for MRO. Elcom.com will manage the system, load it with appropriate catalogs, and help to develop specific rules for purchasing and approvals. The procurement system can have customized links to accounting, project management, and other resources. The enterprise system never has to touch the Internet, so internal security can be very tight. PECOS Internet Procurement Manager provides the same services, but hosted across the Internet.

Extensity, Inc. (`www.largesoft.com`) offers applications that you run on your own network to automate several administrative workflow processes including timesheets, travel planning, and purchase requests. The software provides templates for requests, routes requests for approval according to internal rules, and interacts with other applications such as accounting. The Java interface works with any browser and the application runs on Windows NT/2000 or Solaris server. Concur Technologies, a company that straddles the ERP and B2B markets with its Concur eWorkplace product, includes similar expense and procurement process control capabilities.

Because MRO purchasing is so important, it's also a logical area for the enterprise resource planning companies. PeopleSoft's Business

Network, developed with CommerceOne, is aimed squarely at MRO purchasing in the B2B marketplace model. PeopleSoft's Business Network is a Web-based application providing a single interface for purchasing all types of MRO goods and services.

The PeopleSoft Procurement Community is an Internet-based procurement application designed to link people, content, and commerce on the Internet. The PeopleSoft Procurement Community is based on Commerce One's Commerce Chain Solution, which includes Commerce One BuySite and Commerce One MarketSite. The integration with MarketSite.net provides PSBN customers with access to suppliers of many commodity groups. These include the following:

- Office Depot for office equipment and supplies
- Grainger and Graybar for lighting and electrical supplies and equipment
- PageNet for telecommunications media services
- Nokia for telecommunications equipment
- Wareforce and NECX for computers
- Unisource for cleaning equipment and supplies
- RoweCom for published products
- Standard Register for printing and audio-visual equipment and supplies
- Air Products and BOC Gasses for industrial chemical and gas materials
- Fisher Scientific for laboratory and testing equipment

If You're a Seller

The emphasis in this chapter is on the consumer side. We tell the stories of many large suppliers, but there's room in MRO for smaller sellers, too. You can join the CommerceOne or PeopleSoft systems, but the best approach for a small company is to ask big companies, government bodies, and institutions within the geographical area you serve if they have an automated purchasing system. You can typically join these systems without a charge.

I Need to See Some ID

Security is important in e-purchasing, and a function called *authentication* is a very important part of this kind of security. Basically, you must know that the person placing an order is really the person authorized to place the order. As you just have read, you can start walking the path of e-purchasing simply by creating an account at a vendor's Web site. But good business sense demands more secure procedures.

Buzzwords

Authentication—In this sense, proving a person's identity. The simplest authentication is a username and password.

If you haven't already instituted some authentication techniques stronger than passwords, it's time to start. Personal authentication products are practical today, and introducing them can be one of your initial steps toward establishing a modern e-business infrastructure. How do employees prove who they are regardless of where they are? That proof comes from personal authentication services using ID/password pairs, challenge response tokens, biometrics, or other devices to ensure a positive ID.

We describe authentication and directory services in Chapter 6, "Employee Access and Security," as part of an overall plan for single sign-on. You should check out the information there because the larger your organization, the more you'll need these features.

Buzzwords

Directory Service—A service, often contained in the operating system, that keeps track of the rights assigned to each user, the requirements of all applications and devices, and coordinates between authenticated users and the resources they have the rights to use.

e-Purchasing requires strong authentication. As a part of this, you'll need careful administrative control over passwords and any authentication devices. You'll need to set a good system of administrative practices in place and make them work.

B2B Goes MRO

It's logical for the B2B marketplaces to move into trading in indirect goods along with direct goods. As B2B meets MRO, direct and indirect purchases will still involve different people, types of products, and quantities, but B2B marketplaces can accommodate those differences. A company called ec-Content, Inc., a subsidiary of the venerable Trade Service Corp., specializes in MRO product catalog content. The company, which doesn't sell anything but information, is putting its MRO catalogs and pricing guides on the B2B marketplaces of many vertical market makers. It's also partnered with RightWorks, a B2B marketplace software and service company.

Ariba, one of the major B2B market companies, has a software module called ORMS that routes and applies rules to purchase requisitions and purchase orders, expense reports, and service requests. In a big move toward integrating B2B with MRO, Ariba and Grainger have agreed to make Grainger's catalog available to companies using Ariba's B2B Commerce Platform through the Ariba.com Network.

A new entry in the B2B marketplace arena, Firmbuy, started its service in early February, but its backers include iPlanet E-Commerce Solutions, a Sun-Netscape Alliance (which includes AOL), and other deeply connected companies. Firmbuy focuses on MRO purchases and provides the tools for controlling purchase order requests. An important goal is to consolidate orders among the users of the marketplace to gain better discounts. Setting high goals, Firmbuy manages and maintains standardized electronic catalogs containing over 2 million items from more than 7,000 manufacturers.

Buying common products across the Web isn't glamorous, but e-purchasing can cut costs and impose order while allowing employees to buy the things they need to support their work. It offers more accountability and security and can have a very big impact on the bottom line.

PART III

Business to Employees—Corporate Portals: Talking to Your Employees and Business Partners

CHAPTER 5

Corporate Portals: Multiple Doorways to the Treasures

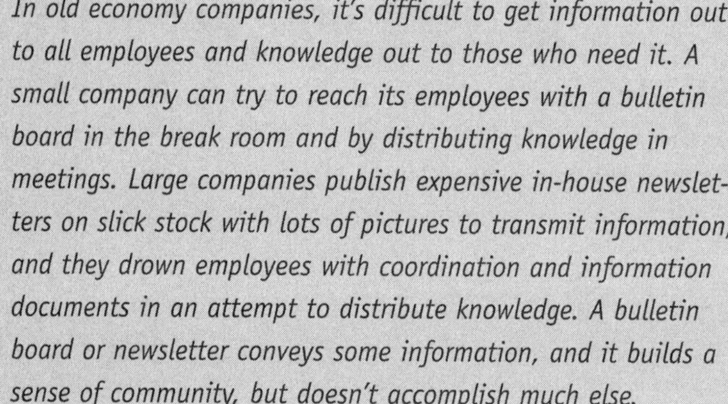

In old economy companies, it's difficult to get information out to all employees and knowledge out to those who need it. A small company can try to reach its employees with a bulletin board in the break room and by distributing knowledge in meetings. Large companies publish expensive in-house newsletters on slick stock with lots of pictures to transmit information, and they drown employees with coordination and information documents in an attempt to distribute knowledge. A bulletin board or newsletter conveys some information, and it builds a sense of community, but doesn't accomplish much else.

New economy companies have a Web-based way to move information and to build community better than a newsletter and to provide knowledge better than a mountain of memos or a week of meetings. Specialized in-house Web sites called corporate portals can do the same jobs as bulletin boards and newsletters, but they can also improve the handling and distribution of corporate publications, aid collaboration between employees, and improve knowledge efficiency. Because they link to email and can include online chat, they at least give the perception of being two-way. And all the employees need is a browser!

But the corporate portal is just the beginning of the leverage that organizations can enjoy by analyzing, coordinating, and facilitating the identification and internal exchange of information. The modern techniques include document management, knowledge management, data mining, email management, and collaboration. Each of these systems is aimed at helping everyone in the company know what they know and at sharing the knowledge. In addition to delivering the basic corporate communications, the corporate portal is the central gateway to these productivity tools.

In Chapter 2, "Vertical Portals for B2B," we introduced vertical portals, or *vortals*. In this chapter, we take the portal concept and bring it in-house for purely domestic consumption. We also use the portal as a gateway to other valuable e-business productivity tools that help manage and transfer information. A corporate portal is a Web site for employees—although it's often useful to give business partners and those with special relationships, such as the corporate accountant or legal firms, customized and limited access to the corporate portal. Think of a corporate portal as an in-house Yahoo! with embedded links to all your applications. In new economy terms, this portal is B2E(mployee). Each employee can receive or create a customized view and use the portal to access email; corporate documents such as memos and reports; policy and procedure manuals; business news; internal news; and corporate applications such as e-procurement, e-CRM, or enterprise resource planning programs. Yes, you can even have chat rooms.

Buzzwords

B2E—Business to employee

Buzzwords

Portal—A Web site that provides a variety of information presented the way you want it. Portals often function as directories for more specialized paths of interest.

Who Needs This?

A corporate portal becomes important when your operation gets so big that a manager can't interact with each employee everyday. A corporate portal is valuable when you want to provide a Web browser front end to your business applications and to make it easier for your employees to use applications. But regardless of the size of the company, a portal immediately becomes valuable when you have more than one operating location or more than two business applications. You should immediately consider establishing a corporate portal if you're engaged in a takeover or IPO to communicate with employees.

A long-term, but important, value of a portal is as an integrated, single point of entry to business applications. The corporate portal can give employees access to all appropriate business applications through a browser. A portal provides a major benefit by allowing a single sign-on step and a consistent user interface that lowers the cost of training and the challenges to employees using the system. This function is so important that we've set aside application integration and single sign-on and cover them in Chapter 6, "Employee Access and Security."

Some companies back in to the job of creating a corporate portal, whereas others meet it head-on, but both approaches meet at the same place: a single yet customized workspace for each employee. Some companies first see a corporate portal as a replacement for the company newsletter and the notices posted in the break room. Other companies quickly understand that a portal provides flexibility, security, portability, and efficient access to knowledge, and they want it all.

From the perspective of corporate management, when you bring all these information access and input points together onto one Web page for easy access, you can also capture, categorize, associate, and search all new and old information so it becomes knowledge. Software running within a portal can create links between pieces of accumulated information and data, and it can point to someone with real knowledge within the organization.

Buzzwords

Document management—This function, performed by special monitoring software, identifies and catalogs documents by key words, titles, or even word-by-word.

Four key portal-related terms are *document management, knowledge management, enterprise application integration (EIA),* and *collaboration.* Document management has been around for a long time. Many of us have at least investigated using products such as AskSam or PC DOCS to index key words or even every word of text in our documents so they become searchable, changeable, and easy to find. Document management tells you what you have and how to get it. Not surprisingly, it's an especially popular application in document-intensive fields such as law, law enforcement, medical record keeping, and library science.

Knowledge management is much newer. Now that it's easy for people to reach a store of information through browsers, it's also easier to categorize, link, and search that information. Knowledge-management software monitoring the corporate portal can tell you who was or is working with similar information and how it's linked to other information. One of the most common quandaries at any corporation, especially large geographically distributed ones, is wondering which employee has expertise and answers in a given area. Knowledge-management software can make finding that person as easy as typing in a keyword such as "surveys" or "statistics."

Buzzwords

Enterprise Application Integration (EIA)—Linking all business applications to provide a single sign-on for users, transfer of information between applications, and a common user interface.

Knowledge management benefits the organization by reducing the time spent searching, researching, and asking for information and expertise already existing in the company. Why spend the day running searches on the Internet or hiring an expert when someone down the hall recently wrote a memo on exactly what you want to know? When you're researching business alternatives, wouldn't it be nice to know that someone else went down the same path six months ago?

You Can Start Slow

In this chapter, we tell you about all the things a corporate portal can be. But don't think that you have to embrace all of this at once! It's prudent to start small, learn some lessons, and grow at a brisk pace. Use a portal as an adjunct or replacement for internal newsletters and let the employees become familiar with the idea.

Growing Your Portal

Backing in to portal creation means starting slow. A corporate portal can start life as just a Web site for company news on your local network. You can create portal pages using standard tools and provide links to Web-enabled applications. You can add syndicated news, weather, and other features using the techniques described in Chapter 2. Links to Web cams on the portal can provide views of the parking lot, the daycare center, and the coffeepot. You want to provide useful things that your employees can't get anywhere else. You can introduce the capability to publish documents and to search documents by adding products such as AskSam or NextPage. These affordable packages allow employees to publish,

Buzzwords

Knowledge management—This function, performed by special monitoring software, links document management, email management, and other similar functions to tell you who was or is working with similar information and how it's linked to other information.

search, and personalize information contained in many types of files.

You can build a nice corporate portal from bits and pieces. However, when you want to provide each person with an integrated and consistent view of all new and legacy applications, with full workspace customization and with single sign-on and tight security, you'll need some help to meet the project head-on. You want what several companies call an *Enterprise Information Portal (EIP)*—a term attributed to Merrill Lynch. DataChannel, Hummingbird Software, Plumtree software, and Viador are leading a pack of vendors with specialized B2E software.

Each portal product is a family of applications with many features and options. Portal security is important, so portal products tie to strong authentication techniques such as smart cards. After authentication, the software creates Web pages customized according to categories of users or by individual user. The products include some type of directory service to link users to resources and to provide the security control to applications and resources—particularly in larger networks. If you have existing business applications, portal designers can use gateways or scripts to bring data into the portal server and to cache and manipulate it for fast access and consistent format.

Across all these actions, the application integration features (discussed more in Chapter 6) provide a single common-user interface to all applications. A user can send email; enter information into a database; set alerts and alarms; search documents, records, and email; and collaborate while seemingly never leaving the portal. These vendors typically use Java and XML to create multiplatform applications providing the services inside the portal.

DataChannel is a relatively new company that used a base of XML expertise to create its DataChannel server. This product emphasizes a single look and a highly integrated employee workspace. The company states that you can't get this look with out-of-box solutions, so be prepared to spend time consulting with its VARs and business partners.

Hummingbird Software comes to B2E armed with strong experience in law offices and with a large family of programs. The venerable, but proven, PC DOCS document-management software, recently purchased by Hummingbird, has grown into a large software suite with applications for image databases, for many operating systems, and for Lotus Notes and Microsoft Exchange.

Plumtree Software, founded in 1996, claims to have started the corporate portal market, and the company has impressive lists of clients and partners. The Plumtree Corporate Portal Server runs on Windows NT/2000 and consists of components installed with a Web server to host the portal for users and a separate job server to process new information from data sources and applications. The job server doesn't depend on users to create links, but rather it looks for relationships between information coming in throughout the network, creates links, and notifies people interested in or working on specific topics. Plumtree has an especially strong set of integration tools that link the portal operation to existing business applications.

Viador, also founded in 1996, is in both the B2C and the B2B portal businesses. The company has special expertise in health care, government, and financial services and offers "ready to use" systems in these areas. The company's E-Portal Framework is a platform for quick development and deployment on a variety of operating systems, including Linux and HP-UX.

Tight integration of applications into a portal doesn't happen overnight. Starting a portal and growing it while getting user feedback is a good development plan. Finding a VAR with experience in your existing corporate systems and line of business is also a good idea.

"Tight integration of applications into a portal doesn't happen overnight. Starting a portal and growing it while getting user feedback is a good development plan."

If you want to get a quick start on a basic portal, you can contact companies such as Digex, Verio, or Exodus. These outsourcing companies can host a portal and handle the security and maintenance for low startup costs. Portals can be portable, so if you need to expand the service later, you can host it on other services.

Knowing What You Know

In today's turn-on-a-dime business climate, knowing what you know as an organization and acting on it are crucial parts not just of excelling but of surviving. Luckily, almost every company has vast stores of raw data and real-world experience. This information can be found in databases, document repositories, email, sales reports, and the heads of staff members. Yet accessing that data and massaging it into usable forms aren't always easy; doing both of these quickly enough to act in a timely manner can be all but impossible without a system in place to manage the information.

Knowledge management is one of those ephemeral terms that seems to mean nothing and everything simultaneously. During the past couple of years, it has been variously identified with document management, business intelligence, collaborative computing, corporate portals, and any number of buzzwords. But rather than a single product, knowledge management encompasses an overarching business strategy aimed at exposing and taking advantage of a company's information, experience, and expertise to serve customers better and respond quickly to changing market conditions. Figure 5.1 gives you an idea of how knowledge management works.

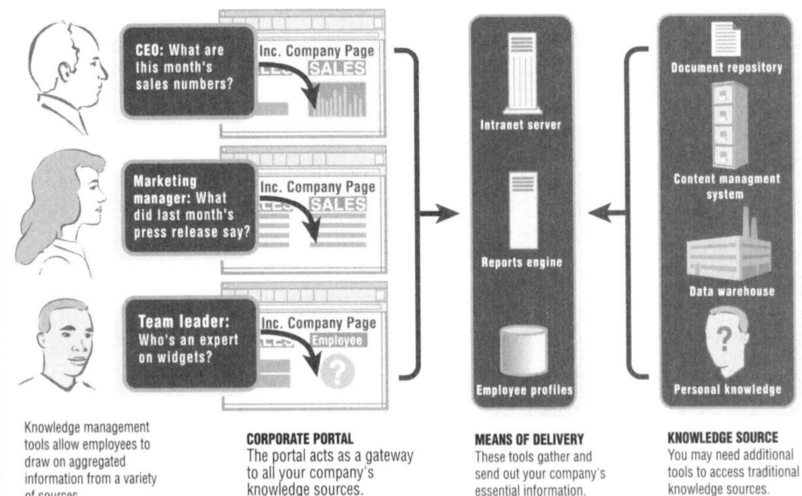

Figure 5.1

Knowledge management takes advantage of a company's information, experience, and expertise to improve customer service and respond quickly to changing market conditions.

"Knowledge management isn't about installing a package," says John Caffrey, director of knowledge management product marketing for Lotus Development Corp. "It's about taking action by leveraging your information resources." Tapping those resources, however, requires a collection of specialized products and platforms.

Business Intelligence

Understanding the external and internal forces that affect your company requires focused, in-depth analysis, which is where business intelligence—a knowledge management bellwether—comes in. Business intelligence consists of tools and technologies that generate surface-level and detailed reports and also provide the capability to drill down into hard-core data sources (this process is also known as *data mining* or *e-analytics*).

Identifying overall trends, especially in terms of sales information, is the unifying principle. High-powered databases are essential to any business-intelligence implementation, as is a well-defined data structure. These data structures, also known as *data warehouses*, are clumps of databases that hold related information. In addition, reporting engines, report-building software, and ad-hoc query tools, which often rely on online analytical processing (OLAP) technology, can be found in any business intelligence arsenal. Though many companies populate this space, Brio Technology, Business Objects SA, Cognos, Hyperion Solutions Corp., IBM Corp., and Seagate Software are market leaders. Ardent Software, maker of DataStage, was acquired by Informix Corp. and has also emerged as a formidable player—as have several e-business–oriented companies such as InterWorld Corp. and NetGenesis Corp.

In addition to providing products for internal business intelligence, such as the Cognos Impromptu and Business Objects' eponymous suite, the established players offer products optimized for delivering reports on the Web and on-the-fly query capabilities over the Internet. These products include Seagate Software's Analysis Suite, PowerPlay Web from Cognos, and WebIntelligence from Business Objects. The obvious benefit is the convenience of providing your employees with access to reports anywhere. The new, Webified business intelligence suites are also transforming data-mining and analysis into customer-facing services—an indication of how the worlds of e-business and knowledge management are colliding.

"Instead of only using business intelligence internally, we're now seeing more and more companies extending it outside of the corporation to their customers," says Keith Gile, an analyst with Giga Information Group. "Companies are starting to use their business intelligence investments to extend customer service by providing direct online information services."

Document, Content, and Email Management

Just as important as the hard numbers found in sales reports are the so-called "soft" knowledge assets buried in text documents, spreadsheets, Web pages, and even email. A range of solutions is available to help manage and make the most of the information in those types of files. The first and most established set of products consists of document-management systems. These products have enjoyed great success in the pharmaceutical and insurance industries, which require massive document-creation processes and document stores for patent and claims filings. Documentum, Open Text Corp., and PC DOCS/Fulcrum, a division of Hummingbird, have dominated this space, offering products such as DocsFusion, Documentum 4i,and WorkSmart.

Typically, document management systems are two- or three-tiered, with all arrows pointing to preserving document integrity and document classification, so the user can find documents easily during searches. The first layer is usually a file server containing both the documents and the classification information. The second layer consists of client software for accessing the system (though this task is increasingly handled by a Web browser). The third tier has to do with the business logic behind how documents are created and routed to the appropriate individuals for editing and approval.

Though these systems are becoming browser-accessible, document management vendors were somewhat slow to address the effect of Internet technology and the increasing need corporations have to manage content on both intranets and public-facing Web sites.

This, in turn, opened the door for companies such as InterLeaf, which is now owned by BroadVision; Interwoven; NetObjects; and market leader Vignette Corp., all of which provide content management solutions. NetObjects's Collage and Interwoven's TeamSite target intranets, whereas BroadVision/InterLeaf's BladeRunner and Vignette's StoryServer are all-in-one solutions for handling both intranet and Internet content on one platform. Increasingly, content management players such as Vignette and Interwoven also specialize in automatic translation of content to other languages. This translation can help automate taking a corporate portal global.

As opposed to focusing on document repositories and routing capabilities, these solutions facilitate the creation of and access to Web-based content through a variety of front-end tools, including word processing programs and Web-authoring tools. Like document management solutions, they do so without requiring users to program or (in the case of content management) know anything about HTML. As of today, many companies still need both a document management and a content management solution for a well-rounded knowledge management implementation. According to a study from International Data Corp., however, this is beginning to change rapidly, as the two categories have begun to morph into one. "Content management and publishing tools have begun to infiltrate the traditional market for document management," said Amie White, an analyst with IDC and author of the study. "The desire to get the most up-to-date information into the hands of the users that are throughout the supply chain is really driving this whole market."

Another knowledge store is email. When you consider the sheer volume of email that flows through your organization, you begin to get a feel for the wealth of information it contains. Products such as IBM's Intelligent Miner for Text can help sort and archive email into buckets of categories based on words found in the text of messages.

> *"When you consider the sheer volume of email that flows through your organization, you begin to get a feel for the wealth of information it contains."*

KnowledgeMail, from Tacit Knowledge Systems Corp., takes a more radical approach to ferreting out valuable information buried in email. The company's KnowledgeMail and KnowledgeMail Plus products aren't email archivers; instead, they use a profiling engine to dig through company emails and figure out the areas in which individuals are experts. Though an individual's profile is built using automated processing, the ultimate approval of its accuracy is left up to the individual, who can also choose whether to make the profile available for public consumption. In addition, these same profiles can be used to route email messages or news stories to the appropriate people within an organization. "The knowledge in people's heads doesn't get stored on a server somewhere, but there's lots of it floating around in email," said David Gilmour, the founder and CEO of Tacit Knowledge Systems. "The kinds of profiles this system builds help broker the right kind of people relationships, which is what makes businesses go."

Knowledge Management Platforms

As you can see, it takes a lot to figure out what you know. There are plenty of solutions that handle portions of your knowledge potential, but tying the components together has proved to be a consistent and daunting challenge. Industry heavyweights Lotus and Microsoft have for years been promoting the idea of knowledge management platforms into which solutions such as the ones previously mentioned can be incorporated. In addition, FileNET Corp., which pioneered the workflow software space in the mid-1980s, has come to market with its Panagon platform and product suite, which has slightly different components but the same theme.

"You want to make knowledge management a seamless, transparent, back plane throughout your organization, which is an organizing principle for our product line," said Bart Wojciehowski, director of strategic marketing at Microsoft Corp. "This helps the principles and practices of knowledge management become infused into a person's day-to-day workings without anyone having to deal with a knowledge management system per se."

In Microsoft's framework, Microsoft SQL Server 7.0 handles data-warehousing and business intelligence responsibilities, Microsoft Exchange accounts for the collaboration and communication piece, and Microsoft Office 2000 has basic content and document management features built in. In addition, Microsoft launched its Digital Dashboard strategy and product offering at the end of last year. Digital Dashboards, which ride atop the Microsoft Outlook client, compose the corporate portal element of Microsoft's approach by providing unified access to various data sources.

Another piece of the system is Microsoft's Web Parts initiative. This initiative extends Dashboards beyond information stores contained within Exchange and SQL Server 7.0. Web Parts, XML wrappers that can be embedded into Digital Dashboards, are consistently displayed windows to other applications and data sources that will be built by individual companies as well as third-party vendors.

The FileNET Panagon product line also leverages a common platform to provide an array of knowledge management functionality. The Image and Content services in Panagon provide standard document management as well as the ability to store and search scanned documents. The FileNET Web-publishing application enables businesses to publish information contained within the Image and Content services repositories to an intranet site or a public-facing Web site. It has catapulted its workflow technology from a means of automating internal processes to a new e-business level.

The latest version of FileNET's workflow engine is built to automate processes across organizations, which Michael Harris, vice president of product marketing, maintains is of paramount importance, particularly in business-to-business scenarios. "If you want to automate your entire e-business process, this isx what next-generation workflow technology can do for you," Harris said. "You can automate the process from the guy who provides materials to the people putting those together in your factory."

At Lotus, the long-awaited Raven platform is the glue that holds Lotus's extensive line of knowledge management and collaboration products together. These include Notes R5, which has text-mining, instant-messaging, and Web-collaboration capabilities built in; Domino.Doc, a document and content management product; and Domino Workflow, among others.

Raven consists of a discovery server that trolls through various information sources and builds a map that clusters related files together, along the lines of Yahoo!'s topical organization of the Internet. In addition, the discovery server watches the way people use the content and begins to build expertise profiles, à la KnowledgeMail, based on these interactions.

e-Business means making standard business practices more efficient through the use of Internet technologies. The most successful businesses become successful because of the talents of their employees and their special skills. Every business needs to understand who excels at which tasks within the organization, how the company is performing, and how that information can help serve customers. And that's where knowledge management tools can help. The phrase "knowledge is power" has never been truer.

Productive Collaboration

Tools such as knowledge management, document management, and business intelligence systems work from the past to the present. But then you must move forward. Collaboration among employees is another important corporate function that can start at the corporate portal. Figure 5.2 shows collaboration in action.

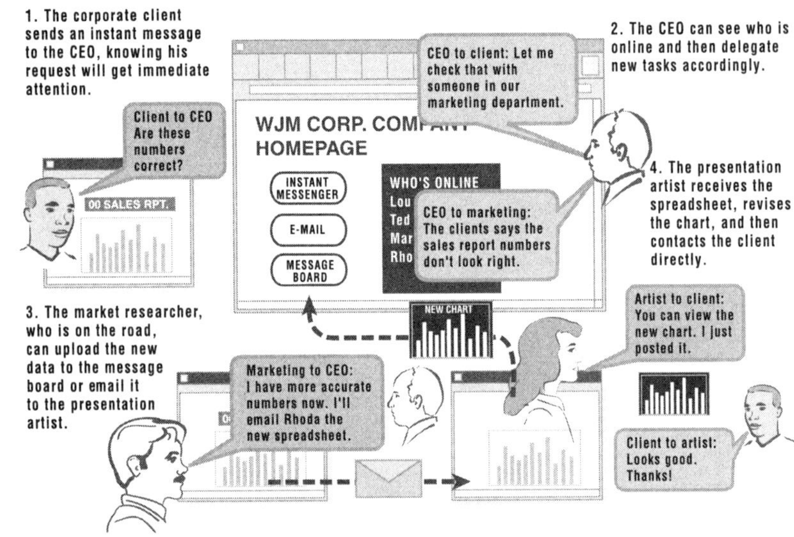

Figure 5.2
Your corporate portal can facilitate employee collaboration.

Arranging for face-to-face collaboration with colleagues is a difficult prospect at best. Odds are that you're busy when co-workers are available, and when you're available they're traveling. The problem is only heightened when you need to collaborate with customers—as a consulting firm does—or with colleagues who work from home. In some cases, you can't even find a moment to schedule a meeting, let alone an opportunity to hold that meeting. Telephones can help, but they don't allow visual or textual interaction. Email discussions provide the textual interaction, but they can be disjointed and disorganized; related messages are invariably scattered throughout in-boxes, and important documents (if not multiple copies of important documents) are often sent floating around a company's network.

You and your colleagues can interact more effectively, and your company can run more efficiently, using a networked collaboration application, also known as *groupware* or *teamware*.

Buzzwords

Groupware—is a term that includes many types of collaboration, conferencing, and discussion software packages.

Consulting Through Collaboration

Halverson Consulting, a small Chicago firm that helps businesses hire and retain employees, uses HotOffice, a Web-based collaboration service. HotOffice gives Halverson a private Web site on which employees and customers can post messages, share files, and schedule meetings. Halverson employees work in multiple locations, and they collaborate with remote customers regularly. "We needed the ability to share documents on an internal level," says Halverson senior director Greg Sekowski, "and also to share documents and meeting notes and meeting schedules with clients." In dealing with such tasks, HotOffice alleviated the company's dependence on email. "It really did cut a lot of time," explains Ron Halverson, the company's principal "to say, 'Go to the site and you'll get the most current information.'"

Five or six years ago, access to groupware required a LAN, high-end client/server software, and extensive IT support, but the Internet has made collaboration software a viable option for even very small companies. Today, Web-hosted collaboration tools are legion. Of course, companies can host their own collaboration tools, be they solutions akin to HotOffice or enterprise-level packages offering a broader range of applications. Each service is designed for a particular market segment but needn't be limited to that segment. Though HotOffice is intended for internal use, any two people can use it to collaborate. "This is rapidly moving toward what I would define as corporate portals for small business," says Eric Klein, senior analyst at the Yankee Group.

Mimicking an Intranet

Typically, we call a tool designed for internal company collaboration a *virtual office* or, somewhat paradoxically, an *intranet*. Strictly speaking, an intranet is an IP-based network used internally; access to a service like HotOffice requires using the Internet. Similar services are available from such companies as Intranets.com, Planet Intra, and Visto Corp.

A virtual office enables collaboration through a strictly defined set of applications. Each person working on a particular project can access folders and read the documents posted; some can make changes to those documents. HotOffice lets you track and control such changes, a crucial feature. The service also includes a bulletin board, a group calendar, personal calendars, virtual meeting rooms for real-time chat, and private email. All are important applications that you'd use over an office network, but HotOffice is cheaper and easier to maintain. In fact, if you're willing to endure banner ads, you can use HotOffice free.

Hosted Extranets

If HotOffice offers intranets, Agillion offers extranets. According to Steve Papermaster, Agillion's cofounder, cochairman, and CEO, his firm "lets companies—especially smaller companies—organize and manage all their customer relationships, customer profiles, customer contacts, customer information, and business partner information in such a way that anybody in the company or their customers can all have access to the same information in the same form at the same time." With a single subscription to the service ($29.95 per user per month), you can create multiple private Web sites and customize those sites freely.

"You're in control of it," said Papermaster, "so the customer can fully engage with you or anyone else you've given access to. They can ask you questions, they can buy things, they can request changes."

Just as HotOffice lets Halverson collaborate with its customers, Agillion can also be used for internal collaboration. And eRoom Technology offers a free-form space much like Agillion's—connecting your employees with one another as well as with customers.

In-House Software

The evolution of software makes it possible to use collaboration tools as hosted services or as applications installed on your own servers. Planet Intra enables you to install its software (Planet Intra 2.3)—document sharing, a calendar, a contact manager, threaded discussions, and other common collaboration tools—on your own servers, if you prefer.

Lotus Development Corp., an IBM company, has long been dominant in the high-end collaboration software market. Lotus QuickPlace, not a hosted service per se, rivals free-form collaboration software such as Agillion. Several Lotus partners do offer QuickPlace hosting.

Lotus's leading collaboration tools primarily use client/server architectures. Lotus Domino for enterprise environments is essentially an application server, with threaded discussions, document sharing, email, and more. Lotus Notes, among other clients, can access the server. Notes can also pull information from the Internet and traditional databases. Direct competitor Microsoft Exchange Server provides similar capabilities.

For real-time collaboration over your LAN, the company offers Lotus Sametime, which includes text chat and whiteboard applications as well as application sharing. With this client/server tool, said Sametime product manager Tim May, "People can remain, for the most part, at their current location and share information back and forth with each other—not only documents and presentations but applications."

Though Sametime provides a much higher level of interaction than an asynchronous collaboration tool (such as Domino or HotOffice), the latter is more advantageous in other situations, letting people collaborate even if they're not available at the same time. The tools are complementary, and both have clear advantages over more typical communication tools.

The High Value of Portals

From myriad solutions, one conclusion is clear. As Mickey Freeman, senior vice president of marketing and sales at HotOffice Technologies, puts it: "A business can't live on email alone." Corporate portals, tied into applications and providing important functions such as document tracking and collaboration, are powerful tools for leveraging the productivity of any organization.

CHAPTER 6

Applications, Integration, and Access

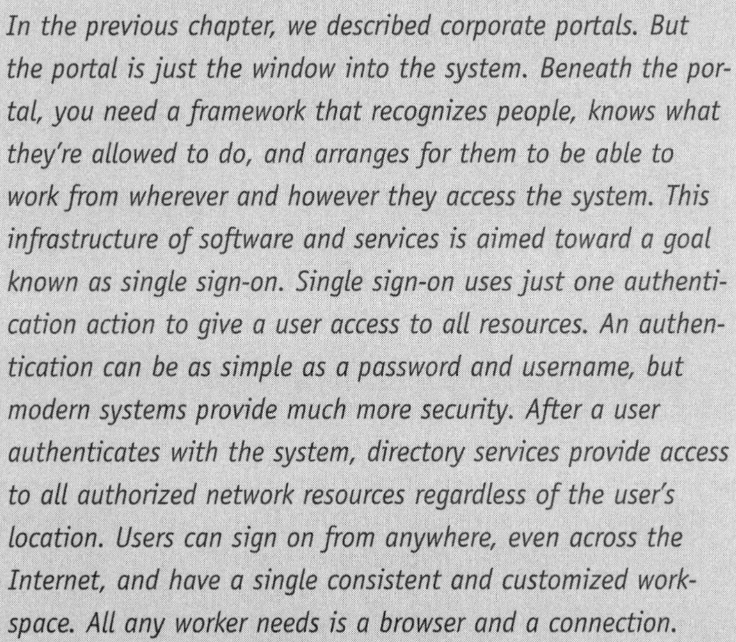

In the previous chapter, we described corporate portals. But the portal is just the window into the system. Beneath the portal, you need a framework that recognizes people, knows what they're allowed to do, and arranges for them to be able to work from wherever and however they access the system. This infrastructure of software and services is aimed toward a goal known as single sign-on. Single sign-on uses just one authentication action to give a user access to all resources. An authentication can be as simple as a password and username, but modern systems provide much more security. After a user authenticates with the system, directory services provide access to all authorized network resources regardless of the user's location. Users can sign on from anywhere, even across the Internet, and have a single consistent and customized workspace. All any worker needs is a browser and a connection.

Making single sign-on possible involves using a single directory service to describe a user's rights and using various forms of authentication, including advanced techniques such as biometrics and smart cards, to ensure identity. You might also roll in certificate services so your company can share information on rights and authentication with its business partners. Virtual private networks (VPNs) bring in the data carefully packaged and encrypted. But competing directory architectures and different certificate services exist. Setting up a directory service is the equivalent of entering into a marriage. It's a big deal.

While you're sorting out the problems of single sign-on, you should simultaneously make it easier for all users to see, access, and change information in applications. Old stovepipe application connections assume that every user is identical and usually demand unique client software, such as the clients for Notes or many database programs. That era is over. People want to use applications through browsers and those browsers might be in cell phones, WebTV devices, or other hardware clients. Modern development tools such as Java or XML provide ways to link applications without massive re-writes.

Bringing Employees into e-Business

Fast companies beat slow companies of all sizes, so your company can either use Internet technology to face the problems of money, people, and crazy business cycles, or be rolled over by those that do. In the previous chapter we described corporate portals that provide employees with access to applications and services such as document management, knowledge management, and collaboration. But successfully integrating all this data for e-business requires more than establishing a portal site. If you want the fullest integration, you and your staff must solve some tough software infrastructure problems.

Who Needs This?

The need for a strong software infrastructure is, unfortunately, a penalty of growth. Bigger companies need better infrastructures simply because they have more employees using more resources.

Small companies can probably benefit most from strong authentication techniques. These techniques can be relatively low cost and potentially they can have a high payback.

It's easy to list the newest challenges in any IS manager's life:

- Cope with the burgeoning telecommuters, mobile workers, and small remote offices.
- Reach your employees and business partners with fast and reliable information and service no matter where they are.
- Maintain security and privacy.

Simplifying everything for your users, business partners, and clients while ensuring reliability is key to a strong software infrastructure. As we said in Chapter 1, "What is e-Business?" e-business is all about facilitating relationships. The description of the perfect e-business system sounds so logical: The network should know each user and provide customized access to everything each user has the right to see or use from anywhere they happen to be. This flexible and customized connectivity should work quickly and invisibly. The common interface to all applications should be through the browser.

Buzzwords

ERP—Enterprise Resource Planning—Large software systems that encompass accounting, human relations (HR), and perhaps functions such as shipping, inventory, ordering, and receiving. The systems include many reports.

But what seems so logical is, overall, the toughest challenge in twenty-first century computing. Today's applications, from email to ERP, are individual stovepipes. What goes down one pipe doesn't impact any other pipe and you often must make a new connection to access each pipe. The whole system must be woven together. A corporate portal is only the visible top of the system, and the larger the enterprise or the greater the number of applications, the bigger the problem.

The Problems Are?

Here are the problems:

- If an application has a sign-on, authorization, and security scheme, it's often proprietary and unique.
- The applications don't interact (except badly) with other applications.
- People want to move around, so it's no longer enough to tie authentication and access to one physical location.
- Some people have rights to one application, but not to others. So you can't have just one security door. You need personalization and selectivity.

Infrastructure Is More Than Hardware

It's interesting to observe how little attention we give to the hardware side of the infrastructure these days. Vendors have worked for a decade or more to make hardware a commodity. Today, the term "infrastructure" involves a spectrum of functionality that includes services provided within operating systems and from specialized directory and security programs. Modern e-business infrastructures should be use standardized and general-purpose products. That's how you design for scalability and flexibility.

Buzzwords

Authentication—The most common form of authentication is a username and password. But this authentication requires strong administrative practices, including secrecy and frequent changes, to be more than marginally effective. More convenient and effective authentication schemes include biometrics and smart cards.

Three Tasks

We've broken down the job of fixing the stovepipe condition into three major tasks that we identify as creating single sign-on, single access, and application integration. Each of these tasks is implemented through the structure of software and services. Single sign-on means one authentication once from anywhere. The buzzword that describes the process of combining application stovepipes for single access is EAI, enterprise application integration.

Creating Single Sign-On

Is this your day? First you log on to your computer, the file server, the print server, the mail server, and maybe even the secure firewall. After that, you log on to the applications you use every day. Add online shopping, more email accounts, and a stockbroker and you can be juggling a dozen passwords. Perhaps your IS manager automated some of those interactions with a logon script, but then how do you get to anything if you're not at your own computer? Single sign-on from anywhere is the hope of users and IS managers, but it isn't easy to do. Figure 6.1 shows how an ideal single sign-on system works across an e-business infrastructure. Personal authentication services, directory services, certificate services, authorization checking, and various forms of encryption all combine to enable single sign-on.

Buzzwords

EAI—Enterprise application integration. Providing a way for applications to exchange information and to use common stores of information.

Looking toward the future, we aren't very far away from providing individuals with an electronic identity bubble in the form of a wireless personal area network that identifies them to any resource from an ATM to a refrigerator. But even then we'll need the back end of directory and certificate services.

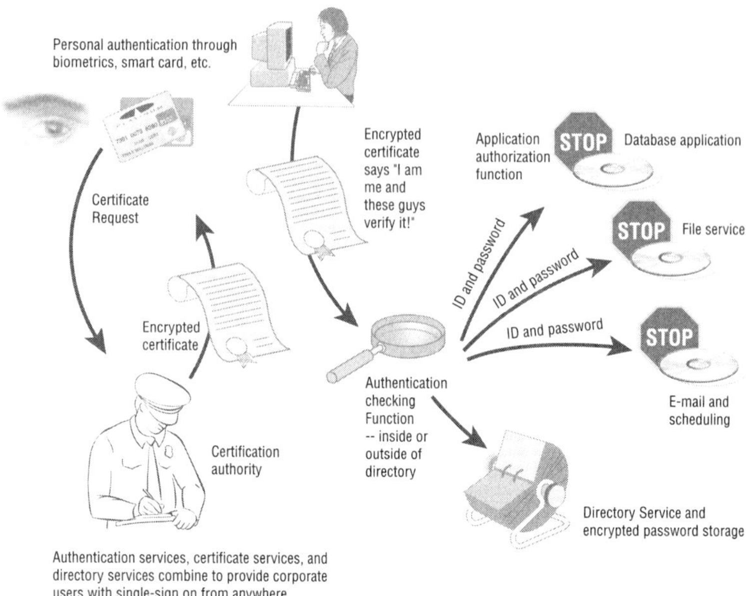

Figure 6.1

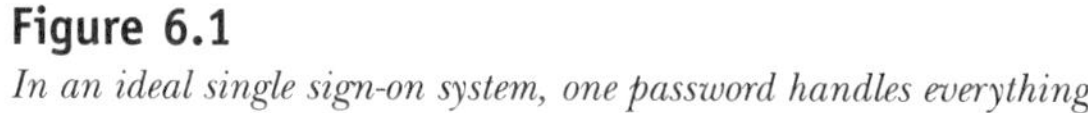

In an ideal single sign-on system, one password handles everything.

Buzzwords

Single Sign-on—The ability for an authorized person to sign on the network from anywhere using only one form of authentication and have access to all resources without any further authentication.

Sage Advice

We think that if you're a smart manager making e-business bets, you should move quickly into strong personal authentication services, particularly smart cards and biometrics. You should also strike a deal with a certificate service, set up a test bed for directory services, and start to invest in encryption wherever there is a threat. Those actions will take you on the road to single sign-on, but strong authentication is the first step.

Directory services have gotten a lot of press because Microsoft entered the market with Windows 2000, but directory technology isn't anything new. A list of companies including Unisys, Computer Associates, Hewlett-Packard, IBM, Bull, and Tivoli have offered directory solutions, but large price tags and lack of interoperability limited their adoption.

In recent years the Novell Directory Service (NDS) and the Novell ZenWorks software family have made inroads as tools hailing from the network-centric crowd. Microsoft's Active Directory (AD), shipping with Windows 2000, entered the market just as managers started to understand or admit the need for universal directory services.

Big Guys Go, Little Guys Hold Back

Bringing a directory service to life is a big project that benefits from experience, but very little of that is around. If you have a network with a few hundred nodes or less, we advise waiting and using existing server naming schemes, access control lists, group policies, and login scripts for a year or so. By then, the industry may build the skills and tools to make installation of a directory system cheaper and easier. If you're expanding like crazy and need directory services right away, then look for experienced help.

Buzzwords

Directory Service—A service, often contained in the operating system, that keeps track of the rights assigned to each user, the requirements of all applications and devices, and coordinates between authenticated users, and the resources they have the rights to use.

Integration between applications, operating systems, and directory services is a problem. That's why we recommend starting with a test bed and, above all, looking for interoperability between your applications, operating systems, and any directory service you choose.

The ideal solution for interoperability, but not for full service, is the Lightweight Directory Access Protocol (LDAP). But do you see the word "access"? LDAP is a standard describing a client/server process for accessing directory services. It isn't the complete model. The LDAP model allows entries to contain information about an object, device, service, or person. The information can include photographs, sounds, and encrypted information such as passwords and encryption keys. LDAP provides standardized ways to store, retrieve, and create this information, but vendors vary in how they structure the authentication and authorization functions.

Right now, we believe that your best bet is to plan on using NDS or AD inside the company and an LDAP directory for connections outside the company with a planned migration to a LDAP in the more distant future. Microsoft and Novell agree on the value of LDAP, but they each add more proprietary features.

Buzzwords

LDAP—Lightweight Directory Access Protocol. An agreement describing how applications and directories will exchange and access information about users, devices, and applications.

Is one clearly better than the other? No, so that's why we suggest starting with a test bed. Windows 2000 contains an LDAP server and applications can use AD's features through LDAP. NDS also offers LDAP access, and Novell's NDS eDirectory is an LDAP-based add-in product for NT, NetWare, and Solaris that has strong industry endorsements. If you want an LDAP standards-based directory today, iPlanet sells the Netscape Directory Server, which is popular with the e-commerce Web crowd and extranets. In times of confusion somebody must prosper, and Oblix is an example of one company that is calming the waters and providing products to build e-business solutions on LDAP. The company offers tools for managing users and integrating information within directory architectures.

Linux/Open Source

With less than 2% of total retail sales being done on the Web, and business-to-business exchanges still in embryo stage, commerce sites of all kinds will be expanding their own technology platforms in the years to come. So will ISPs, ASPs, and Web hosting providers. The expansion will be expensive, in what are seen as some of the world's most competitive markets. Free platform technologies from the Linux and Open Source arenas may flourish.

Buzzwords

Metadirectory—A metadirectory is actually a process that translates between various types of directory entries. Since we don't have agreement on entry formats, a metadirectory provides the Rosetta stone.

One of the practical problems of creating a directory service is that people in different parts of the organization might not agree on a naming scheme, might already have a naming scheme, or might bring one with them through merger or acquisition. If you're in this fix then you need a software product called a *metadirectory*. A metadirectory can synchronize between two or more existing directory services. One directory can act as the master or the metadirectory can act as a master. Metadirectories can also be used to add secure access to applications such as HR or ERP across the enterprise. These solutions should leave the server security routines alone and offer an easier migration path to future LDAP directories.

However, metadirectories, like most things in the directory market, are still young products. The big three directory companies have announced their meta-directions—Microsoft's ZoomIt Corp's technology integrated with Active Directory; Novell's announced DirXML metadirectory; and iPlanet's Netscape Meta-Directory. Isocor has its MetaConnect product, which also forms the basis for IBM's SecureWay, an integrated directory, connectivity, and security platform. The tools and expertise are out there, but they're both still rare and expensive.

RadiantLogic offers its RadiantOne Virtual Directory Server that provides access to different corporate databases through an LDAP directory entry the company calls an *Information Resource Locator (IRL)* interface to different corporate databases. Implementing a metadirectory can be an expensive multiyear project and still too much proprietary technology exists to make most managers comfortable; however, the long term return on investment should be very high on big networks.

Buzzwords

XML—Extensible Markup Language. XML is the most popular and practical language for e-business, although it now has many extensions and special libraries.

Encryption

Encryption is a specific technology that you should apply at several levels. But, because it carries its own costs and penalties, the key to using encryption is to judge the threat. Encryption is critical to virtual private network communications channels, authentication services, and certification systems. Directory services are encrypted and they might contain stores of encryption information. You can protect files in servers using encryption in the operating systems and even encrypt communications down to the desktop using a product like 3Com's Typhoon Encryption NIC. But encryption soaks up bandwidth, throughput, and processing power, so our advice is to use appropriate encryption to meet the threat. If you are only protecting inventory and shipping records, 40-bit encryption will keep you safe from a casual system crasher. If you're guarding large amounts of money or corporate secrets, 1024-bit encryption of files isn't too much.

Many companies are working on more robust security technologies and standards. A wave of new approaches to security technologies is expected in 2001 because the patent on RSA's ubiquitous public-key encryption algorithm will have expired, allowing it to slip into the public domain. Also, Congress passed legislation to allow far-reaching, easy authentication of digital signatures on the Internet, which should help commerce sites of all kinds more easily consummate contractual agreements and eliminate paperwork. Meanwhile, the World Wide Web Consortium is backing many standards—such as SDML and XML-based schemes—for implementing digital signatures.

Buzzwords

Digital Signatures—The U.S. Electronic Signatures in Global and National Commerce Act of 2000 paved the way for the use of digital signatures. This act gives the force of law to digital signatures affixed to broad categories of documents. But digital signatures depend on strong authentication services.

Importantly, if you don't take steps to provide strong authentication, strong encryption hardly matters. Although today's most common use of encryption is SSL used with secure Web servers, it uses strong encryption without strong authentication. Business-to-business e-commerce demands both strong authentication and encryption. So let's see how people authenticate themselves.

Buzzwords

SSL stands for secure sockets layer. The term describes a method of encrypting the data stream between a browser and a Web server. People use SSL everyday to retrieve financial information and for ordering through Web sites.

Directory services identify users and resources, but certificate services and the public key infrastructure (PKI) assure that the appropriate people use them in e-business. Inside a network, each major operating system has an internal network authentication service based on what is called the Kerberos client/server authentication protocol. Although Kerberos works well inside a corporate network, it is complex for e-business, and PKI has a brighter future. Think of PKI's trust management much like the government granting a passport or the division of motor vehicles granting a driver's license. In both cases, a trusted entity issues a document that identifies a person and some associated rights. As long as you believe in the trusted entity, you can believe in the individual. In the PKI realm, an organization called the certificate authority (CA) serves as the trusted entity that identifies individuals or companies and issues a digital certificate that is tied to those entities.

Buzzwords

CA—Certificate authority. An organization that people agree to trust. The CA issues certificates of authenticity for identities, software, and transactions.

What is PKI?

The term public key encryption describes a process for exchanging the keys used to set encryption and decryption engines. In PKI, two closely related keys are used together (they're often called a key pair). Typically, the public key is used to encrypt the stream, and the private key is used to decrypt the stream. You can publish the public key freely, and in fact, current directory services often come with an integrated public key infrastructure (PKI) for just this purpose. This form of encryption is also called asymmetric encryption. Unfortunately, asymmetric encryption is many times slower than symmetric. In situations where two different parties want to exchange data using the vastly more efficient symmetric encryption, they typically use public key encryption first to pass a secure one-time-use symmetric key to both parties.

Would You Know It If It Happened?

Would you even know if intruders have been in your site?

Keep in mind that the greatest security threat isn't from vandals who do damage; they're just the ones that make the news. The greatest threat is from the silent thief who leaves no trace.

Security breaches of corporate networks don't get the same kind of attention as denial of service attacks or public vandalism. After all, a company that has suffered a security problem doesn't want the event publicized and might not even know that a problem has occurred.

The effect, though, is no less worrisome. The security holes prevalent in the networks of U.S. companies and the government "have the potential to do serious damage to U.S. economic competitiveness," says Richard Power, editorial director of the Computer Security Institute (CSI).

Of the 643 network security managers surveyed for the recently released 2000 CSI/FBI Computer Crime and Security Survey, 70% reported experiencing unauthorized use of computer systems. Corporate Internet connections have been increasingly reported as a point of attack, and the incidence of internal systems used as point of attack has dropped over the five years CSI has conducted the survey.

One encouraging sign: The number of respondents who reported that they didn't know whether their systems had been infiltrated dropped from 21% to 12%, indicating, according to Power, that organizations are no longer living in denial. Rather, they're looking more closely at activity on their networks. Remember, the most dangerous crooks don't let you know they've been there at all.

Certificate Servers

Your company will need recognized certificates to authenticate business documents of all kinds, to place orders, to transfer funds, and to take many other kinds of actions. You have many CAs to choose from, but we think you should make a choice. Today, the vendors of directory services and more specialized companies such as Entrust, RSA Security, Verisign, and Xcert function as CAs. If you're in a very large corporation, your corporation might become its own CA. Almost all of us have seen the certificate notice asking if you want to trust Microsoft. You should pick a public CA that is widely accepted in your business-to-business e-commerce activities.

In the coming years you'll see CAs emerge along industry or trade lines whereas banks and credit card companies will issue certificates for the general public to use in retail commerce. Because of the great convenience they provide, the authentication and CA architectures will probably grow more quickly than the directory architecture. This is an area to look at early.

When an individual establishes identity with a CA, the CA's server generates a unique signature key and encryption key pairs in the form of certificates that include the individual's name. The certificates are signed by the CA's private key, which passes along the trust implied by the CA's name and procedures for granting certificates. From that point on, people can rely on the signature certificate to confirm the individual's true identity.

Personal authentication products are practical today and introducing them can be one of your initial steps toward establishing a modern e-business infrastructure. How do you prove who you are regardless of where you are? That proof comes from personal authentication services that use ID/password pairs, challenge response tokens, biometrics, or other devices to ensure a positive ID.

Buzzwords

Biometrics—The use of images of the eye, the face, fingerprints, voice prints, and other physical inputs to authenticate the identity of a person.

Hardware-based challenge/response mechanisms from Enigma and SecurilD use electronic card devices that generate unique one-time pass-codes. When the cards are issued, they're associated with an ID that triggers a password request. They provide excellent, but somewhat expensive, authentication.

We like these cards because they provide a single and portable location for an individual's private encryption keys. A security administrator can physically hand an individual the card to start the security chain. Because the information stays with the individual and isn't on a computer's hard drive, there is less chance of someone compromising the private key. The American Express Blue credit card is one of the first commercially available smart cards. Expect other credit card companies to follow.

A broad area of technology called *biometrics* uses encoded versions of your physical voice, eye, face, or hand attributes to uniquely identify you. The installation process associates your ID with your biological attributes. The system uses those attributes to verify your identity. For example, Key Tronics offers a complete keyboard with a built-in fingerprint scanner with a street price under $100. We expect to see the biometric function appear in many more devices and we expect biometrics to become more tightly integrated with LDAP and PKI. Add biometric patterns to the smart card and you'll have a two-way authentication mechanism in a very small device.

Digital Signatures

Strong authentication has been thrown into the limelight by the creation of a U.S. law known as the Electronic Signatures in Global and National Commerce Act. This law, passed in mid-2000, gives electronic signatures and documents the same force in law as those done with ink on paper. The act eliminates legal barriers to using electronic technology to form and sign contracts, collect and store documents, and send and receive notices and disclosures. When President Clinton signed the bill into law—electronically—on June 30, 2000, he said "Under this landmark legislation, online contracts will now have the same legal force as equivalent paper contracts."

It's nice that the federal government is out in front on this issue, but unfortunately the government is not in front of standards and many related potential legal complexities. The law requires that consumers consent to doing business online and that they are assured consumer protections equivalent to those in the paper world. It also ensures that government agencies have the authority to enforce the laws, protect the public interest, and carry out their missions in the electronic world, the White House said in a statement. But many things are still to be ironed out and they'll certainly affect the way that your e-business uses or accepts digital signatures.

Digital, Not Digitized

Don't get a digital signature and a digitized signature confused. A digitized signature is simply a scan of that scrawl you call a signature on paper. It doesn't mean much except for historical purposes. A digital signature is affixed to specific types of documents after proper electronic authentication. As we keep saying, strong authentication is a foundation technology for e-business.

At this point, a few companies are driving the digital signature technology, and they are still contending for leading roles in the development of the technology. Companies such as VeriSign and Entrust Technologies are leading the technology in authentication servers. They have laid strong foundations in developing the public key infrastructure that is the basis of most digital signatures. The biometric companies, such as Litronic, are pushing forward with links between biometric authentication and digital signatures. Interlink Electronics is also linking biometrics to digital signatures.

It's not clear how digital signatures will come into use. It seems likely that the days of using the fax machine for real estate and other important exchanges are numbered. But strong authentication must be in place before people really feel confident in digital signatures.

Technologies such as authentication and digital signatures are important to e-business. Creating single sign-on from anywhere is important to businesses and employees. But, after corporate users are identified and authenticated, what do they see? How do you provide simple access to applications after you're past the sign-on phase?

Developing for B2B & EAI

You've created a great foundation for secure e-business using single sign-on, but are your applications still scattered in isolated clumps all over the network? Your typical Web-enabled corporate offices will have some processes on the Internet proper and others safely hidden on your private network. Business-to-business applications need to be on the Internet to bring the largest groups of suppliers and consumers together. You'll want to give your business partners secure access to shared applications and files while keeping them out of internal corporate data. Your internal systems will probably also leverage Internet technology to reduce the number of special client programs and to take advantage of emerging broadband connections in hotels, airports, and homes.

Significant changes are afoot for business-to-business automation. When new Web startups threatened entire bricks-and-mortar markets, we heard that disintermediation (doing away with the middleman) was the new watchword. Now, competition is bringing back new kinds of e-commerce middlemen with software tools and network services to grease the e-supply pipeline and to offer complete business solutions for all aspects of the business.

Some of the tried-and-true vendors from the early software markets are redefining themselves as e-business entities aimed at helping you leverage your existing systems onto the Web. If you're in a larger company with established internal business software systems, you should look at Enterprise Application Integration (EAI) software to help the migration. EAI focuses on webifying what you already have through special software tools.

Tool Time

You can buy B2B market software and services, customer relationship management applications, portal software, or external services, but how do they link together and how do they link to your existing applications?

Companies that sell application development tools haven't stood still and the industry is rolling out open standards to integrate applications. LDAP plays an important role in directory services for e-business. Another important development is the eXtensible Markup Language, or XML.

Get the Staff Up To Speed

Companies of almost every size have a programming staff, whether they know it or not. The programmers might be on the payroll of a value-added reseller or consultant selling you services, but they're there. The question is, are they up to speed?

Although Microsoft's Visual Basic was the staple for client/server applications; Perl, C, tcl, ASP, NSAPI, and ISAPI were early Web content development standards. That's probably what your programmers know. But your development staff needs to understand what XML and its various extensions and subsets can do for you and your industry.

Not only does XML provide methods for rendering content to many devices, but it also provides the framework for B2B commerce and trading of all kinds of traditional data. There are already XML specifications for directories (DSML), commerce (cXML), ad insertions (adXML), electronic catalogs (ecXML), wireless devices (WML) and many more, detailed at `www.xml.org` and `www.biztalk.org`.

Select Carefully Up Front

Web sites provide internal information, public information, and public commerce. Each type of site must be reliable, fast, and accessible, but they have different requirements for services, security, and privacy. Many tools are available for Web site development and management, but often you have to keep riding the horse you bet on. It's difficult to start a project with one set of directory software tools and then change tools.

Buzzwords

CORBA—Common Object Request Broker Architecture. A program that helps transfer messages to and from objects between various platforms in a distributed environment.

Many of the latest integrated development environments (IDEs) leverage reusable components in their final assembly process. A sampling would include XML as a data-interchange format, Enterprise Java Beans as a server architecture, CORBA and DCOM as programmatic methods for processes to call each other, message-queuing systems to let systems communicate asynchronously, and transaction monitors to ensure that operations complete properly.

You'll want to grow high-level programmers that can build these reusable objects in one of the three object models. (DCOM—Distributed Component Object Model, CORBA—Common Object Request Broker Architecture, or EJB—Enterprise Java Beans). These objects' properties will then be available in the integrated program development environment to perform important functions. The real plus here is that the process can be handled by less skilled programmers or savvy end-users themselves.

Buzzwords

DCOM—Distributed Component Object Model: A Microsoft programming architecture for communications between applications across a network.

A typical integrated application system for e-business, shown in Figure 6.2, offers a series of generic services for security management, protocol management, data mapping, and other functions. These services define the functionality and flow of data in your application. Software connector modules that let these services communicate with specific outside systems or in-house or proprietary systems are also generally required. Outside systems might include IBM's MQseries or Microsoft MSMQ for message queuing; DB2, Microsoft SQL Server, database products from Oracle; and products from Baan, PeopleSoft, or SAP R/3 for ERP.

XML Really Is Important!

I know that we sound like we're harping, but it's practically impossible to overstate the importance of XML to e-business. Companies use it as a fast-setting universal cement to build all sorts of e-business structures from different components. Various dialects of XML link directories to applications, link applications to Internet services, and voice-enable everything. Those who create or support your applications really do need to be on top of the world of XML.

Although this approach lets any system connect to any other system (as long as there are connector modules), it also requires that you and all your partners run the same B2B system, such as

Brahms B2Bengine, from Bridges for Islands. The B2BEngine and similar systems are not meant for smaller companies (unless furnished by an application service provider), because they are expensive, and implementing them requires a knowledgeable IT staff.

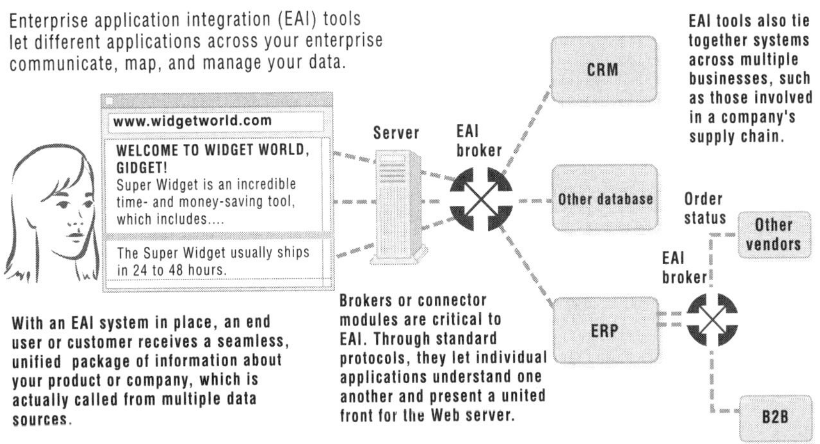

Figure 6.2

A typical e-business integrated application system offers services for security management, protocol management, data mapping, and other functions.

Mercator Software offers a series of enterprise application integration products for different environments: Mercator Commerce Broker for B2B, Mercator Enterprise Broker for application-to-application integrations, and Mercator Web Broker for customer-to-business integrations. The company's data transformation, mapping, and workflow technologies are at the core of all three products.

The products use a series of graphical tools to display data as seen by various applications such as ERP systems, transaction monitors, and databases—even some types of COBOL programs—and let you build rules graphically.

XML is fast becoming the unifier among integrated systems. Brahms B2BEngine is typical in its use of XML as the *lingua franca* among participants in a B2B exchange. An integration wizard ties applications that are not XML-enabled into the process. XML is also the basis for SOAP (Simple Object Access Protocol), a new way for processes on different systems to communicate using standard, open protocols. SOAP could greatly simplify interoperability among systems because of the openness and simplicity of XML. SOAP is at the core of Microsoft's BizTalk Server 2000, which lets you build B2B networks on Windows in collaboration with any system that supports SOAP.

SOAP is a communications protocol, not a description of the data in your e-business system. The fact that SOAP can run over any transport protocol such as HTTP, SMTP, or message queuing means that any two SOAP programs can communicate without another layer of middleware. Sagavista, from Saga Software, can often accomplish the same goal through the use of multiple native adapters for popular systems such as Baan, CICS, PeopleSoft, and SAP. Sagavista is a visual environment in which you connect data sources from one end of your network to the other.

XML is also at the heart of document-interchange networks such as Microsoft's BizTalk.Org and RosettaNet (a self-funded, nonprofit consortium), which provide repositories for or collections of standard formats for communication of common elements such as purchase orders and part numbers.

Sun's Java, and particularly Enterprise Java Beans (EJB), the company's Java-based application server platform, is a popular platform in the EAI space. The portability of Java is its main selling point, because large parts of any program will be binary-compatible between systems on which the Java2 platform, Enterprise Edition, is implemented.

Brahms and webMethods B2B both use EJB as their architecture. This gives them interoperability with other EJB platforms, in addition to their operating-system portability. For example, transaction-based applications written for one system should work on another EJB-based system with little or no adaptation.

CORBA/IIOP and DCOM are the two main protocols for object communication across networks, including the Internet. These are low-level programming concepts, but often dictate compatibility between applications in a complex system. DCOM is used for Windows-based applications, and CORBA is found on many platforms. Because both have wide support in the market, you'll find that many EAI systems, including those from Bridges for Islands and Saga Software, support both.

Not all calls between programs need an immediate response. Message queuing is a long-established technique that lets programs call each other using connections over which responses are not necessarily immediate—Internet connections, for example. Message queues deal with these calls asynchronously and can resend them if necessary. Message queues are an excellent means of connecting disparate systems, especially across the Internet. Support for the most popular message-queuing systems such as IBM's MQSeries and Microsoft MSMQ, is common.

Transactions are a critical part of all e-business. They let a system designer ensure that all parts of an operation complete successfully—or that none do. Take a simple Web-based credit card purchase as an example. You need to debit inventory and charge the customer's credit card, but if either process fails, you don't want the other one to occur. Transaction-processing systems, such as IBM's CICS, Microsoft Transaction Server (now part of COM+), and Tuxedo, from BEA Systems, are built for such tasks.

EAI is a linchpin that lets e-business work. If your applications across the enterprise can't all talk to each other, your organization will fail to realize the cost savings of the e-business model and your business could get left behind.

Calling in from Anything

You will get pressure to extend services to employees and clients who want to be in touch from anywhere and seemingly from anything. Again, you will need some specialized development tools. We recommend learning more about special extensions to XML and about the wireless access protocol.

XML extends the service of applications into the wireless device and microbrowser area with the wireless markup language (WML) specification. Web phones and wireless palm devices will be the best client devices for many distributed applications. These mini-clients speak the wireless access protocol (WAP) in conversations with their WAP gateways. The gateways do all the heavy lifting and translate between the small devices and the rest of the Internet. Unwired Planet maintains an interoperability testing lab for WAP Forum members at `www.wapforum.org`. If your company embraces open-source initiatives, you'll want to review the work done at `www.mobilelink.org` where their mobile application link (MAL) source code resides in the latest release.

According to Mark Bregman, general manager of pervasive computing at IBM, 70% of wireless devices will be Internet-ready through the Wireless Access Protocol by the end of this year. e-Businesses will use such devices to acccess corporate databases, pay bills, and make airline reservations, among other tasks. Through WAP gateways, the devices will be used to access customer data, mine marketing data, and find services and products from suppliers and merchants. Consumers will use the devices to shop.

"The wireless phenomenon is going to trigger an acceleration of e-business growth."

"The wireless phenomenon is going to trigger an acceleration of e-business growth," Bregman said. As wireless devices perform transactions and other complicated tasks, according to Bregman, technologies will come from IBM and others to make wireless devices more secure and reliable, with better store-and-forward capabilities, more robust instant messaging, and improved data synchronization.

Among non-WAP wireless protocols that could become significant for ubiquitous e-business are GPRS (General Packet Radio System), Universal Mobile Telecommunications Systems, and various versions of CDMA (Code Division Multiple Access).

Part of the technology challenge in extending e-business applications to new devices consists of facilitating truly cross-platform access to data. Sun Microsystems, along with IBM, would like to see Java and XML work together to facilitate such cross-platform access. Sun recently expanded support for XML in its J2EE (Java2 Enterprise Edition) and announced the development of a Java API for XML messaging. An IBM technology called WebSphere Transcoding Publisher, and Sun's iForce Solution Set for Mobile Wireless Internet, reconsitute Web data into formats that handheld devices can display, and many kinds of content are being repurposed into WML format for display on handhelds. These kinds of technology efforts are driven by a desire to allow e-business to take place untethered, from anywhere, across multiple platforms.

Crossing Borders

If you're doing business online, you're doing business everywhere. Translation and site globalization technologies loom large for the e-business world over the next several years. Right now, the English-speaking world dominates the Web, but Europe and Asia, among other regions, are becoming big forces. XML and XHTML are among technologies being used as platforms for multilingual sites capable of automatically drawing content from databases and feeding the content into a translation engine that can generate the right character set and syntax for non-English speaking site visitors. Idiom, with its WorldServer technology, and Translation Experts, are among many companies that provide technology for automatic translation and site globalization based on extensions to HTML such as XML and XHTML.

For example, Idiom's WorldServer technology (`www.idiominc.com`) employs customizable, rule-based software scripts to properly replicate and translate content across globally partnered sites. E-commerce content management software suites are quickly offering integration with these translation and globalization technologies. Vignette and Interwoven offer Idiom's WorldServer as part of their product suites. A Working Group at the World Wide Web Consortium is developing many internationalization technologies.

A company called Speak Globally (`www.speakglobally.com`) uses live people to do much more than translation. Speak Globally's staff of linguists does *localization* on an entire Web site or any content within the site. Localization includes adapting the site for local customs and idioms.

Calling in from Anywhere

You want your employees and business partners to use your corporate portal and to access productivity applications, but how do they accomplish that despite their location? A virtual private network (VPN) is the answer to providing secure and flexible access for traveling and work-at-home employees. It also works for secure office-to-office connectivity.

Buzzwords

VPN—Virtual private network. A way to create a secure link across a private network or the Internet so that authorized users can reach the corporation's assets from anywhere.

The phrase "virtual private network" seems imposing, but it boils down to special software in client PCs connecting across a corporate intranet or the Internet to special software in a dedicated box or in a server in your server room. Figure 6.3 shows how a VPN connects users to the corporate network across a managed network or the Internet. VPNs are becoming increasingly important as employees gain fast Internet access through cable modems and DSL connections. Encryption at both ends keeps data safe and you can choose from several options for user authentication. Installing a VPN requires a substantial up-front effort for configuration and software deployment, but after everything is running it offers much lower connection costs than traditional remote access servers and it provides excellent management control and information.

You can elect to create your own VPN system or to outsource it from one of many ISPs, VARs, and connectivity vendors. The choice depends primarily on the talents and capabilities of your own IS staff. Measured over years, outsourcing costs much more than the cost of the equipment and software, but outsourcing provides skilled and experienced help that you might not get in any other way. An outsourced VPN is often part of a larger package of Internet, intranet, and security services.

An alternative way to provide remote access for employees is a conglomeration of modems, telephone lines, and a central processor known as a *remote access server (RAS)*. RAS devices were the brick and mortar of the industry for a decade, but VPNs seriously challenge their importance. The downside of an RAS system is in high circuit costs and daily management chores. On the other hand, a good RAS system offers reliability and security that are more difficult to ensure while drilling through the Internet. Savvy network administrators will probably keep a small RAS system operational as backup for when the Internet VPN has a bad day.

Many companies offer VPN products. Altiga Networks; Checkpoint Software Technologies; Lucent Technologies; Shiva, a division of Intel; and TimeStep are among the best known. Additionally, Microsoft's Windows NT/2000 and Novell's NetWare operating systems can provide VPN services.

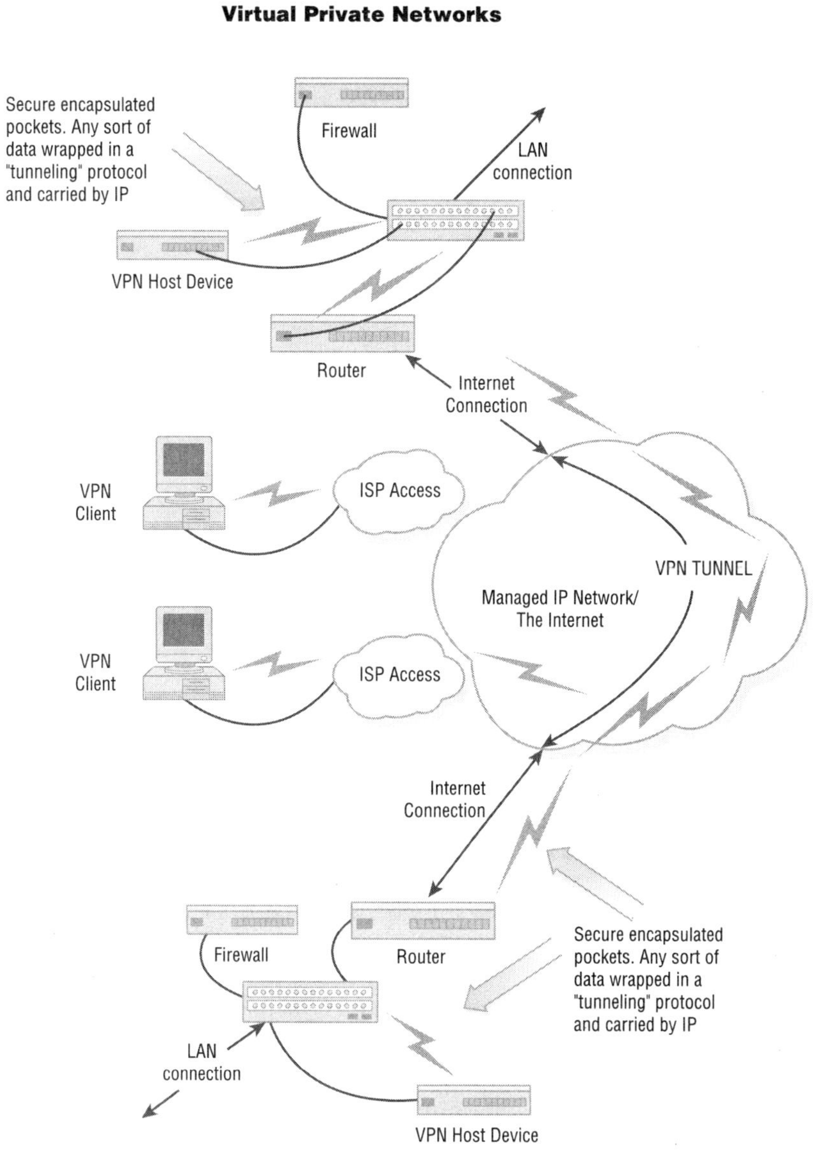

Figure 6.3

A Virtual Private Network (VPN) connects users to the corporate network across a managed network or the Internet.

You can also lease VPN services from all but the smallest ISPs. The ISP will charge a monthly fee, probably based on the number of clients, and will probably set up and maintain equipment within your facility. This option gives you a predictable cost, reduces your internal workload, and should provide a system with expert support 24-hours a day.

However, like all outsourced services, you need to judge the quality of the expertise you're buying, set standards for performance, and demand accountability.

VPN Decisions and Options

How much security do you need? What's the threat? How many people need remote access? What are their computer skills? How much traffic do they generate? Are they all employees? Are they geographically dispersed? What kinds of client computers do they have? These are all questions you need to answer before you enter the process of buying a VPN.

All the popular products use IPSec encryption between the clients and the host system. IPSec is an encryption and authentication architecture that provides security for IP packets.

IPSec is flexible and powerful. Some speculation has been that processing strongly encrypted IPSec can overload client computers, but our tests in *PC Magazine* Labs didn't turn up any unexpected or unusual problems. If you start 1.5 Mbps IPSec encrypted FTP file transfer with a 166 MHz computer, you'll notice a difference in the speed of other applications, but they still work. At slower speeds and less intense tasks, or with more computing horsepower, operation is normal.

IS managers know that remote users generally consume more support time than local users. The support problem escalates when you load something a little different such as VPN client software on their computers. Deployment of the client software is a problem largely ignored by all the equipment vendors. The general failing of the equipment vendors to help with client deployment makes outsourcing a total service more appealing.

As cable modem and DSL connections proliferate, employees will have high-speed access to the VPN, but they might find a constriction at your corporate network connection. You'll need a large enough Internet connection to carry the load presented by your employees coming in through VPN connections.

Weave It Together

Success in e-business demands an investment. Using a portal is a good way to start to tie your applications together. Other early and relatively easy steps include adopting new strong personal authentication techniques and looking into an outsourced certificate services. You should study your need for and approach to directory services. You must give close attention to your development staff and provide modern tools for system integration. Step-by-step you can build the software and application infrastructure you need for a flexible and responsive e-business system.

PART IIII

B2C: Business to Customer—Customer Relationship Management (CRM)

CHAPTER 7

Find Them And Keep Them: e-CRM

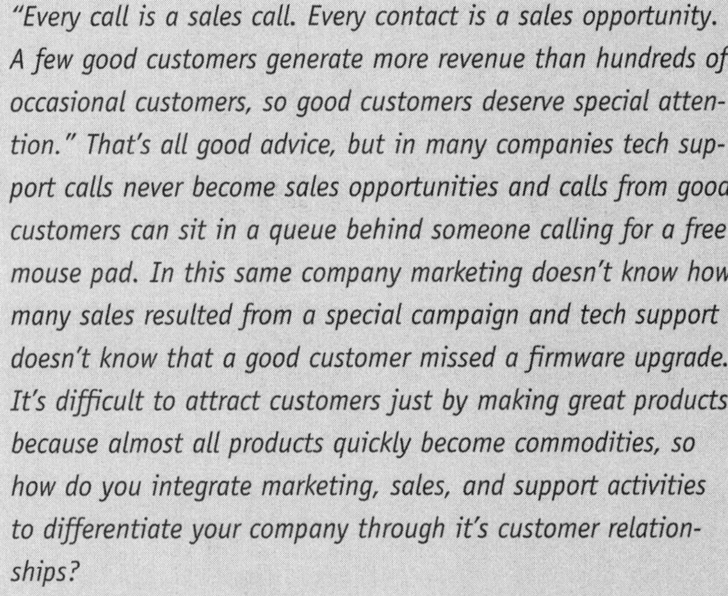

"Every call is a sales call. Every contact is a sales opportunity. A few good customers generate more revenue than hundreds of occasional customers, so good customers deserve special attention." That's all good advice, but in many companies tech support calls never become sales opportunities and calls from good customers can sit in a queue behind someone calling for a free mouse pad. In this same company marketing doesn't know how many sales resulted from a special campaign and tech support doesn't know that a good customer missed a firmware upgrade. It's difficult to attract customers just by making great products because almost all products quickly become commodities, so how do you integrate marketing, sales, and support activities to differentiate your company through it's customer relationships?

The answer to the problem of finding and keeping customers and leveraging their goodwill into sales is in a big bag of technologies called customer relationship management or CRM. CRM is many things and it has several roots, but the general goal is to create a synergy between the sales, marketing, and customer service activities within an organization to get and hold customers. CRM on the Internet, e-CRM, leverages Web technology to create team relationships between sales, marketing, and support, and between that team and its clients.

e-Business is about using Internet technology to further relationships, and no relationships are more important than those you have with your customers. The term we use to define modern relationships with customers is *e-CRM*. Any description of e-CRM is like the classic parable of the blind men describing an elephant—it depends on where you start. Some companies enter e-CRM through the traditional contact management software such as GoldMine or SalesLogix. Many companies see e-CRM as a natural extension of their call center, now renamed "contact center" activities. Finally, larger companies with corporate enterprise resource planning (ERP) systems see e-CRM as a natural part of computer-facilitated corporate management.

In terms of benefits, this means that if tech support has a problem at a vendor's site, the sales team knows about it before they make the next sales call. If a product update comes from engineering, the sales and support teams receive actions concerning customers with that product. Engineering, sales, and marketing can collaborate to target upcoming products to potential buyers. Messages and screens of data "pop" between responsible managers based on rules established in the software by the users.

Buzzwords

Call center—A place where agents use automated tools to interact with customers. When integrated with a full CRM solution, contacts are logged, categorized, and tracked as customer histories.

Arranging this interaction can teach lessons in how your company actually works and it often calls for customized software. The lines between marketing and sales, for example, are different in many companies and you want the software to match the way you work.

One of the primary benefits of e-CRM software is that it generates regular reports enabling management to carefully track sales efforts and results. Managers can see data on proven and potential customers and how they respond to specific sales approaches.

Classic CRM grew from the benefits that companies such as Digital, IBM, Wang, and Xerox found in exchanging information about customers between field technicians and sales groups. They moved out of carbon paper forms and into email and automated reports in the early 1990s. Field support for sales and service employees is still an important e-CRM driver, but today the tools include browser-equipped phones and laptops using VPN links to large database systems.

Who Needs It?

The nice thing about e-CRM is that you can start small and build. You can start with outsourced services or with a small contact center and work up to full integration with your ordering and technical support systems. Also, unlike corporate portals or other elements of e-business, e-CRM can make a very prompt contribution to the bottom line. The catch is training. The best e-CRM system provides little benefit if the people using it don't have proper training. Practically any organization with something to sell or support can benefit in e-CRM, but you must train people to use the system and to follow through on customer contacts.

Buzzwords

CRM—Customer relationship management. This isn't a new idea. Business has always been about relationships with customers. But when you try to prioritize and control the important actions, it becomes a management science. Most CRM software packages are front-office products that sit on top of databases to track all forms of customer contact.

To understand the current situation, it helps to get some historical perspective on e-CRM. The first wave of e-CRM solutions, which many large companies have in place today, surfaced en masse in the late 1980s and early 1990s. These systems came from companies such as Clarify (which is now owned by Nortel Networks Corp.), Onyx Software, Oracle, Vantive (acquired last year by PeopleSoft), and the now-colossal Siebel Systems.

All these vendors provided packaged solutions that were focused on automating and standardizing the internal processes associated with capturing, servicing, and retaining customers. These processes ranged from capturing sales leads to creating scripts for customer service agents to enable consistent service and support across product lines and divisions. Though these applications addressed a pressing need, they did have a significant gotcha: They were very expensive and onerous to implement and maintain.

Buzzwords

e-CRM—Automating CRM.

"The main emphasis of CRM used to be around how can we improve our processes internally to make our customers an asset," said Robert Duffner, formerly of Vantive and now a senior product manager at Vignette who is helping that company develop its own e-CRM product strategy. "It was about automating around customer support, then sales, and then the way in which field sales and service representatives worked with customers."

But then in the mid-1990s the Web came along, and with it both the CRM market and customer-related business requirements of all-size companies changed completely. Not only did the widespread embrace of the Internet mean that existing and potential customers had yet another channel through which they could interact and communicate with corporations, it also meant that the client/server architecture behind existing e-CRM applications would eventually be rendered obsolete. Figure 7.1 show how e-CRM promotes customer contacts and general business.

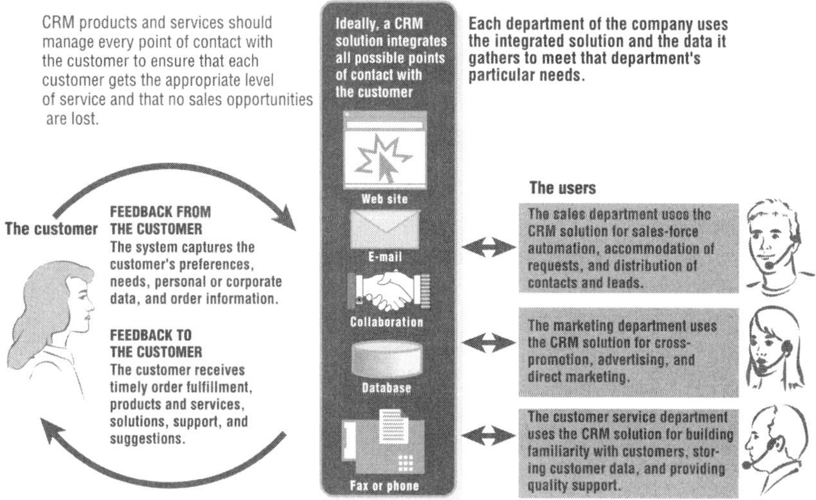

Figure 7.1

e-CRM is your tool for promoting customer contacts and general business.

The characteristics Lucent uses to describe e-CRM built on its CRM Central 2000 software pretty well describe the best of e-CRM. It uses telephone, email, voice-enabled Web site, and other types of customer contacts; it manages and delivers business and customer information; it automatically triggers the work required across different areas to fulfill customer requests; and it monitors service levels to ensure quality. In an ideal system, actions and data screens can be triggered based on historical information—such as customers' buying preferences—or circumstantial information—such as customer contract volumes. And everything ties into corporate ERP and database applications. Whew!

Getting to Know You

Though e-CRM goals, implementations, and strategies fluctuate wildly from company to company, at the root of this recent e-CRM revolution is the desire of all businesses—regardless of size—to know their customers better. And pulling the electronic communications media mentioned here into an overall e-CRM strategy is one way companies can do that. Not only do these channels offer untold efficiencies when implemented smartly, but electronic interactions with customers allow organizations to capture massive amounts of information about how individuals behave when purchasing products, whether they are buying books or wholesale auto parts. By understanding that data, businesses can market their products more effectively and provide an unprecedented level of service.

At the end of the day, no matter how sophisticated or confusing the underlying technology might be or how many competing players there are, e-CRM is an incredibly simple concept that all companies must understand. "Everything old is new again, and the same is true with CRM," said Mark Bartin, vice president of marketing at OfficeLand. "When you get down to the basics, CRM—even on the Internet—is as old-fashioned as the barber on the corner remembering your name."

Conventional wisdom holds that Siebel and its ilk were slow to respond to the Internet in terms of providing solutions centered around electronic communications. This left the gate wide open for a smattering of enterprising start-ups that understood the implications of the Web. Almost overnight, they created a new market segment to deal with e-CRM.

The e-CRM space includes players like eGain, Genesis, Octane, Silknet (acquired by Kana), Talisma, and others. The first products from these vendors—which began to surface about three years ago—mostly helped companies deal with customer service requests through email and, in some cases, through chat or Web-based forms. But the market has progressed rapidly, and many of these vendors are starting to offer product suites that enable businesses to integrate multiple communication channels, including voice. Some, such as Octane, are accomplishing this by building their own technology; others, such as eGain, are doing so through acquisition. Even Cisco has jumped in, with its recent purchase of WebLine Communications, which provides a wide range of electronic customer service offerings, including a call-center application.

"One of the bets we took when we started the company is that businesses would eventually want to build across multiple channels, such as email, chat, Voice-over-IP, telephone, and even video," said Gunjan Sinha, president and co-founder of eGain. "And we knew this kind of system would have to be intelligent enough to keep a consistent view of the customer, regardless of the channel."

Though e-CRM players such as eGain have made impressive strides, the traditional CRM vendors are fighting back hard. Siebel, for example, announced its eBusiness suite in early 2000, which includes applications for selling, marketing, and providing customer service over the Internet. Personalization features have been built in, as well as software that will let field personnel access sales and service information through cellular phones. Onyx also made a string of announcements this spring about its portal product line, which was built to address direct-to-customer as well as partner interactions. This suite represents a complete reinvention of the product, which now has a Web-based architecture.

Also in early 2000 came Clarify's eFrontOffice, which includes software components for managing Web interactions with customers—and integrates those elements with call-center applications as well as fax to create a universal queue for email, voice, and fax requests. Oracle has launched an e-business suite, which includes marketing, sales, and services modules that enable businesses to deal with call-center, Web, and email channels in an integrated fashion. Industry-specific e-CRM modules are available for the communications, financial, and high-tech markets.

"Companies like Siebel and Clarify are running to catch up—especially Siebel—to make sure they can provide the Internet part of their CRM systems," said Robert Morani, an analyst with The Yankee Group. "However, they will be formidable in their plays to this new market, especially Siebel and Oracle. And you also have to remember these are companies with lots of market share and very large organizations using their systems."

Will VRM Replace CRM?

In the e-CRM world, companies such as Siebel have made great strides in tracking every point of customer contact, but new VRM (visitor relationship management) technologies in the category are focusing on analyzing every point of site visitor contact. Recent market research from McKinsey Corp. has shown that fewer than 5% of visitors to commerce sites buy anything, and recent data from Forrester has shown that about half of first-time site visitors abandon commerce sites because they find them too difficult to navigate. VRM technology is seen by some as the solution.

One of the early VRM technologies is CommerceTrends Server from WebTrends, which produces intricate click-stream analysis and visitor behavior reports that site managers can analyze to observe things such as which visitors to a site responded to or at least read about a marketing promotion. A new VRM-related technology from a company called eHelp works on the thesis that commerce sites should have built-in help, just as productivity applications do. eHelp's technology lets site managers build pop-up help into every part of their sites, and provides "heuristic" predictive technology that observes how a site visitor initially behaves and then makes suggestions that could prevent a site visitor from abandoning the site. Players such as Kana/Silknet, Broadvision, and e-CRM providers themselves are also building VRM solutions to extend the CRM and personalization concepts.

Buzzwords

Contact management center—The traditional call center expanded to handle email, online chat, and other forms of customer contact.

Clearly, both segments of the e-CRM market are pushing hard on the notion of integrated e-CRM suites, but the truth is that these application suites are, for the most part, just now becoming available. Take Siebel and Oracle, for example. Both have announced e-business product lines but haven't yet delivered all the pieces. And it may take some time for companies like eGain and Cisco to figure out how to integrate the solutions they've recently acquired with existing platforms. All of which poses an interesting question for businesses, none of which have time to wait: Should they get their e-CRM needs filled by one vendor, which can mean waiting for pieces to become available, or look to buy best-of-breed point solutions and deal with the integration issues later?

You can start a little less grandly and build your system in reasonable steps. The experienced contact management companies such as Commence, Corp.; GoldMine Software; Multiactive Software; and SalesLogix provide a good start for companies of any size. For example, GoldMine 5.0 is aimed at teams of as many as 50 users who want to track, refer, and take action on telephone and email contacts from customers. The users don't have to be on a local network to coordinate an action; all each user needs is an IP address. GoldMine FrontOffice 2000 handles more users and ties to a SQL Server database for larger operations. GoldMine offers templates for specific industries that define roles and relationships and include rules for workflow processes. Similarly, SalesLogix has a multilayer product family including ACT! and SalesLogix 2000 that can integrate the activities of sales, marketing, and support teams.

Because the software from these companies isn't customized to your operation, you should examine each product to find the one that forces the smallest organizational shift in your company. Because you don't need custom programming, these packages will get you online within weeks instead of months. Each company has a large established base of supporting VARs and partners who can assist with installations. These products don't have all the options and reports available in the more expensive and integrated software suites, but they can create very effective e-CRM systems with a cost well below $1000 per seat.

Smaller organizations can also leverage the services of dot-com companies such as salesforce.com and UpShot.com. These companies will start your basic e-CRM services completely online for under $50 per user per month. On the downside, you don't get much customization or integration. You might have to organize your company to match the software instead of the other way around.

The newer e-CRM companies have fewer VARs and fewer options than the more established companies, but they're eager. They often drill into vertical markets for somc wins. Janna Systcms Inc., for example, specializes in e-CRM solutions for the financial services industry. Some companies, such as eGain and Talisma can help you with email campaigns and offer both hosted and online services. Socrates Technologies Corporation takes the online ASP approach to offer the SalesLogix 2000 suite online along with other e-business and ERP applications.

~~Call~~ Contact Center

The providers of classic call centers, including Lucent and Nortel, come naturally to e-CRM because they provide the desktop infrastructure: call routing systems, headsets, and pop-up screens linked to the client's telephone number and account information. The push to e-CRM has changed the name from call center to "contact center" or "interaction center." The traditional headsets still hang in agents' ears, but now agents also use email, fax, fax and voice-over-IP, Web site enhancements such as shared browsing and chat, and several methods of electronic document exchange to work with customers. Figure 7.2 shows some of these customer interaction features at work.

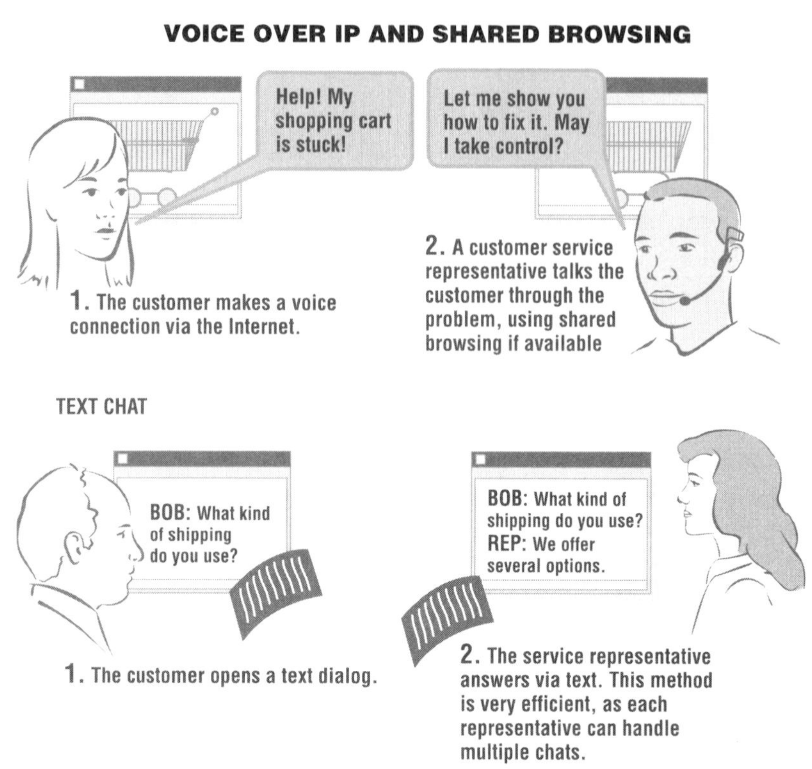

Figure 7.2
e-CRM customer interaction features include the traditional headsets, but also email, fax, fax and voice-over-IP, Web site enhancements, chat, and several methods of electronic document exchange.

Talking to Your Customers

Many companies are enhancing their sites with support features that enable real-time communication over the Internet. The tools available range from text chat to page pushing, voice-over-IP (VoIP), shared browsing, call-back technology, or a combination. In most cases, you needn't install a new set of servers to handle these solutions. Several vendors offer these tools as hosted services, for which you pay a monthly fee, and add a few lines of HTML to the code for your site.

A company called Click2Talk is one of the most aggressive in providing voice-enabled Web site services. Click2Talk is HTML code that is embedded in your Web site. The HTML code is associated with a specific telephone number that you select. When a customer who is surfing your site clicks the Click2Talk icon, a Java applet initiates a phone call from their PC. Of course, the PC must be equipped with a sound card, IP telephony software, and a handset. The Click2Talk service is free, but the company makes money through advertising, so you're trading a voice service for some ad real estate.

At `zapdata.com`, a site specializing in sales and marketing data, customers can contact the company in real-time through text-chat software hosted by LivePerson. Customers using zapdata.com who need a question answered can just click a text-chat button and the site launches a new window. Visitors can type questions and continue to browse while a zapdata support rep answers. Erik Ekwurzel, the zapdata.com director of operations, said that about 60% of the people who need support or have questions gravitate to that chat engine…Under 10% use the phone.

Ekwurzel's team had originally decided to install an engine on zapdata.com's own servers, but this proved expensive and impractical. With LivePerson, zapdata.com paid a one-time start-up fee of $500 and now pays $250 per month for each zapdata.com service rep using the product. Because Zapdata.com didn't have to purchase new servers, using the LivePerson's service doesn't create a new demand for more information technology staff.

"Real-time interaction isn't just for the Dells of the world, the QVCs, the EarthLinks—our big customers," said Robert LoCascio, president, CEO, and founder of LivePerson. "It's for the mom-and-pops, and everyone who wants to interact with their customers." You integrate LivePerson with your site—just by pasting one line of HTML and a few lines of JavaScript into your code. This creates a button to click that links customers to LivePerson's chat servers, which then link each customer to a support rep at your company. This not only enables customers to get help without interrupting their Internet sessions but also enables each of your support reps to help several customers at once through multiple chat sessions.

With LivePerson, your service reps can also push pages to customers. The user will ask a question, such as "How do I get VPs of marketing from your database?" If after the rep answers the customer still can't find the information, the rep can simply send the customer the page.

With voice-over-IP engines, such as the ones that are provided by Lipstream Networks, customers can literally speak to support reps without a telephone. As with text-chat solutions, the leading engines are hosted services and, to integrate with your site, simply require you to add a few lines of code. When a customer clicks a button on your site, a small piece of voice client software auto-installs into the customer's browser. Through that client, users can have verbal conversations with support reps. Of course, voice-over-IP might not be an option for every site. Accordingly, Lipstream has chosen to offer its service direct and through partners. "We came to the conclusion that the way to provide live voice over the Internet is as part of a broader application," said Lipstream's president and CEO Matt Jones.

Browsers Better Than Callers?

When looking over the voice-enabled Web site applications, some members of our *PC Magazine* staff have observed that they can't get a live person with good knowledge when dialing an 800 number, so, they ask, why should they get one when they click a Web site? The answer they get is that Web clicks will have a higher priority in the contact center than incoming 800 numbers.

"You'll always see our services integrated in or embedded in something larger, and live voice is just a piece of it," said Matt Jones. Lipstream has a partnership with LivePerson, for instance, letting you purchase both text chat and services.

Shared browsing, from such companies as Hipbone, enables a support rep to post pages to a customer's Web browser and type information into those pages as well. As with page pushing, shared browsing can supplement text chat, VoIP, or telephone support. While explaining a task, a support rep can literally show the customer how that task is performed.

Like LivePerson, Hipbone provides a hosted service for a small start-up fee and $750 per year for each support rep. Because the service is best used in tandem with some other form of real-time communication, Hipbone partners with several other customer-support vendors, including LivePerson, so that Hipbone can provide more complete solutions.

An alternative to using text chat is call-back technology from one of Hipbone's other partners, Net2Phone. When a customer clicks a Net2Phone call-back button, the service presents a window that lets the customer ask a support rep to phone immediately or to schedule another, more convenient time. Hipbone offers its shared-browsing service with Net2Phone call-back technology for $1,500 per seat per year.

If having one form of live support is good, having many to choose from is better. Those with deep enough pockets might want to purchase support tools from unified-software platform players such as Cisco Systems or eGain Communications Corp.

Having recently acquired WebLine Communications Corp. and GeoTel Communications Corp., Cisco currently offers text chat, shared browsing, call-back technology, email management, all from a single platform. Cisco won't host these services, but several of its primary customers will, or you can use your own servers. You can load eGain's software on your own servers, or eGain will host its services for you beginning at $3,000 per month. This might seem expensive, but the cost can be worthwhile in the long run. "Most customers who come in want to have an integrated collaboration framework, as opposed to trying just one subset of it," says Ashu Roy, co-founder and CEO of eGain. "They might start with one, but very quickly they need everything else. The efficiency of collaboration goes up with multiple touch points."

Rockwell Electronic Commerce (`www.ec.Rockwell.com`) targets smaller companies with its Transcend product line. Rockwell will install everything from headsets to servers running a suite of software that provides online collaboration, video, and a host of actions, rules, and reports. As a ballpark figure, 30 seats in a turnkey business would carry a list price of about $65,000. But everything is negotiable and customization is extra.

New Standards

Another trend at commerce sites that is expected to grow in the next several years is giving customers the option of talking through a Web-enabled device with a live customer service or support representative even as the customer is navigating a Web site. Many Web retailers already facilitate this through voice-over-IP technologies such as Click2Talk, Net2Phone, and VocalTec's Surf&Call plug-in.

For example, VocalTec's Surf&Call plug-in appears as a button on a commerce site, and the plug-in loads automatically when a potential customer arrives at the site, enabling live communication with a customer service rep. However, many Web shoppers have found existing solutions lack transparency, are difficult to use, are unreliable, and suffer from poor quality.

Two emerging standards that might change that in the world of VoIP are SIP (Session Initiation Protocol) and MGCP (Media Gateway Control Protocol). Many existing implementations use H.323, the ITU standard for packet-based multimedia communications systems, and there has been much haggling in the technology world over VoIP standards.

The Internet Engineering Task Force-backed SIP specification is a signaling protocol developed by telecommunications service providers to render VoIP services more transparent and simple to use. Lucent, Cisco, and other companies are building SIP technology into their products. MGCP is similar to SIP and also has big backers.

Many observers expect these new standards to usher in the era of live personal support as users navigate commerce sites, and Instant Messaging technology is also emerging as a way for real people to interact with Web shoppers. In addition to the benefits these technologies can bring to consumers, commerce sites can reap support savings from eliminating some of the phone-based and other kinds of support they provide, and being able to outsource Web-based support away from in-house call centers.

Buzzwords

ACD—Automatic call distribution. Equipment that routes incoming calls to appropriate agents.

Center Partners provides outsourced multimedia contact center services for technical support and customer service for companies of all sizes. They sell support by the minute, by the agent hour (approximately $26–$32/hr), or by contract. Center Partners is part of the huge WPP Group PLC and can expand its contact center services into all areas of e-CRM and e-business.

Lucent's CRM Central 2000, an e-CRM development system resulting from Lucent's acquisition of Mosaix, Inc., rolled out its first modules in September 1999 and many new integrated installations are underway. A software sub-set called iCOSM is designed for small businesses and departments.

Nortel bought its way into a more established e-CRM development system by purchasing Clarify, Inc. Clarify is a decade-old CRM vendor that now embraces e-CRM in its proven and extensive Clarify Front Office Suite development system.

CASE STUDY

CRM Outsource

Servtek—a division of $1.6 billion plastics-processing and metalworking behemoth Milacron—was facing a CRM crisis. Servtek consists of an inventory-planning group, a warehouse center, and a shipping group, all devoted to filling and servicing orders for the plastics-processing–related industrial products that Milacron manufactures. Because of the close ties among these groups, the opportunity to provide great customer service was within the division's grasp. But Servtek's antiquated call-center technology was an obstacle hard to ignore.

"When we bought our call-center system a few years ago, it was state-of-the-art," says Steve Hayden, Servtek's business unit manager. "But it required lots of manual intervention; we had to ask callers about their history and then go run reports, and we had no way of tracking them." In addition, Servtek's agents spent loads of time answering calls about order status, a less than efficient use of manpower.

After some CRM soul-searching, Hayden and his staff determined that they had to do three things: Get rid of their call-center system, find a way to use the Internet as a customer contact channel, and let someone else figure out the technical ins and outs of implementing this. Servtek did land on one company that could supply the new-fangled e-CRM system it wanted: CRM outsourcer Synchrony.

This decision not only took the burden of figuring out unfamiliar technology off Servtek, it also enabled the company to get up and running faster and make improvements to its customer interactions and business plan that Hayden had never dreamed possible. For starters, customer service reps are now rewarded with what e-CRM enthusiasts call a "screen pop." Whenever they get a call, all the calls are routed through Synchrony's data center in Cincinnati. This screen pop tells the representative who's calling and provides a link to that person's buying history—a big improvement over the old system. The agent also immediately gets information as to whether any co-workers are dealing with the customer's problem already.

"Often the same person will call five different times and talk to five different agents about one problem, which means we have people running around doing the same work," says Hayden. "Eliminating that will help us work better and will in the end let us serve the customer much better."

With this system, agents are also able to keep tabs on how many of the quotes for equipment they pass out each day are actually converted to purchases, something the old system was incapable of providing.

Last, Hayden plans to take care of the company's nasty order-status problem by implementing advance shipping notices through Synchrony's email management offerings. He anticipates that this move will cut down on customer service calls by up to 20%, which obviously will result in significant cost savings for Servtek. The email notices will tell customers when their orders were shipped, who the carriers were, and the arrival dates.

Hayden isn't the only person concerned with trying to put an e-CRM system in himself. In line with larger industry trends, a veritable cottage industry is springing up around outsourced e-CRM.

In addition to Synchrony, eConvergent, iSKY, Neteos, RainMaker Systems, safeharbor.com, and Talisma are also hawking e-CRM services for rent. Also, many packaged-application e-CRM vendors, such as eGain and Oracle, are partnering with hosting companies such as Exodus, or using their own infrastructures to offer e-CRM-for-rent solutions.

"All kinds of businesses are realizing that the technology now exists and is mature enough to put CRM and e-CRM applications in place, but they don't know how or don't want to deal with implementing them," says Karen Smith, an analyst with the Aberdeen Group. "So there's a big shift towards outsourcing, and you're going to see a whole new class of application service providers emerging to handle these types of business solutions."

Buzzwords

Screen pop—Displays forced to agents in association with an incoming call.

e-CRM for Small Companies

Much of the e-CRM buzz has centered around what larger companies are doing, and with good reason. Until recently, e-CRM has been the almost exclusive domain of big business because of the cost and expertise required to maintain the applications. But this is yet another rapidly changing area, as companies that are traditionally associated with the contact management world—such as GoldMine Software Corp., Multiactive Software, and SalesLogix—jump into e-CRM with both feet. Not surprisingly, pure-play start-ups are in this arena as well, including salesforce.com and UpShot.com.

Early in 2000, GoldMine announced a new CRM division that will focus on what the company calls front-office solutions for sales, marketing, and customer service. At the core of this initiative is GoldMine FrontOffice 2000, which has modules to address the needs previously cited. Goldmine's customers have been moving from contact management to sales force automation, so the company is serving their needs.

GoldMine isn't alone, however. Multiactive Software, maker of the contact management package Maximizer, is also hoping to capitalize on the e-CRM needs of small and medium-size businesses with its Entice! and Maximizer Enterprise product lines. And Commence Corp., a contact management company, is offering a product road map for small businesses that want to move to e-CRM with its Commence 2000 offering. Similar to GoldMine FrontOffice 2000, this product provides contact management, sales force automation, and service and support functionality. In addition, Commence provides an outsourced Internet piece of its product line, called Allure, through a partnership with Exodus Communications. Allure enables Commence's customers to put forms on their Web sites that integrate with the Commence database.

As the Allure service clearly illustrates, outsourcing isn't just for big business. Some providers mentioned earlier (including Neteos and safeharbor.com) intend to serve the small to midsize market exclusively. And many of the e-CRM vendors such as eGain and Talisma provide hosted options for their applications.

Traditional CRM players are also starting to offer solutions that are suitable for relatively small businesses. Onyx's various CRM portal solutions, for example, are turning out to be highly palatable to smaller businesses, as evidenced by the implementation of its customer relationship portal at Creativepro.com, a graphic design portal based in Portland, Oregon, and its Extensis Products Group division, which makes graphic design software.

When Creativepro.com decided to get rid of its homegrown system, which supported Web-based customer interactions but wasn't up to the rigors of Web traffic, it opted for Onyx's product. The results have been astounding. In about six months, the company realized that a large chunk of its sales—especially to individuals and small graphic design shops—could be handled on the Web site. But just as important, the information captured in Onyx is helping Creativepro.com and Extensis to build substantial self-help sections on their Web sites, which result in fewer customer service reps and lower support costs.

"We knew that people liked electronic information, and this is one way to provide it," says Max Brammer, director of sales for Creativepro.com and Extensis. "The self-service parts of our site are still new, but we're already feeling positive effects internally, because our staff can concentrate on other areas."

Custom Jobs

The major e-CRM products are development environments and big sets of tools used to create customized systems. For example, Clarify's eBusiness Solution is one of six major modules in the Clarify family of e-CRM software. Under this one module you'll find applications called eBusiness Framework, Customer Portal, eOrder, eConfigurator, eMerchandising, eResponse Manager, and Support. The other five major modules have similar subgroups. Typically, you start with a few selected applications and build a system over time. Because e-CRM is about the integration of teams and processes, it changes corporate cultures, so employee indoctrination and training are as important as the design of the database structures. It's clear that you'll want an experienced VAR involved in the planning, configuration, and installation of any highly integrated e-CRM system.

Another old-line CRM company, Siebel Systems, with sales running over $300 million per quarter, is the powerhouse in the e-CRM business. Even IBM, no slouch in e-business software, is deploying Siebel's software to serve more than 55,000 internal IBM users, 30,000 business partners, and millions of IBM customers directly over the Web.

Siebel *e*Business 2000, released in April 2000, is the sixth major release of the Siebel eBusiness Applications. The new suite includes several dozen application and development modules. One subset, called Siebel.com, is a suite of pre-built applications including user customization, email response, Web portal, esales, and

CASE STUDY

NAME: NANTUCKET NECTARS
LOCATION: NANTUCKET, MA
WEB SITE: WWW.JUICEGUYS.COM

co-founders Tom First and Tom Scott, a.k.a. The Juice Guys.

CRM Nantucket Nectars Online

Nantucket Nectars (`www.juiceguys.com`), which is renowned for the pithy sayings and advice on the underside of its bottle caps, decided that an integrated platform from one vendor made the most sense for its e-CRM needs. This decision came about a year ago, after the company faced up to what had become a customer relationship nightmare. Drew Farris, the company's director of IT, maintains this was mainly because of the older, disconnected systems that Nantucket Nectars was using.

"Last year we ended up in desperate straits, because our customers, who are mostly small beverage distributors, were extremely upset. We couldn't get them the products or information they needed," said Farris. "We have a fantastic operations and manufacturing center and a great sales and marketing organization, but it became apparent that our software systems were a big problem."

After this revelation, Farris made some bold moves. He and his staff tossed out the Solomon software that was being used to track sales numbers, the Access database that held marketing projections, and the ERP system that simply wasn't robust enough to handle the company's needs. After reviewing offers from several companies, Farris decided on an Oracle solution. On the manufacturing end, Oracle's ERP modules are now in place, and sales and marketing information is stored in Oracle databases. The next phase involves popping in Oracle's CRM modules, an initiative that's currently under way, and building what Farris calls Nectar Net.

When Nectar Net is complete, both sales representatives and customers will be able to log on through the Internet. Customers will be able to check on order status and eventually place orders online (these are now received by fax and entered into the system manually), while the reps can determine whether emarketing, among many other modules. Again, you'll typically install this software using the services of a Siebel VAR or business partner.

The most ambitious e-CRM systems tie into enterprise resource planning (ERP) systems, so it's natural for ERP vendors such as PeopleSoft, SAP, and Oracle to start from the ERP management core and build out to e-CRM. PeopleSoft's large family of applications with the Vantive name blankets every area of e-CRM from field service and help desk to automation of sales and marketing. My.SAP uses a role-based model to create highly structured e-CRM Web pages for eleven different types of managers and engineers, four types of purchasers, and several categories of browsing consumers. Oracle's e-Business Suite contains an eclectic mix of e-business

they're meeting sales and marketing goals. The CRM modules will pull the information that populates Nectar Net from the Oracle back-end systems.

According to Juliette Fulton, Oracle's vice president of CRM product strategy, many companies are just like Nantucket Nectars with older tools in place that prevent them from moving into the customer-centric Internet age. Fulton maintains that more and more businesses are looking for suites of products that handle the front-office processes of sales, customer support and services, and marketing as well as the back-end duties associated with inventory and manufacturing.

"Corporations are struggling to move from point solutions to suites," said Fulton. "They are realizing that they need to be totally unified across all their customer touch points, but this is hard to do with point solutions because of the integration piece."

On the other end of the spectrum from Nantucket Nectars is Tradient, based in Alameda, California. A start-up B2B marketplace that launched this spring for the transportation industry, Tradient didn't have any legacy systems to discard, because it was only a few months old. But like Nantucket Nectars, this company concluded that a one-vendor solution was needed for serving a far-flung and highly diverse customer base, which includes shippers, suppliers, and shipping intermediaries of all shapes and sizes.

Because Tradient exists solely on the Internet, a CRM solution that had been architected for the Web from its inception was crucial, according to Greg Johnson, Tradient's director of product marketing. This ultimately led the company to Octane, whose product and platform enable Tradient to handle all its Web-based, email, and call-center customer interactions. Tradient has also completely integrated its marketplace database—which captures information from all areas of Tradient's Web site—with the Octane customer database. For now, this information is being used to drive prospect lists into the Octane applications including e-CRM. Oracle offers software product groups in procurement, supply-chain management, marketing, and interaction center, among many others. Each of these ERP vendors also drills deeply into specific industries with specialized e-CRM applications packages.

Interestingly, even the biggest e-CRM systems have comparatively modest hardware needs. Clarify and Microsoft have publicly benchmarked Windows NT Server and SQL Server platforms, running on a single Compaq ProLiant 6500R, with Clarify Front Office Suite supporting the equivalent of 5,000 concurrent users. Your e-CRM systems must be responsive, but it's doubtful that you'll need a full server room full of equipment to make them run. The software's the high hurdle in the e-CRM infrastructure.

A company called Aristasoft takes to the online approach in a big way. Aristasoft wants to be the whole IS department for e-business companies. The company offers a complete online ERP plus e-CRM solution using J.D. Edwards and Clarify software products.

Modern companies need e-CRM to be with their customers around the world. Adopting e-CRM involves some imposing options and potential changes. Taking a step-by-step approach with the help of an experienced VAR makes good sense.

system, which will provide fodder for electronic marketing campaigns.

"A big part of our market expansion plan is the ability to capture and retain new customers, which means we must capture knowledge about our existing customers and their questions and problems and use all that information to pivot on a dime and serve them better," said Tradient's Johnson. "This also meant that when it came time to choose our underlying systems we needed to nail it from the beginning, because the name of the game is growth, and you have to invest in systems to allow for that."

Along with the customer service basics of dealing with orders and answering general questions, Tradient is using Octane to create knowledge bases about all corners of its business. These knowledge bases are being used to populate self-help portions of Tradient's Web site, and customer service representatives are using them to answer questions even in areas they are unfamiliar with and to ensure that the responses are consistent across the business.

CHAPTER 8

e-Tailing: Selling Your Wares on the Web

Money changes everything. Five or six years ago, as the Web started to attract attention as a medium for commerce, predictions about how much buying and selling would take place in cyberspace seemed nothing more than lofty pipe dreams. In retrospect, many of those predictions look like pocket change.

Cash registers are ringing all over the Web, and some of the biggest business-to-consumer success stories are coming from companies that have taken their long-standing brick-and-mortar businesses online. Sound easy? It's not.

You can have a retail site on the Web within 20 minutes. But creating an effective site with integrated marketing takes much longer. Online services allow you to build and maintain a site for free or for a low monthly charge. Generally, the online services provide a good way to get started, but they top out when you need a database or integration with enterprise applications.

When your retail operation needs more capabilities, companies like Microsoft and IBM offer extensive development environments.

Focus For Success

Today the focus for smart site managers is not on ever-more glitzy technology, but on delivering better search results, avoiding site failure, organizing sites intuitively, facilitating intelligent product comparisons, making purchasing recommendations, and personalizing the customer experience. In many cases, efforts in these areas are leading to seismic improvements in both site traffic and bottom lines.

Build the Basics

The first step in e-tailing is planning and then carefully building your online store, as shown in Figure 8.1. Storefront services abound on the Internet for companies wanting to be the next Amazon.com—or just the Web version of the corner hardware store. With some investigative work you can find a service that's right for you. Smaller stores can choose from among a variety of services. Two free sites, Bigstep.com and freemerchant.com, have good reputations for helping Web storefront startups.

If you prefer to get your store exposure through an online shopping mall, consider Yahoo! Stores or Amazon.com's zShops. eCongo.com's FreeCommerce Builder is a solution targeted at ISPs, small-business associations, and other organizations interested in hosting a variety of storefronts under a common umbrella. As the name implies, this is a free service for all parties. See Figure 8.1 for some functions of an e-tailing Web site.

Buzzwords

e-Tailing—Selling online.

If you want to get started on a storefront fast, here are the basic details for some of the most popular Web e-retail services. Each of these services is extremely easy to use and powerful. You really can establish a storefront on the Web in one afternoon. The prices shown are the minimum to start. As you add more products and services, those prices will climb.

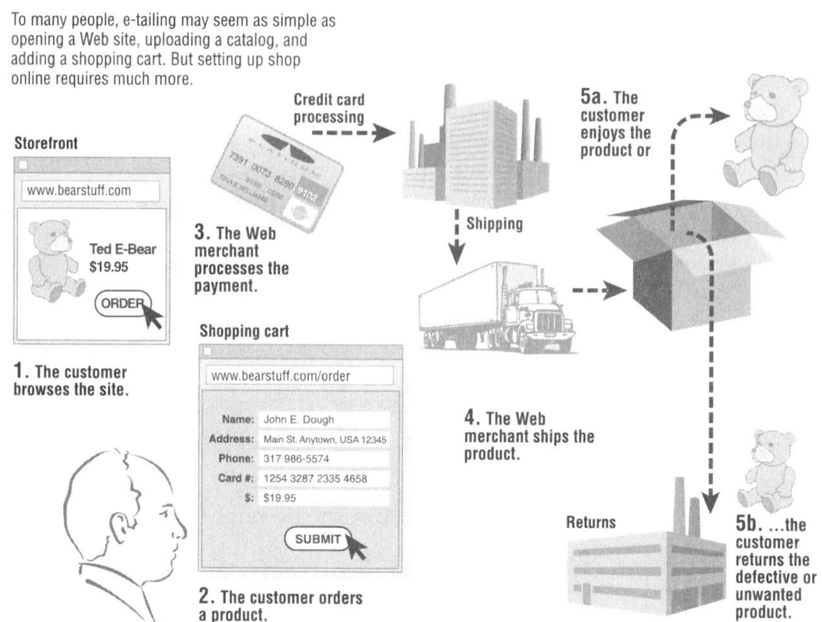
To many people, e-tailing may seem as simple as opening a Web site, uploading a catalog, and adding a shopping cart. But setting up shop online requires much more.
Storefront
www.bearstuff.com
Ted E-Bear
$19.95
ORDER
1. The customer browses the site.
Credit card processing
3. The Web merchant processes the payment.
Shopping cart
www.bearstuff.com/order
Name: John E. Dough
Address: Main St. Anytown, USA 12345
Phone: 317 986-5574
Card #: 1254 3287 2335 4658
$: $19.95
SUBMIT
2. The customer orders a product.
Shipping
4. The Web merchant ships the product.
5a. The customer enjoys the product or
Returns
5b. ...the customer returns the defective or unwanted product.

Figure 8.1

e-Tailing involves a more complicated start-up process than you might expect.

bCentral

Microsoft Corp.—$19.99 per month—

www.bcentral.com

Essentially a portal for small to medium-size businesses that want an all-in-one solution for doing business online, bCentral offers a potpourri of services (many of which date back to the familiar LinkExchange). If Microsoft's FrontPage 2000 is your primary tool for developing a Web site then bCentral is set to work for you. In many ways, the site is an extension of FrontPage 2000. But bCentral doesn't offer much room for growth. It lacks such important features as customer membership, inventory control, and detailed sales-reporting features available even in some free programs we reviewed.

bCentral is organized into three groups of services: Start (Site Manager, to set up and run the store), Market (to promote the store), and Manage (to support store operation). You begin the Start package with a well-paced wizard that helps you create the

Web site and store. When the wizard is finished, however, a barrage of prompts and tips can leave you confused about the big picture.

Site Manager plays triple duty, providing a single spot for building your site, building your store, and managing your store. As with most entry-level products, Site Manager isn't a true WYSIWYG design program. But there's a long list of themes to choose from, and you can control the layout of each page. Site Manager offers an immediate and dynamic link to Microsoft FrontPage 2000, a unique feature. We found that this worked very smoothly, enabling more advanced design capabilities.

Constructing our store catalog was very laborious. We had to create department pages one department at a time, and then product pages one page at a time, with only one product per page. We then linked each product page to the appropriate department. For shoppers, navigating through these pages is slow, especially if the store offers many products. Solutions like Bigstep.com and FreeMerchant enable you to place more than one product per page—much better for both store owners and customers.

Buzzwords

WYSIWYG—What you see is what you get. In this case, the Web page looks like what you see on the editing screen.

For the operations side, the Order Manager provides basic features, including shipping and tax tables, order review, and editable payment rules. The shipping options don't let you specify tables by carrier or charge by weight.

Ironically, despite bCentral's emphasis on site promotion, there is very little in the way of in-store product promotion or merchandizing. For instance, there are no discounting or featured-product tools. bCentral doesn't even offer sales reports.

Overall, bCentral is a great place for FrontPage 2000 users to start, but you can quickly run out of resources.

Bigstep.com

Bigstep.com—Free—www.bigstep.com

With an excellent combination of features and control, Bigstep.com makes the transition from a traditional business model to the online world as painless as it can be. Add the fact that basic service is free and you've got a combination that's difficult to beat.

Getting a site started with Bigstep.com is surprisingly simple. A wizard guides you through the initial steps needed to build a basic site. From there, you move into the back-office management features that let you micromanage every aspect of your storefront. We were able to get quick yet tangible results before moving into the heart of the application.

"One of Bigstep.com's great strengths is its flexibility; you can fine-tune every component of your storefront layout."

One of Bigstep.com's great strengths is its flexibility; you can fine-tune every component of your storefront layout. You can select from a series of site-wide templates, define vertical and horizontal layouts, and apply any color scheme you want. As you build your site, you can control the layout of each page in your catalog with a seemingly inexhaustible range of options.

To add items to your catalog, you fill out a form for each item. Though this requirement is frustrating if you already have your data stored electronically, the form is designed to let you enter data quickly and easily. You can add an unlimited number of items to your site and ease navigation by creating any number of sections.

The manager lets you expand any aspect of your site in a sophisticated development environment. You can publish sections separately as you finish them. And as you progress through the creation of your site, all of the tasks you have yet to complete are automatically added to your to-do list. Icons show you the status of tasks, indicating whether they are started, completed, or published.

Bigstep.com goes well beyond mere shopping cart capabilities. You can, for example, create surveys to collect useful feedback from your customers. Creating and distributing newsletters is also easy. Because Bigstep.com keeps track of information on all customers who have placed orders, content can be personalized to each customer's specific interests.

Bigstep.com clearly understands the needs of small businesses and has put together a solution that is sure to make even the most demanding business owner happy.

eCongo Powered Commerce

eCongo.com Inc.—Free—www.econgo.com

An entry-level solution should let you build an online storefront quickly without sacrificing quality for speed and simplicity. eCongo powered commerce accomplishes just that, letting you create a high-quality site while providing the management tools to nourish and promote your business and your site.

Getting an eCongo site started is very simple. The Store wizard guides you step by step through the initial stages of site design; you provide basic information about your company and then establish a layout. When you have completed the wizard, the basic site is published, giving you a Web presence in a matter of minutes.

You are then taken to the real meat of eCongo: the Store Manager. This is a powerful application where you can drill down into and tweak any aspect of your site.

You can add departments and categories very quickly using simple forms. Adding products is similarly easy, though they must be entered one at a time using the forms provided. As with Bigstep.com, entering each item could be an arduous task if you have a large inventory, but the forms are designed to minimize the potential headaches.

Support for tax and shipping tables is built in seamlessly. You need enter only a minimum amount of information on sales tax to get that aspect of your site working correctly. Shipping is slightly more complicated but still quite simple to maintain. You select some generic terms—Ground, Second Day, and Overnight, for example—that your users will see when they choose shipping options. You then indicate which carriers will handle your shipping and enter the shipping tables for the carriers you have selected. When the user selects a shipping method, the appropriate carrier is chosen and the correct shipping charges (based on the shipping table for that carrier) are added in.

In an interesting move, eCongo is partnering with some other businesses, creating a series of portals that allow eCongo partners to provide commerce to eCongo storeowners.

When your site is published, your store is added to an online mall provided by eCongo. Search features built into your storefront are extended, allowing your customers to search throughout the entire mall and making your store accessible to shoppers throughout the mall.

eStoreManager

estoreManager Inc—$149 per month for basic services plus $99 to set up; $49 per month plus 25 cents per transaction for credit card processing—www.estoremanager.com

One of the more pricey services, eStoreManager includes many important advanced features—particularly for product merchandizing. Though the package delivers solid operational capabilities, its page-design tools are too complicated for many novices.

Unlike the majority of storefront solutions, eStoreManager doesn't let you start instantly. You first contact a sales representative, after which eStoreManager.com creates your store and sends you an ID and password. Although you have to wait for these clearances, we found this approach efficient.

The Administration Center is downright sparse—simply a column of buttons for the various elements and features of the program. Despite its straightforwardness, many users will find the interface awkward and unintuitive, with little in the way of hints or guidance. Be prepared to read the manual or online help.

Compared with a service such as Bigstep.com, eStoreManager's ability to design and customize store pages is limited. Store design templates are bland, and unless you are versed in HTML, visual customization is limited to images and plain text. eStoreManager lacks a WYSIWYG editor, but you can preview the store in a browser window.

Its promotion and merchandizing features distinguish eStoreManager from most of the competition. We were especially impressed by the sophisticated discount and personalization modules that let a merchant design customized promotions. The

Personalized Content module ($99 per month) allows you to establish shopper groups, set targeted content for them, and develop promotions for select customers.

In the back office, eStoreManager is quite comprehensive. It supports inventory control, order tracking, and credit card processing, and provides a fair amount of standard reports and statistics. Although it doesn't link directly to databases or accounting applications, you can download or upload files to them.

Buzzwords

Affinity group—A group of people who have demonstrated similar behavior.

We were impressed with the integration and security of eStoreManager.com's hosting package; the company owns its network operating center and does its own credit card processing. On the other hand, it needs a Web community that supports its online stores more actively, as eCongo and Yahoo! Store have.

FreeMerchant

Network Commerce Inc.—Free—

www.freemerchant.com

FreeMerchant is a great deal for would-be online merchants. It enables you to create an electronic store quickly while allowing decent control over your ultimate design. Unfortunately, its store-building interface has also changed little and feels a bit amateurish.

Obviously, one of FreeMerchant's most appealing features is that the service is free. There are no hidden costs, and nobody takes a percentage of your sales. Note, however, that you'll need a separate merchant banking account to accept credit card purchases online. FreeMerchant offers discounted rates if you sign up with U.S. Merchant Systems for banking.

FreeMerchant lets you choose from a series of well-designed templates. You can add categories and products within categories. Adding a new product is easy, with little of the tedium that other services put you through. Even better, you can edit all products in a category from a single Add/Edit screen. Here, you can also change the product order on the list. One shortcoming: Categories are added one at a time.

Design choices are somewhat limited, a problem accentuated because you can't do much of your own HTML coding. Still, for a quick and useful storefront, FreeMerchant's design tools will more than suffice.

The service offers some especially nice features. You can, for example, create a variety of coupon types to offer free shipping or percentage discounts. You can even create discounts that increase at higher price points.

Intuitive screens give you the ability to set up shipping parameters, tax options, and shipping and return policies. You can set default international currencies for your products, and you can have orders faxed to you if that's how you prefer to keep track of them. An equally usable inventory system notifies you when you're running low on products.

FreeMerchant has a variety of service partners to enhance its offerings. You can auction items on eBay, use TeamOn for collaboration, and use CompuBank for banking and payment processing. Furthermore, WebTranslator.com (which offers a 5% discount to FreeMerchant users) can help you enter international markets. These partnerships help make FreeMerchant a well-rounded small-business service.

You can't go wrong with FreeMerchant. The design system, merchant tools, and vendor community are all strong, and the price is definitely right.

GoBizGo

NetObjects Inc.—30 days free, then $19.95 per month—www.gobizgo.com

An entry-level solution must make technology readily available to its customers without forcing them to become experts. Focusing on the small-business market, NetObjects' GoBizGo succeeds with an extremely simple interface that allows users to build online storefronts with great ease.

The service features three levels of hosting, with the top tier offering commerce functionality. Building a site is notably simple. You can build a complete site using the trial version, with the option of activating your membership and your site up to 30 days later.

GoBizGo's site-creation tool is designed to let you build a full, commerce-enabled site. Unlike the wizard-driven creation processes offered by such products as Bigstep.com and eCongo, GoBizGo provides a great level of control over details when initially creating your site. Though it can take longer to get a tangible result, the end product is fairly complete. Once you have a site built, the commerce features become available.

Entering items into your catalog is fairly simple. As with other services, there is no way to bulk-import your data from an existing system. Rather, you must complete the forms provided online. GoBizGo lets you enter approximately 100 items in your catalog. We were impressed by the tremendous level of detail that you can bring to any item in your catalog. Similar to FreeMerchant, GoBizGo helps you sell items from your catalog on eBay. This is a useful way of promoting merchandise and your store.

Setting up departments in your catalog, however, is not very intuitive. The same tool that lets you add pages about your company, your location, or your links is also used to add catalog pages to your site. Each section of your site requires a new page, so you must give careful thought to your site's navigation before you begin to build.

As with the other products in this roundup, GoBizGo handles tax and shipping calculations automatically. You set up tax information through a single form, entering the rates for each state. After you save the form, GoBizGo takes care of the rest for you. Setting up shipping preferences is also simple. A couple of options are provided by default, and each of your shipping tables can be customized to calculate charges using a variety of methods.

Although GoBizGo isn't the strongest solution in this roundup, it does provide an intuitive design tool. If you need to set up a noncommercial site immediately and then enable commerce at a later time, GoBizGo is worth a look.

HyperMart

Go2Net Inc.—$19.95 per month and up—www.hypermart.net

HyperMart is a relatively new service that promises to become one of the more interesting services to watch. HyperMart is owned by Go2Net, the company that also owns Authorize.Net, an online credit card payment system. The result is that HyperMart offers built-in credit card authorization, a great convenience for online merchants who are just starting out.

HyperMart makes it much easier than other storefront services to establish a full domain name. From the initial sign-up screen, you have the option of using the tailored hypermart.net domain name, registering your own domain through Network Solutions, or transferring an existing domain name. In all cases, HyperMart hosts the domain name free of charge. The best idea is to find the cheapest service for registering a new domain name and then transfer it to the HyperMart servers. Nonetheless, this feature is extremely useful.

Building the store, however, isn't as easy as it could be. Because HyperMart's tool isn't WYSIWYG, you don't see the fruit of your efforts until you either preview the site or save it and visit it. You change the colors of links, table lines, and backgrounds on a color chart; unfortunately its interface requires you to keep scrolling back to select another item to edit. Font choices and templates are limited. HyperMart-based sites are bound to look similar. Fortunately, you can use third-party HTML tools to build the site and count on HyperMart primarily for its shopping cart features.

Adding categories and products is similarly tough. Lacking a WYSIWYG interface, the process is difficult, but you can upload your product catalog from a spreadsheet.

Reports and statistics are available but limited compared with those offered by such services as Bigstep.com, FreeMerchant, and Yahoo! Store. Signing up for a cart-based site improves the service's design, reporting, and cataloging features. But even then, HyperMart is not the most elegant service available.

Card authorization is available in two price categories. For manual order processing, the cost ranges from $19.95 per month to $84.95 per month. Monthly fees for real-time card authorization range from $49.95–$114.90. The Web hosting is free, or $8.25 per month for an ad-free site.

HyperMart has great potential, but it is still young (even in Internet time) and changing frequently.

Web Store

iCat, A Division of Intel Online Services—Fees vary by service provider—`www.icat.com`

iCat's Web Store offers more catalog management and back-office options than most other services. Its impressive back-office features offer such key capabilities as inventory, promotions, and reporting. Yet despite its many offerings, Web Store manages to retain a clean and simple organization that's easy to use.

Interestingly, you do not purchase this service from iCat (or even Intel). Instead, you sign up through a service provider; British Telecom, LaSalle Bank, and PNC Bank are the current options. We signed up with LaSalle Bank for our testing.

The online installation process requires your valid credit card. When signing up with LaSalle Bank, we were given a survey asking for considerable detail about the merchant and store. The formality of this procedure is intimidating compared with the somewhat breezy approach taken by many other products.

In developing the catalog, you pick the layout and style, but you don't have an option to add extra pages. This isn't the most flexible of store design programs, but the outcomes look good.

The catalog options are excellent. You can specify properties (such as size and color) and the appropriate values (blue, green, large, small, and so on). You also have control over which combinations are available.

Web Store is one of the few packages that lets you define the fields you want to appear in your product information, including the standard items (name, SKU, price) and as many as 17 additional fields. Also unusual for entry-level stores, you can batch-import product items into your catalog from data files. The protocol, however, is so picky that batch imports are worth the effort only if you have a large number of items.

Like its catalog, Web Store's order processing is polished, including a full battery of reports for customers, sales, and inventory. Site analysis information, however, is scant. Sophisticated merchandising options enable cross-selling, up-selling, discounts, and featured items. Additional services and merchant communities (like those offered by Microsoft bCentral and Yahoo! Store) are dependent on the service provider and are thus limited.

Fees for Web Store are based on the number of items in the store catalog and vary among the providers. LaSalle Bank charges $49.95 per month for 50 items.

In some ways, iCat's Web Store takes a more businesslike approach than many other services. It is relatively formal and emphasizes the actual operation of the store. This is a sophisticated solution that is well suited to merchants who want flexibility in pricing and first-rate promotion tools.

Yahoo! Store

Yahoo! Inc.—$100 per month and up—store.yahoo.com

Yahoo! Store is probably the most visible and most established storefront system on the Net. For those reasons alone, it is worth considering for your storefront solution.

Creating a store is easy, and Yahoo! Store includes an excellent tutorial to help newbies get up and running. The page layout has improved since this service first appeared. A Variables button gives you a wide range of control over fonts, colors, image dimensions, and other details. We like the fact that you can embed HTML tags inside text. Even so, many of the stores created with this service look similar, and controlling the design isn't nearly as easy as we would like it to be.

Store management is handled through a well-designed screen that is the heart of your store. It provides access to order processing, statistics, site settings, and promotional functions. Order tracking and order summaries are highly useful features. You can view a variety of statistics, including hits per page, orders and sales per page, searches, click trails, and how people arrived at your site. From this screen, you can also set payment methods, shipping rates, tax rates, and other details.

The administration page is solid and useful. We were impressed with the fact that if you run an inventory database on your own server, you can tie it and Yahoo! Store's inventory system together with a bit of programming.

Yahoo! Store really exploits the concept of vendor community. Yahoo! provides an extensive and searchable listing of stores (`shopping.yahoo.com`), as well as a rewards system that encourages customers to buy from Yahoo! vendors. Community is also promoted through the gift registry. Customers can search the registry for friends and family to find out what they want. Yahoo! then provides a list of stores that sell the desired products. These community aspects can really help drive people to your site and strengthen your online presence.

> *"Customers can search the registry for friends and family to find out what they want... These community aspects can really help drive people to your site and strengthen your online presence."*

All this isn't free by any means; fees start at $100 per month for a store with 50 items for sale. In addition, Yahoo! takes 2% of your monthly sales over $5,000 if you participate in Yahoo! Shopping. And for credit card sales, Yahoo! requires that you establish a merchant account.

After you've created your online store, you'll need to concern yourself with orders, shipping and handling, and taxes. Yahoo! Store makes all of this almost as easy as assembling your storefront, though perhaps not as fun. Through its management interface, you can determine whether you would like your orders emailed or faxed to you, or you can retrieve them through a Web browser. And you're presented with a vast array of acceptable payment methods, including credit cards. Yahoo! Store's automated wizard steps you through creating shipping tables, determining how you want to charge for shipping, and choosing your delivery methods.

Taxation is handled in similar fashion. And when you're done, Yahoo! Store lets you test out the whole thing.

After you're up and running, you can watch the traffic using Yahoo! Store's rich reporting and analysis tools. Slice your daily statistics any number of ways, determining the most popular pages, the sites from which your visitors hail, and the search keywords generating the most sales. You can also generate a report that summarizes trends on your site.

Yahoo! Store is a terrific e-commerce tool and service for small and midsize businesses. With tough competitors such as iCat Commerce Online and MerchandiZer, Yahoo! Store is no longer alone at the top, but it deserves serious consideration.

Using Yahoo! Store, you can easily create a storefront using just your browser. A navigation bar lists available commands, and you can display an explanation of each function.

Who Needs It?

It's well known that a good Web storefront can make a small company look like a multinational corporation, but a small company might pass up the efforts to personalize its site. That would be a mistake. Personalization is key to online retail success. Companies of any size can benefit. At www.personalization.com, you'll find a vertical portal for the personalization market.

Five Tips for Getting Started

Step 1—Web Server

You'll host your Web storefront on a Web server either in your own facility, in the facility of a local ISP, or in a large Web hosting service. Regardless of where it is, the server system consists of the software that will serve your application to site visitors and the hardware that will host your server and application. If you need to specify the server, the average hardware should have 128MB of RAM and anywhere from 150MB–1GB of free harddisk space. Server software options vary depending on which storefront application you've used, but Microsoft Internet Information Server, Netscape Enterprise Server, and the freeware Apache are all good solutions.

Step 2—Payment Services

To accept credit cards, you must open an Internet merchant account with a bank. Most Web site hosting services will do this for you.

The payment process sounds complex, but it works for businesses every day. You can't communicate directly with your bank, so you need to submit secure credit card transactions to a transaction-processing service such as PaymentNet or CyberCash.

These services will, in turn, send transactions to a payment-processing network such as FirstData with your merchant account information for authorization. After the product ships, the transaction is submitted for settlement and the payment-processing network charges the customer's credit card and submits payment to your bank account.

Step 3—Order Fulfillment

Depending on the type of products you are selling, you'll fulfill orders either by download, for electronic goods, or by physical shipment, for hard goods. One benefit of downloadable products is that you can submit the credit card for authorization and settlement immediately. For shipped products, credit cards can be authorized but not submitted for settlement until the product ships.

Real-Time

If the products you are selling can be downloaded over the Internet, you will need a mechanism such as an FTP site. Your Web server likely includes FTP capabilities.

Shipping

For hard goods, you will need to fulfill the order and ship it directly to the customer. You might want to tie your system into FedEx or UPS so that customers can get live shipping estimates when placing their orders and can use your site to check the shipping status of their orders.

Step 4—Site Promotion

For your site to be successful, people need to visit it. Generating traffic can sometimes be a daunting task, and you might want to avail yourself of tools for search-engine submission and monitoring, such as WebPosition Gold.

Banner Exchange

A banner exchange service such as Link Exchange is a low-cost way to generate site traffic and make your site look more professional. In exchange for displaying other companies' banners on your site through the exchange service, your banner will be displayed on other participating company sites in kind.

Step 5—Site Monitoring and Analysis

Keeping track of who's coming to your site, how they're navigating it, and how they found it (through a banner ad or a search engine, for example) is key to determining how your site promotion efforts are faring. You'll need a log analysis tool, such as WebTrends, that will give you reports analyzing your traffic so that you can make any changes to the site or tweak your marketing efforts.

If you already have a marketing Web site that describes your products or services, Digital StoreFronts' Retail Pro is one of many services that allows you to commerce-enable your site without learning an array of programming skills. If all you need is a shopping cart added to your site, Digital StoreFront's InterCart provides that very service for $19.95 per month. The Retail Pro service ($49.95 per month) goes beyond the shopping cart: Such features as inventory control, search tools, sales support, and reporting validate the additional cost. Either solution provides SSL encryption for transactions and the capability to handle online credit card processing.

Customers Complaining

The Boston Consulting Group recently produced research data about online buying habits, illustrating how unhappy e-shoppers are. The research was based on a survey of 12,000 online consumers. According to the results, 48% of online shoppers gave up trying to buy some products online because Web pages took too long to load. Another 45% gave up because they found particular commerce sites too confusing to navigate. In cases where a listed product was not in stock, 32% of respondents said that they gave up trying to buy the product online. Four percent of respondents said they had ordered products online that were never delivered.

That kind of growth adds to the urgency of delivering a good customer experience. "The first online purchase experience is the moment of truth for consumers and retailers. It is the beginning of a brand connection," said Boston Consulting Group senior vice president Michael Silverstein. "The frustrations that are commonplace in these early days of electronic retailing could be the kiss of death for the brands of Internet retailers."

The dissatisfaction results reported by the Boston Consulting Group can seem surprising, but should they really be? After all, the Web has only reached its full volume of welcome in the past few years, and is still in its infancy as a communications, shopping, information-delivery, and trading medium. Wouldn't it be more accurate to call it the Wild West? Online shoppers seem to think so.

Midrange Solutions

Larger stores require a more powerful solution that provides their customers with a richer experience and integrates with their existing systems. Keep in mind that you or an outside contractor will typically build the site and then host it on a Web site hosting service. The picture gets more complex in that many of the hosting services have their own e-commerce development systems and site development services. However, although a hosting service might help with site creation, creation and hosting are two different things. You can create a site or have it created for you and then host it practically anywhere. Here are some examples of products and services you can use to build very robust e-commerce sites.

Microsoft Commerce Server 2000

Microsoft Corp.—$8,499 per processor ($12,999 per processor includes Commerce Server 2000 bundled with SQL Server 2000)—`www.microsoft.com/commerceserver`

Formerly Microsoft Site Server 3.0 Commerce Edition, Microsoft Commerce Server 2000 offers a compelling e-commerce solution for the Windows platform. This new version, which is currently in beta, greatly simplifies installation and administration overhead, letting managers control virtually every aspect of their sites without relying on programmers to do the dirty work.

In the past, Microsoft provided all the tools for successful e-commerce but required you to apply all the proper service packs to install and configure the tools—a very time-consuming process. So we were pleased to find that Commerce Server 2000 has a truly streamlined and integrated install.

In the older Site Server, Microsoft employed a wizard that generated a default store, along with a separate set of pages for administrative tasks. Now, Commerce Server 2000 offers a new, more powerful method. Rather than run a wizard, Commerce Server 2000 bundles sample retail stores in single package up (PUP) files.

PUP files represent an important step forward in managing Microsoft-based electronic stores, because they let you collect everything in your store—from SQL data and ASP pages to images and COM+ components needed to run a site. First, this is a nifty way to distribute model stores. Second, it lets you package up an entire store and re-deploy it on a new Windows server along with all the necessary components. Any administrator who has faced the intricacies of COM+ and Microsoft Transaction Services (MTS) will recognize this new feature as groundbreaking.

To create a simple custom store, we added a theme and tweaked some of the HTML and ASP scripts. By default, the working store was entirely functional, with a shopping basket and access to order tracking. The only missing feature, as with most of the products in the market today, was the ability to work with your bank to set up credit card processing; you'll need a merchant account for that. Out of the box, the credit card processing does a checksum for a valid credit card.

Commerce Server 2000 has a very sophisticated administration tool in the form of a DHTML-based browser application called Business Desk. Adding new products, editing shipping tables, changing tax options, and otherwise administering our site were all very simple. You can even manage auctions and view bids.

Business Desk's reporting capabilities are notable as well, with more than 20 canned reports on all types of traffic and site analysis. Because Commerce Server 2000 relies on OLAP Services in SQL Server 2000, you get a built-in data warehouse for your site free, along with all the analytical power for analyzing traffic and customer behavior.

One of the most immediately useful features in Business Desk is the Campaigns tool. This lets you create promotions for particular products and build targeted direct-mail campaigns for selected customers based on any criteria, all without writing a line of code. You could, for example, target shoppers who spent over $100 in the past six months.

For developers, Microsoft uses Visual InterDev 6.0 (part of Visual Studio) along with VBscript or JavaScript on the server side to generate Web pages dynamically. Visual InterDev is a powerful developer tool that provides a visual environment for designing pages.

In addition to creating or modifying ASP scripts, Commerce Server 2000 also exposes the innards of e-commerce business rules through its Commerce Pipeline Editor. Using this convenient visual model, developers can attach script code to any section of the pipe, representing steps in an online transaction. Using Commerce Pipeline, you can integrate your electronic store with your inventory and accounting systems. With the forthcoming BizTalk Server 2000, Microsoft will extend Commerce Server 2000's capability to communicate with other vendors in your supply chain. This will involve advanced XML support and message-based processing for business-to-business scenarios. Commerce Server 2000 offers a more manageable solution on its own, however, ideally suited for selling to consumers.

This release offers a rich B2C solution that is quite easy to get started. And in case you want to move into the B2B realm eventually, you have plenty of room to grow. To keep your store running, you'll need some Windows administrative expertise on hand, but for the business side, Commerce Server 2000's broad toolset and customizability will impress managers.

Buzzwords

B2C—Business-to-customer.

WebSphere Commerce Suite (with WebSphere Commerce Studio)

IBM Corp.—$9,500—

www.software.ibm.com/commerce

IBM's e-commerce solution, WebSphere Commerce Suite Start Edition, provides all the tools any business will need to succeed online. When testing this very capable product, we were pleased to find that it let us roll up our sleeves and really dig in. Meanwhile, IBM's experience with traditional brick-and-mortar business solutions is evident, with excellent support for managing multiple stores and a realistic approach to role-based security for the multiple players that need to interact with your site.

The Commerce Suite package includes 11 CD-ROMS. A single utility manages the setup process, installing the various pieces of a fairly integrated set of tools. We tested the default tools and configuration with Windows NT 4.0 as our operating system, IBM HTTP Web Server powered by Apache for the Web server, and db2 for the database back end. We used two server packages: IBM WebSphere Application Server 3.1 (with support for Enterprise JavaBeans, servlets, and JavaServer Pages), and IBM Commerce

Server 4.1 (which manages the resources needed to run a store). Although the Start Edition runs on Windows NT 4.0, the Pro Edition ($38,000) supports a variety of platforms including AIX, AS400, OS390, Solaris, and Unix, and adds support for features such as auctions and reporting.

You'll need to configure the various server-side components using separate tools. Nevertheless, our test store was up and running reasonably quickly. Two Java-based modules are used to administer both WebSphere Application Server and Commerce Server. IBM HTTP Web Server can be accessed through a Web browser for common options, and db2 has its own native-code administration console and tools. We got Commerce Studio up with the default installation, but we must point out that you will probably need in-house expertise to administer all these modules properly.

When building your own store, Commerce Suite offers two options. First, you can purchase IBM WebSphere Commerce Studio 3.1, which is available as an add-on. This commerce-enabled version of IBM's well-known WebSphere Studio Web development tool provides an impressive wizard for store creation. By selecting options on a series of screens, we built our own default store in a matter of minutes. The wizard lets you select visual styles for your store and choose where to place the navigation bar, among other options. It also features excellent support for international markets, with over 20 built-in currencies, and it supports dual currencies (an option required by European countries transitioning to the Euro).

Tweaking the underlying HTML and scripts used by Commerce Suite is fairly easy. We were a little surprised that although IBM WebSphere Application Server supports industry-standard JavaServer Pages and servlets, the product relies on IBM's Net.Data scripting language. Of course, developers can still write their own JSPs and servlets. Commerce Suite 5.0 should improve matters by delivering full support for JSPs in the default commerce store. IBM also claims that version 5.0 will ramp up from Sun's JDK 1.1 Java standard to Java 2 on the server side.

The other choice for getting started doesn't require Commerce Studio. Instead, you can customize one of the sample stores provided in the package. Though this requires little HTML expertise, more extensive modifications will require a programmer who is familiar with Net.Data script. We had no trouble creating our test store using this approach, and we ran the wizard-created store alongside the second, customized store.

Regardless of which method you choose, you will need to use the Commerce Administrator application after your store is up and running. This is, undoubtedly, one of the best parts of Commerce Suite. This command center can be used by managers to control virtually every aspect of stores and malls, including defining roles, specifying tax rates and shipping options, and creating discounts. As a Web-based tool, Commerce Administrator has a few quirks, particularly with catalog and product entry. But we found it to be an entirely capable solution. If you need better control over products and catalogs, your organization should consider the $3,000 Catalog Architect add-on (bundled with Pro Edition).

The Start Edition of Commerce Suite does not include a reporting module. We recommended using Seagate Software's Crystal Reports. Commerce Suite Pro Edition bundles its own reporting module. If your company needs these features, consider the higher-end product because it will probably pay for itself in development costs in only a few months.

As a maturing e-commerce solution, IBM Commerce Suite offers a powerful set of tools and it is certain to see even more integration and ease-of-use in the upcoming 5.0 release. The Start Edition offers an affordable and powerful solution for your organization to get up and running. You should consider the Pro version, however, if you do not want to invest in developer expertise to supplement the base package with custom functionality, that is, functionality that's readily available in the full version.

OpenSales AllCommerce

OpenSales Inc.—Free—www.opensales.com

Along with the right hardware and developer know-how, OpenSales AllCommerce lets you put up a store with virtually no start-up software costs. A freely distributed open-source solution, this program truly surprised us with its maturity. AllCommerce was developed for Apache and mySQL running on Linux. But being a

Perl-based solution, it is compatible with any Web server running Perl and a SQL database.

Although it is available free, you will undoubtedly have to hire a Perl expert or two to customize your store. If you have access to such talent, you should definitely consider the extremely capable AllCommerce as your e-store solution.

> *"Unlike the other products in this roundup, AllCommerce uses a command-line script to define common options for your store."*

Unlike the other products in this roundup, AllCommerce uses a command-line script to define common options for your store. After answering a few simple questions, you generate the HTML pages for the store by running some Perl scripts. On a Linux system, the other parts of the puzzle—Apache Web server, the Perl module for Linux, mySQL, and the DBD/DBI Perl database connectivity library—are installed separately. A solid knowledge of Linux is useful when getting up and running.

We also tested AllCommerce on Windows NT 4.0 using Win32 versions of mySQL and ActiveState Perl, with Microsoft Internet Information Server 4.0 as the Web server. Though the Windows installation took more work, AllCommerce did prove itself as a cross-platform solution.

After your store is running, few of the managerial and administrative tasks require Perl expertise. The administrator front end let us add and manage catalogs and products easily. One minor quirk: You must copy an object ID (a unique ID assigned to each data item in the database) manually between pages. The administrator module enables managers to tweak business rules for the store.

We like the way AllCommerce lays out products on the page intelligently. A camera bag, for example, wouldn't appear before the camera it holds. Our test store functioned well and looked very professional. We were particularly impressed by the shopping basket and customer access to order information.

The AllCommerce package contains technology derived at least in part from real sites, including MyHome.com. As a result, it's ready to manage complicated product lines and support variants. AllCommerce can also track inventory from multiple warehouses. You'll want to tweak the look and feel, of course. This is done through HTML templates, saving you from having to rewrite Perl scripts.

One of the great things about AllCommerce's open-source model is that as customers add whiz-bang features out in the field, the new features can be integrated back into the main product. This includes scripts like our favorite, which imports the current UPS and USPS shipping rates directly from the Web into AllCommerce's shipping tables.

As a result of feedback from real customers, the reporting capabilities are comprehensive and provide truly useful data. Available reports give you a quick snapshot of site activity over the past 24 hours. These include total orders and the 25 most popular pages and items, as well as more detailed reports of site traffic and customer activities. You can even view click trails.

AllCommerce's only obvious limitation is its inability to automate promotions. OpenSales plans to include this in a future release. In the meantime, you must use Perl to add promotions yourself.

For developers, OpenSales relies on well-documented Perl program interfaces to perform common functions. Unlike IBM's WebSphere Commerce Studio and Microsoft Visual InterDev, AllCommerce's development lacks a visual interface. Still, there's no denying Perl's elegance and power as a Web development language.

OpenSales proves that with a Perl guru and a little more up-front work, you can get a powerful electronic store for free. Following in the footsteps of Linux, the AllCommerce package shows off what's best in the open-source movement: Continual updating from some of the best programming minds in the world.

Which Development Tool?

Each of the midrange solutions we list above is impressive. They offer different approaches and different strengths, though, so no one product is right for every user.

Microsoft Commerce Server 2000 makes the midrange much more approachable. Although you will need a knowledgeable administrator on hand, the product is far from difficult to get up and running. It also provides the best administrative tool in this roundup, allowing business users to manage the site easily without involving developers. Commerce Server 2000 also introduces the revolutionary PUP file format, which lets you bundle up entire sites and move them to another server.

IBM's WebSphere Commerce Suite Start Edition offers more customizability, allowing you to really get into the code. The sample stores that you see are impressive and easy to tweak. And like Commerce Server, WebSphere Commerce Suite provides a nice administrator interface.

OpenSales AllCommerce is quite different from the IBM and Microsoft offerings. This extremely powerful and scalable solution is free and Perl-based. Your options are limitless, provided you have a talented developer or two on hand to write and edit Perl scripts.

Integration with legacy systems is another consideration. Many products have hopelessly inadequate data-import facilities. Hooking into existing accounting systems, the ideal scenario for truly putting your existing business online, is effective with Microsoft Commerce Server if you're using Microsoft BackOffice systems.

In defense of most of the vendors, however, legacy systems are usually databases and can be integrated by using the scripting or language capabilities the products offer. But again, that means that your buying decision is colored by the level of programming or Web expertise you have on hand or need to hire.

The purpose of your Web site is to drive business, whether by direct online selling or by steering traffic to real-world stores. The tools we review here offer you the best platforms for growing your business online—that is, scaling it up from something modest, and then delivering more and more options and services as time goes by.

Billing

Handling billing is a complicated matter. Any kind of credit card processing requires a merchant bank account. Your e-commerce host should provide you with assistance on setting up this account. But your business might have billing needs that go beyond one-time transactions. ibill, one of the leaders in the billing industry, has a turnkey solution designed to integrate with your site seamlessly. Most of ibill's solutions also require a merchant account, with ibill providing the interface between your site and the merchant account. In case your customers require billing options other than credit cards, ibill also supports online checking and payment through its Web900 telephone billing service, which lets customers pay by calling a 900 number. Many of the sites that enable you to build your own e-commerce site and then have it hosted, such as Freemerchant.com, also let you automatically sign up for different billing choices and credit card strategies.

Many items come with the option of extending their warranties. That procedure was easy enough to handle in your brick-and-mortar operation, but how do you do this online? Enter WarrantyNow. When you sign up for WarrantyNow, you gain the ability to provide warranty service and support directly through your shopping cart. Your customers have the ability to sign up for extended warranty service, and WarrantyNow provides and supports the warranty services with live 24-hour telephone support.

Beyond Credit Cards

The current trend, which many companies are betting on as the future of e-money, is electronic bill presentment and payment (EBPP)). EBPP takes your site miles beyond the mere capability to accept secure credit card transactions, letting you present bills and collect payments over the Internet. Figure 8.2 shows you the EBPP process.

No more checks lost in the mail. Customers can review statements online and transfer funds instantly. They can even contact customer service reps electronically, substantially cutting down on the number of calls going through the call center—and reducing the cost of your company's customer support.

Buzzwords

EBPP—Electronic bill presentment and payment. Electronic billing and collection that also facilitates collection of marketing information. You get your money faster and potentially learn something about your customer.

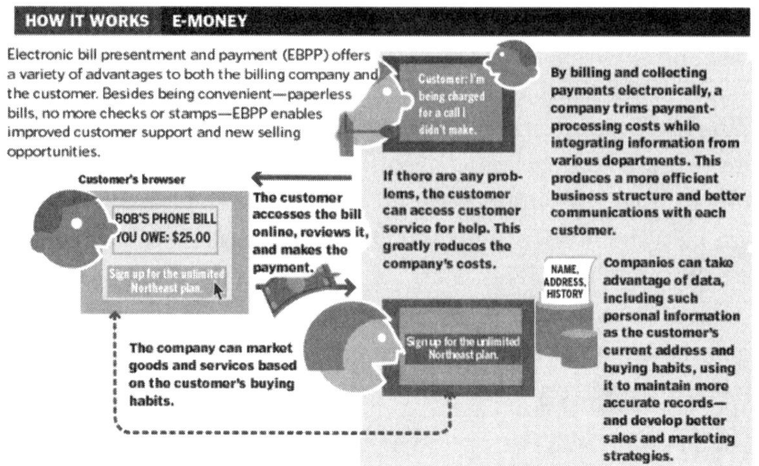

HOW IT WORKS E-MONEY
Electronic bill presentment and payment (EBPP) offers a variety of advantages to both the billing company and the customer. Besides being convenient—paperless bills, no more checks or stamps—EBPP enables improved customer support and new selling opportunities.
Customer: I'm being charged for a call I didn't make.
By billing and collecting payments electronically, a company trims payment-processing costs while integrating information from various departments. This produces a more efficient business structure and better communications with each customer.
Customer's browser
BOB'S PHONE BILL
YOU OWE: $25.00
Sign up for the unlimited Northeast plan.
The customer accesses the bill online, reviews it, and makes the payment.
If there are any problems, the customer can access customer service for help. This greatly reduces the company's costs.
NAME, ADDRESS, HISTORY
Companies can take advantage of data, including such personal information as the customer's current address and buying habits, using it to maintain more accurate records—and develop better sales and marketing strategies.
Sign up for the unlimited Northeast plan.
The company can market goods and services based on the customer's buying habits.

Figure 8.2

Electronic bill payment can be faster, more convenient, and more secure than paper bills and checks.

Micropayments

Micropayments are very small payments made at commerce sites for transactions that would be too small to be feasible as credit card transactions. For example, a Web shopper might buy an online product for as little as a fraction of a cent. A working draft for micropayment technology and standards is The Common Markup for Micropayment Per-Fee-Links, available at `http://www.w3.org/ECommerce/Activity.html` and information on micropayment technology from IBM is at `http://www-4.ibm.com/software/webservers/commerce/payment/mpay/index.htm`.

The obvious benefit of EBPP to your company is cost savings. Traditional paper billing methods typically cost a company about $1–$1.50 per invoice, which includes printing and sending a bill and receiving and processing the payment. Billing electronically typically saves a company about 25%–30% per statement, according to most players in this market.

These savings, though, have been outweighed by the prohibitive expense of EBPP systems for all but the largest billers—utilities, telcos, and financial institutions—which routinely send out millions of invoices each month. Derivion Corp., an ASP, enables companies to outsource EBPP—making it more affordable. The Derivion system converts a company's invoicing and accounts-receivable data into data that can be shared with major bill presentment systems.

Costs tend to be about $30,000 for setup and about 30 cents per transaction. This significantly expands the potential EBPP market but remains beyond the reach of many small businesses.

Derivion is working with several small-business portals to provide a more automated, less expensive solution that should be available later this year. Some claim that estimates of EBPP cost savings are exaggerated. The Internet Research Group's 1999 Bill Payment and Presentment Report states that EBPP "doesn't save its users money." The report does not dismiss EBPP, though, stating that the value "comes from business improvement rather than cost savings." Customer data becomes more available and therefore more useful. When a customer moves and notifies the billing department, the information is automatically shared throughout the company, establishing an important building block for a successful CRM strategy. Ultimately, EBPP gives you the opportunity to foster better communication with your customers.

Traditional billing methods present lucrative opportunities to stuff statements with ads. EBPP, through its improved data collection, facilitates marketing that is tailored to a customer's individual spending habits. For example, AT&T electronic statements can offer new service plans that match the customers' usage patterns. As Jim Moran, co-founder and executive vice president of sales and marketing at Internet billing platform provider edocs, said, there is a "strategic value of being able to very precisely cross-sell your customers with very specific content that you weave into the bills and statements based on a customer's actual usage patterns and spending habits."

Powerful solutions, such as edocs and TriSense Software's PaySense, are ideal for companies that want in-house programs that integrate tightly with their customer care systems. Currently, edocs targets large, Fortune 500-caliber companies such as American Express, General Electric, and Sprint.

Recognizing the larger scope of these technologies, edocs eschews the term EBPP in favor of Internet billingbilling and customer management. To the customer, EBPP means access to account data at any time, from anywhere. But to the company, Moran explains, Internet billing means that customers can access their data without burdening the call center. edocs and PaySense both support multiple distribution models, including direct billing—posting data on the company's own Web site—and indirect billing—distributing bill content to portals. Personal finance portals such as CyberBills and Quicken.com enable customers to access and manage all their finances in one place.

But most businesses don't need a solution of edocs' scope. Companies such as CheckFree Corp. and billserv.com offer hosted solutions. With CheckFree's outsourced solution, merchants and billers pay CheckFree for distributing bills and receiving payments. CheckFree recently acquired BlueGill Technologies, now called CheckFree i-Solutions, which is positioned to compete with edocs' in-house solution.

Of course, the business benefits of EBPP are moot if the consumer has no incentive to be billed electronically. Fortunately, like merchants, customers reap the cost savings and convenience of not having to send checks through the mail. Often, the consumer's credit card can be billed directly, or funds can be deducted from a bank account. Best of all, customers don't have to deal with the clutter of incoming bills and trips to the post office.

One of the big questions, though, is whether consumers will prefer to deal directly with each vendor or with a centralized system. Most people in the industry agree that customers will ultimately demand a single point of billing. "After all," said Read Ziegler, Derivion's chief marketing officer, "you don't have 15 mailboxes in front of your house."

EBPP means different things to different people. To the billing department, it means less paper and less overhead. To the marketing and sales departments, it means better data collection and data mining, as well as better cross- and up-selling opportunities. For customer care, it means fewer incoming calls. And to the customer, it means better service and easier maintenance of personal finances.

Ship It

Getting the customer to place the order is only half the battle. Next you need to fulfill it. How you handle shipping is an important part of your commerce solution. Your good reputation as a merchant can hinge on this very process. The product must arrive on time.

One of the greatest challenges a product-oriented business will face on a daily basis is shipping. Stamps.com is an excellent tool for handling your shipping needs. Rather than entering and maintaining shipping tables yourself (or worse, looking up shipping costs manually), Stamps.com will keep up-to-date tables for you. To determine the cost of shipping, you simply provide information about the size and weight of the package, along with handling and insurance costs. Stamps.com will then return the correct shipping charges for a variety of carriers and options. After you have selected the best option for your package, you can generate a shipping ticket. Stamps.com also provides tracking tools, adding peace of mind that your package was delivered. Beyond handling packages, Stamps.com offers a complete postage meter service, which lets you print postage directly onto envelopes or labels.

Take It Back

As much as you might wish otherwise, you'll need a strategy for handling returns. As online sales continue to grow, returns of merchandise sold online will grow as well. Less than half of the returned merchandise can be resold as new, and the rest is liquidated. And be aware that as returns grow, so will the number of customers seeking to abuse your returns policy. Are you ready?

If you can't take care of returns adequately, check out The Return Exchange. Customers click the return button and are presented with a form to fill out. The Return Exchange checks its databases: If the customer has a history of abusing return policies, The Return Exchange flags the return for your consideration. Otherwise, the customer receives a return authorization number. The easy returns are solved automatically, leaving your team to handle only special problems. The customer can ship products to The Return Exchange's regional center, which will restore as many of the products as possible to resalable condition and add them back to stock. If a product can't be salvaged as new, the company will auction it for you.

Most of the familiar retail services are migrating to the Internet. Ultimately, service is what separates the stellar companies from the mediocre ones. By ensuring that your Web customers receive the same high level of service your walk-in customers expect, you go a long way toward succeeding at e-tail.

Be Found!

Hopefully, they'll seek and find you online, but you can do many things to help. Advanced search technologies and more intelligent shopping tools are among the most important tools for many commerce sites. You can see various tools and their relative success rates in Figure 8.3. According to Nick Valente, vice president of e-Commerce at AT&T's Worldnet site, targeted search technology and intelligent product comparisons have made a big difference for Worldnet-based shopping and communications tasks. Part of the charter of the Worldnet site is to attract users who want to search and shop across the Web, while at the same time the Worldnet site is designed to help position and sell AT&T's products.

How Are *They* Finding *You*?

• E-tailers finding customers is one thing, but which media best drive customers to merchant sites? According to BizRate.com, Web referrals are the top source, followed by alternative sources, which include previous experience with a merchant, recommendations, and word of mouth. Yet TV ads result in the highest average amount spent per purchase.

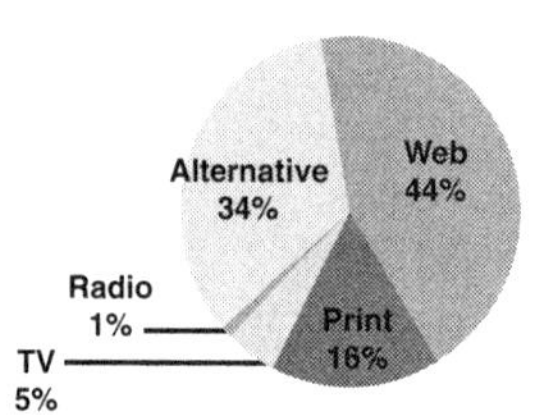

Medium	Average spent
Web	$99
Print	$100
TV	$139
Radio	$84
Alternative	$127

Figure 8.3

Search engines aren't the only technology driving customers to your site, but they're too important to ignore.

Valente chose to use search technology from DirectHit, which has been acquired by AskJeeves, to provide a more targeted search. He also used technology from AskJeeves to build a shopping center based on "popularity search," which sends back product comparison results where the products most popular with other consumers in various categories are delivered as most relevant. Chrysler is another company that uses popularity search to tell customers which models of cars were most popular with other online customers, and Chrysler also uses the technology to track which Frequently Asked Questions online are the most frequently asked.

"Our site has been up for four years," said Valente, "and has been through several redesigns. The technology we added that has produced the most bang for the buck was adding DirectHit search technology last year. Immediately after adding the DirectHit technology, we saw about a 40% boost in page views and increases in customer satisfaction. Better search really pays off." The Worldnet site has about 3.8–4.2 million unique visitors per month, according to MediaMetrix, and is rapidly growing as a shopping medium for not only AT&T's products but for offerings from other providers.

The Worldnet site is based on back-end Unix systems with a few Windows NT systems mixed in. The site has increasingly featured custom content, which is often associated with the shopping features at the site, and Valente manages the content at the site with DreamWeaver from Macromedia. He describes DreamWeaver as a great product for using visual tools to organize and update a commerce site. Dreamweaver defines HTML behavior by browser level and can check a remote user's browser level when loading a page to customize what is delivered.

In addition to targeted search technology from AskJeeves, through DirectHit, and popularity-based Jeeves Shopping technology, the Worldnet site takes advantage of the Open Directory Project. The Open Directory Project allows any person to become an "editor" in what is billed as the largest targeted search effort ever on the Web. Keywords are associated with categories in intelligent ways through the project.

As part of the DirectHit search technology at Worldnet, people who search at the site can specify their gender and age in a dialog box, for "personalized search." Any commerce site can incorporate this DirectHit technology. According to Eric Newman, Product Manager of Webwide Navigation Services and Personalized Search at AskJeeves, knowledge of gender alone can dramatically help target shopping offerings and search results for any commerce site.

> "The issue of "search abandonment" is so important to many managers of commerce sites that a number of companies are working on new technology in this area."

"For example," he said, "our research shows that women searching on the term 'flowers' at a site are about twice as likely to want gardening-related results than men, who would be more likely to want to know how to buy flowers as gifts." Likewise, said Newman, a music site might help target suggestions for music to buy based on knowledge of a site visitor's age.

The issue of "search abandonment" is so important to many managers of commerce sites that a number of companies are working on new technology in this area, specifically targeted to help commerce sites boost revenues and increase customer satisfaction. Among many companies offering such technology are Inktomi, Verity, Oingo, and Northernlight.

On top of helping customers find what they want, better search technology can help the many commerce sites that provide advertisements to better target ads, which is of great importance to advertisers. According to Gilad Elbaz, CEO of Oingo.com, "one important ROI metric I can give you here is that in advertising, if you compare the value of an ad impression that's been targeted appropriately based on recognition of what a keyword means, that's generally accepted to be about ten more times valuable than leading the keyword searcher to a 'run of site' banner ad. So advertisers are obviously very keen to see better search tools and better personalization tools, and commerce sites can benefit from putting these in place."

Oingo.com provides a search technology called BroadSense to commerce sights. "Typically a site will give us categories such as product categories—as many as hundreds of thousands—and then we have linguists and some automation tools that look especially for typical co-occurrence of various terms go through the categories, creating relationships between keywords and categories."

One advantage to BroadSense, said Elbaz, is that it can help sites with many diversified kinds of properties direct searchers to those properties before they go elsewhere. As an example, at 4Anything.com, Oingo search technology is used to help searchers find products within 4Anything sub-sites such as 4Books, 4Music, and so forth.

Your End Of The Bargain

What if all your virtual store dreams come true, and hordes of online shoppers flood your site? Site stability and performance were cited by e-shoppers as huge concerns in the Boston Consulting Group survey mentioned at the beginning of this story, where nearly half of respondents said they had abandoned online shopping trips because of poor site performance. Site stability was also cited as a major concern by many of the technology managers we talked to for this story. When shoppers leave, they take their money with them.

Two companies that specialize in load-testing Web sites (replicating the activity of thousands of users to identify when and why a site will fail or suffer degradation) are Velogic and Mercury Interactive. Both companies can help identify bottlenecks and pinpoint the most likely ways for a commerce site to lose customers. For more information on crash-proofing your commerce site, see Chapter 10, "Crashproof Your Web Site."

Though Web site usability has been mostly pooh-poohed as too hard to quantify, it's getting increasing attention lately as Web sites try everything to keep customers hooked. Many firms now offer services to help you assess your site.

WebCriteria (`www.webcriteria.com`), whose customers include Delta Airlines and IBM, has a slew of offerings. Alistair Williamson, CEO of WebCriteria, says, "Companies are learning that how they offer their products and services online is as important—if not more important—as what they offer."

Gomez.com helps companies fix their usability problems through Gomez Advisors, its professional services arm. And Keynote Systems (`www.keynote.com`) has unveiled its Transaction Perspective service, which measures how long it takes users to conduct multi-step transactions, such as signing up for an online brokerage account.

Any business seeking to win over customers on the Web must have, to use Hallmark's Paul Inman's words, "a ruthless focus on the customer." That means delivering the right search results, delivering relevant product information and comparisons, choosing the right technology platform, stabilizing the commerce site, and personalizing it.

PART V

The Infrastructure for e-Business

CHAPTER 9

Keep Them Coming Back

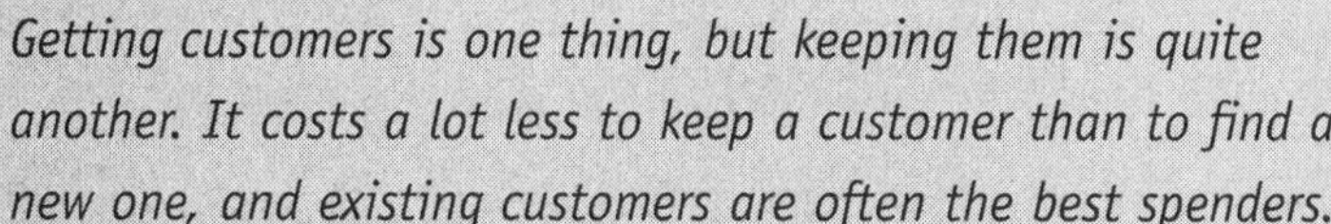

Getting customers is one thing, but keeping them is quite another. It costs a lot less to keep a customer than to find a new one, and existing customers are often the best spenders.

Earning customer trust and providing a good customer experience are major business and technology challenges. Any business starting up on the Web needs to meet the needs of frustrated online shoppers. The primary techniques include good execution of the fundamentals: having a good catalog, the right prices, and good delivery. But the difference is seen in the companies that personalize Web sites for their users. Making shopping a personal experience is the primary advantage of the Web.

But personalization has a dark side. It's imperative to keep a balance between personalization and privacy. Violating privacy can ruin your business. Fortunately, you can take several specific steps to enforce sound privacy and business practices.

Knowing the name of every customer isn't enough. You need detailed information on the effectiveness of your marketing, the needs of your customers, and the appeal of specific products. Modern tools allow you to stress, test, and analyze every aspect of your Web site and design and business plan.

Keeping Customers Is the Key to Success

Finding and keeping customers is a basic business challenge. But the keeping part of the proposition is what Web retailers are just now focusing on. The motivation is clear: Repeat customers spend more than first-timers or one-timers, and it costs more to acquire a new customer than to maintain the ones you have. Now the emphasis is on building strategies into sites that will keep customers coming back again and again. As it turns out, the best way to make money, even in the new economy, is with a downright old-fashioned idea: Build and maintain a loyal and long-term customer base. You can get your retail site on the Web in an afternoon, but the investments in personalization techniques and in analysis tools will keep you in business for years to come.

Please Come Back!

It costs money—and lots of it—to acquire new customers. According to a recent report from McKinsey & Co., an international consulting and research firm, e-commerce companies spent as much as $250 last year to acquire a single customer yet made only about $24.50 on each deal. As expensive as that first date can be, a loyal customer makes good on the initial investment over and over. A study by consulting firm Bain and Co. found that repeat customers at ten popular retail sites, including Gap Online, spend 57% more (per purchase) than first-time customers—and twice as much as those making their very first online purchases. The study also found that return shoppers were much more adventurous in trying out new products or new categories, as long as they were buying from a company they knew and trusted.

"For most businesses, the shortest, most direct route to profitability is by holding on to customers, plain and simple," says Don Peppers, a partner at Peppers & Rogers Group and coauthor (with his colleague Martha Rogers) of several books on the subject of one-to-one marketing and customer-centric business strategies. "Likewise, the capital market realizes that the long-term customer base is what will, in the end, give a Web business its value."

And that's why the world of Web shopping is at last realizing that just because everybody knows your name doesn't mean everybody will buy your stuff. The result is a sea change in both business strategies and infrastructure, as companies start to combine systematic and sensible marketing techniques with breakthrough technologies in an attempt to follow their customers into the black.

Personalization

To paraphrase Amazon.com's Jeff Bezos, if your site attracts a million visitors, you must offer a million local newspapers and a million shops around the corner. Such an obstacle requires a personalization engine and, perhaps, an e-analytics tool. The latter, the Internet-centric successor to traditional data-mining software, helps you understand who is visiting your site and how the visitors are using it. You can feed this information to a personalization engine, which will customize your site on-the-fly, so it can serve up content or merchandise that is likely to appeal to each visitor's particular tastes.

e-Analytics

An e-analytics engine gives you information to help you update and improve your site. Such engines collect specific data about your site's visitors, observing what pages they access and what items they purchase, and occasionally asking them direct questions. It then analyzes that data and generates reports that explain the site's effectiveness—or lack thereof.

The hosted analytics tool provided by Net Perceptions, known as Intelligence Channel, costs about $10,000 a month. Administered through Web browsers, it seamlessly hooks into your site, collects information, and provides a daily report. Steve Larsen, Net Perceptions' senior vice president, said, "It helps you identify who are your best customers, what are the characteristics of those customers, and how can you better serve those customers—as well as who are your mediocre customers, who are the customers who are maybe costing you money." Accrue Software and NetGenesis Corp., among others, provide similar tools.

These analysis tools can help you customize your site's content. Larsen cites Garden.com, a Net Perceptions customer, as an example: "They found that when customers buy certain products on a first-time visit, the chances of them becoming repeat customers went up ten times. Obviously, if you're a first-time visitor, they want to make sure you're seeing one of those products."

Companies such as Webtrends.com and Andromedia also offer personalization products that deliver rich analysis tools. For ongoing coverage of this space, see www.personalization.com.

Rules-Based Personalization

One way to make use of the information from an analysis tool is to install a rules-based personalization engine. Available from BroadVision, Vignette Corp., and others, rules-based engines customize a page's content not by determining the personal habits or interests of a current user but by consulting a set of rules defined by the site's designers.

For example, one rule could be that your site shows product B to any customer who purchases product C, the two products being related in some way. "Even without understanding who this person is as an individual," stated John Roberts, senior product manager at BroadVision, "we can still try and tailor the site based on some of the anonymous observed patterns."

Rules-based engines have two drawbacks. First, they require constant care. "Someone always has to reset the rules," said Jonathan Gaw, research manager at IDC. Additionally, they often play more to the needs of the Web site than to the preferences of the customers. But after asking questions of a visitor (during registration or the purchase process) and assigning that visitor a cookie, some rules-based engines also provide a bit of personalization.

BroadVision, for instance, can modify a site's rules relative to particular users and avoid offering content that isn't likely to interest them. "Say you're on a boating site," explains Roberts. "You can go in and say, 'I'm a sailor, I live in the San Francisco Bay area, and these are the kind of things I want,' and then be rewarded for that as you use the site."

"[Garden.com] found that when customers buy certain products on a first-time visit, the chances of them becoming repeat customers went up ten times. Obviously, if you're a first-time visitor, they want to make sure you're seeing one of those products."

Collaborative Filtering

More extensive personalization is available through collaborative filtering, which determines a user's preferences, identifies groups of individuals who have similar preferences, and then serves the user additional content enjoyed by members of those groups. Net Perceptions and Macromedia license their collaborative filtering

"We can translate your behavior into preferences and based on those preferences make recommendations for other things you would like, or even change the menus on a site so that it's more personalized."

engines, and Be Free provides a similar hosted service. "We can translate your behavior into preferences," said Larsen of Net Perceptions, "and based on those preferences make recommendations for other things you would like, or even change the menus on a site so that it's more personalized to you."

Initially, this type of engine collects data much the way an analytics tool would but on a simpler level. When someone visits your site, the engine learns about that user on-the-fly and keeps a detailed record of what it's learned for future use. It typically collects data in two different ways. "One of the ways," said Paula Dieli, director of program management for LikeMinds, Macromedia's collaborative filtering engine, "is of course to ask them, 'What do you think about the following products?' 'Rate the following CDs,' or 'Tell us what you like to do for the weekend.'"

Typically, this is done when the user is registering at the site or is making a purchase. Mainly, however, the engine records the pages users access and the products they buy. "We simply watch where you're clicking," continues Dieli. Whenever users visit, the engine learns more, and eventually it develops a fairly accurate representation of the habits and tastes of each. When a user returns, the engine compares the user's profile with all the other collected profiles and identifies a group of individuals with similar habits and tastes. It then assumes the user will respond to additional pages or merchandise that have gotten a response from other members of this group. "If you seem interested in buying a coat, and you're looking at leather jackets, as soon as you make a few clicks, we can find other folks in the database who have looked at coats and leather jackets," said Dieli. "We ask: 'What did they end up purchasing? What other things were they interested in buying? What other content were they interested in looking at?' We call those groups of likeminded individuals *affinity groups.* And it's to a group of about 50 users we assign you—based on your tastes and preferences—and those 50 people in your group can change as your tastes and preferences change."

Instant Personalization

Of course, with collaborative filtering, you can't provide personalization at the moment a user visits your site for the first time. You must wait until a user makes a few clicks or answers some questions. For immediate personalization, you need a tool such as the one from Angara.

Buzzwords

Affinity group—A group of people who have demonstrated similar behavior.

At GreatCoffee.com, which sells coffee and related equipment all over the world, site developers recently adopted a personalization engine from Angara. Even when you're visiting GreatCoffee.com for the first time, Angara's engine can personalize the site's home page to suit you. If you access the site from New York, for instance, you might see an offer for a free coffee maker or grinder, but if your friends log on from northern California, GreatCoffee.com will offer them tickets to a San Francisco Giants game. This kind of offer, meaningless to most of the site's audience, has greatly improved business within small segments of applicable users. "It's roughly doubled the number of customers we could have attracted with the default home page," stated Ron Walters, GreatCoffee.com president.

Angara's service relies on a vast database of information collected from various third parties. "We have developed a network of online data providers," explains Rich Clayton, vice president of marketing for Angara. "They include a major portal, marketing services companies, a free ISP, a free e-mail service, and firms that sell Angara anonymous profiles." Odds are, if you have browsed the Web, you have visited one or more of these data providers, and they have collected information about you that Angara has purchased.

When companies tie their sites to Angara, Angara divides all potential users into a certain number of categories and builds a home page for each of those categories. "Let's say [the companies] have a high-income segment; let's say they have a male over-45 segment, and they have a female California segment," said Clayton. "Those are the three affinities that they think are in their visitor traffic. They then define, through their merchandising process in-house, what content they think should match with those." In theory, whenever a user accesses that site, Angara pulls that user's profile from its database and tells the site which of the categories the user falls into. The site then serves the home page that corresponds to that category.

"Let's say you go to one of our customers, Netmarket.com," explained Clayton. "You will actually be redirected to our site. We'll identify whether you've been cookied by any of our data network providers, and if you have, we'll score you into a consumer segment and pass Netmarket back a segment ID so that they can then tailor the front-page or home-page content to your interests."

The upshot of this or any personalization process is that more users stay at and return to a site. "Because of personalized content, people get excited," said the president of GreatCoffee.com. "They feel like we're a local company. It draws them in, and ultimately not only do they register with the site more often, they purchase more."

Personal Hallmark

Paul Inman is the site manager for Hallmark.com who brought Hallmark's 90-year brand heritage from the brick-and-mortar world to the Internet in 1996, playing the central role in developing and launching Hallmark's commerce site. The site did well, which Inman attributes partially to the fact that Hallmark carried to the Internet a lot of existing brand equity and trust. For example, Hallmark did not have to initially cut a portal deal to drive traffic to its site because many consumers found the site based on their long-standing familiarity with Hallmark's business. However, Inman concedes that keeping consumer trust and interest online is a great challenge, and he has attacked the problem by concentrating on personalization and relationship-building online. In late 1999, he was able to kick this effort into gear by implementing personalization and site organization software tools from BroadVision.

BroadVision's personalization-focused e-business applications dynamically capture information about a Web user's specific activities online, such as buying habits and preferences. The goal is to start personalizing a customer's experience the minute the customer logs on. BroadVision also offers links to customer relationship management (CRM) software tools, such as Siebel's. Within BroadVision, customized business rules can be set, so that online product offering categories can be related to each other to make relevant suggestions to consumers, for example. BroadVision also does profiling of consumers, to match product offerings to, say, a consumer's gender or age. And BroadVision does click-stream analysis so that an online commerce site can analyze the paths consumers follow as they navigate a site. In Hallmark's case, one use of this feature in the BroadVision software is to help direct users to Hallmark's e-reminder service, which e-mails ongoing reminders to site visitors about birthdays and other events which can be appropriate for a Hallmark gift or card.

As special feature of the site, Hallmark launched a free "e-card" service allowing consumers to build and customize electronic greeting cards. This had an explosive impact on traffic, and since last fall Hallmark.com has sent more than 11 million e-cards, averaging more than 400,000 per week.

"Community aspects of BroadVision help us segment types of content that we offer, and lead consumers to the product offerings most relevant to their needs. For example, we can intelligently lead people from several locations to our reminder service that can remind the consumer when it's time to send a card or buy a present to mark an occasion."

Personalization is tricky, according to Inman. "If you think about a search an individual does on a site and you say, 'I want to predictively offer up some relevant suggestions,' that's one level of complexity. But when you think about the whole gift angle, the consumer might be shopping one time for a wife and the next time for an aunt, and the best approach here is to have a dialogue with the consumer. Our hope is to serve the content and product offerings up in the most consumer-specific way possible, making relevant buying suggestions to consumers wherever possible."

"All of this works on the same theme," said Hallmark's Inman. "You have to have a ruthless focus on the customer's needs and customer's history to do well. Doing it online means using good tools."

Privacy

We can't let all this discussion of personalization go by without a discussion of privacy. If you're not careful, privacy can be the victim of customization. People are, rightly so, becoming very sensitive about what they give away in return for customization. Maintaining the privacy of your employees, clients, and business partners is very important. Abusing privacy is an abuse of trust.

Privacy on the Web is a matter of basic Web design principles. It's a matter of KISS—not Keep It Simple, Stupid but Keep It Safe And Sensible. You can choose to highlight privacy as part of your trusted brand—a key element in building and sustaining your customer relationship. Conversely, you can choose to handle it as just another subset of security and data management—an administrative add-on and a bit of a nuisance.

If you are simply designing a Web site, you'll probably take the latter view. But if you think instead in terms of designing the customer experience, privacy will be right up at the top of your list of key features. We've come up with some rules of thumb for achieving appropriate e-business privacy.

- Have a privacy policy in place. Make sure you have an explicit and formal company policy in place and that you highlight it in all business interactions. Make it prominent and easy to understand.
- Don't ask for too much: Don't ask for more private information than you need.
- Affiliate with privacy organizations. Associate your business with organizations such as TrustE, BBBOnLine (Better Business Bureau), and CPA WebTrust. Affiliation certifies that you follow specific practices and audit processes.
- Let users opt out: Allow customers to easily opt out of allowing you to share information with other parties.
- Stay away from trickery. Don't be tempted by easy technology tricks that deceive your customers. There are various pieces of code available that can inventory and grab information from client sites. Don't use them.
- Use audit controls: Most breaches of privacy happen far away from your Web site. Access control, audit logs, and formal rules for the use of information are the tools that keep all of your information safe.
- Be optimistic: Privacy is generally discussed in negative terms. Everyone's for it and violating privacy for commercial purposes is universally a bad thing. In practice, maintaining the privacy trust is a matter of common sense, sound practices, and informed consent.

Privacy Through P3P

A long-standing World Wide Web Consortium-backed specification for safeguarding the personal information of Web surfers now is gaining momentum in the wake of Microsoft's announcement that it will support the standard in its next version of Windows and the next version of the Internet Explorer browser.

For some time now, the World Wide Web Consortium (W3C) has backed an effort called the Platform for Privacy Preferences Project (P3P), which lets Web sites express their privacy practices in a standard format that can be retrieved automatically and interpreted quickly by user agents. P3P user agents, based on XML (eXtensible Markup Language), will inform Web users of site practices and automate privacy protections when appropriate.

For example, users can set up templates indicating privacy lines they don't want crossed as well as personal information they are willing to give out. This information is then automatically compared with a site's privacy policies. The main hope with P3P is to free users from reading a privacy policy at every Web site—and to prevent users from unwittingly providing personal information.

The W3C's Privacy Activity Statement explains how privacy policies should be viewed: "When a user arrives at a Web site, the idea is that their browser will receive a privacy policy from that site, explaining what information it would like and how the data would be used."

Microsoft's Windows and Internet Explorer will incorporate technologies based on the P3P specification. P3P will show up in the Whistler version of Windows, which will include a Privacy Statement Generator—Microsoft's version of the XML-based privacy policy generator that the W3C's P3P specification calls for. The P3P technology within Internet Explorer will enable automatic comparison of a user's privacy preferences template with the policies at Web sites. AT&T and other companies have expressed support for P3P, but some privacy observers say that the standard doesn't go far enough to protect privacy.

According to a recent report from the Federal Trade Commission (FTC), 92% of Web users expressed concerns about having their personal information misused by Web site operators. The FTC also recently studied how commercial sites are responding to concerns about online privacy, and it found that sites aren't doing enough to protect privacy. As a result, the FTC recommended government-driven privacy regulations.

As you can see in Figure 9.1, although privacy policies aren't the most important factor in influencing customers to return, they're ranked nearly twice as important as product price, selection, and ease of ordering.

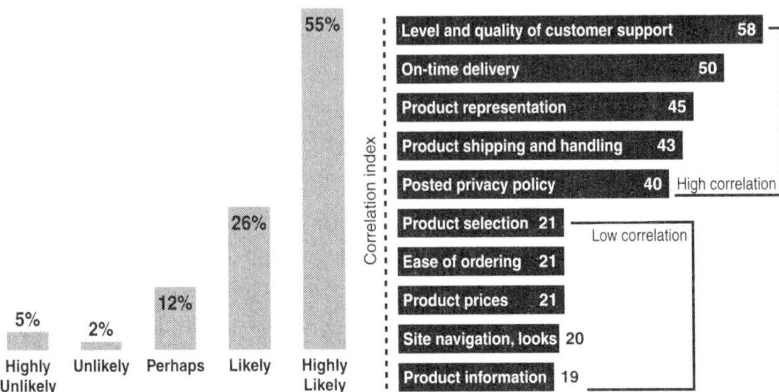

Figure 9.1

An accessible privacy policy ranks among customer support and on-time delivery as factors that keep customers coming back.

Watching the Store

Of course, personalizing the user experience at a commerce site, and boosting efficiency through things such as advanced search and intelligent shopping technologies can only take a site so far. At the end of the day, commerce sites need to deliver products on a timely basis, treat inventories efficiently, run stable sites, and leverage the Web in supporting customers. Much of that process is managed by technology on the back end of the B2C flow chart, where everything from order entry, database logging, and analysis tools comes into play. The back end is also where many of the commerce sites are rushing to put in business-to-business supply chain management solutions, such as those offered by Ariba, and CommerceOne. See Chapter 3, "Business-to-Business Markets," for more information.

Few long-standing businesses on earth have had to adapt to faster growth in Web sales than Cisco Systems. Cisco now manages over 70% of its revenues through unassisted sales from its Web site, totaling tens of millions of dollars per day and billions of dollars per year. Customers also have direct, online access to technical support and order-status information at Cisco's Web site. As Cisco has moved all this product buying and support to the Web, it has saved hundreds of millions of dollars.

To facilitate this focus on selling and supporting on the Web, Cisco uses Oracle Database Applications, Oracle Applications ERP software, Oracle e-Business Applications, and Oracle Financials on backend powered by Sun servers. When these applications were implemented together, about 5,000 backlogged product orders were immediately converted in only one weekend. According to Cisco CIO Peter Solvik, the applications have had an enormous impact on getting products to customers efficiently and quickly. Speed in delivering products not only has an impact on customer satisfaction but also reduces inventory write-offs for Cisco.

Djangos.com is a Web site that sells used CDs and videos. The company has had a small but successful chain of retail stores in operation around the United States for 27 years. The Djangos.com Web site was brought live only this year, and Jon Alder, vice president of technology, is working to put in place an infrastructure that centralizes the company's distributed inventories.

The company's Web site (`www.djangos.com`) is based on a back end of Windows NT servers running Microsoft SQL Server and Microsoft Site Server Commerce Edition. Site Server Commerce Edition, like Oracle's e-business suite, is a platform on which many commerce sites are based, including Dell Computer's site. Through a Wide Area Network, inventories in all of Djangos' stores are kept track of at this back end in real time. Alder is also working to put in place a 10,000 square foot warehouse to centralize much of Djangos' inventory.

According to Alder, putting in place a solid infrastructure on the back end for getting products to customers quickly is important. However, for a company new to doing business online, it's also very important to use reporting tools to watch the virtual store itself, who's coming to it, and how the customers got there in the first place.

Alder uses WebTrends Enterprise Reporting Server for NT to track traffic and to analyze what the company is doing right in terms of pages and events. Importantly, he stated, the WebTrends software also helps him identify what the virtual store is doing wrong. For

WebTrends tells us whether users went through the two pages necessary to enter the contest, or whether they visited the main contest page and then left. Because our online business is new, these promotions matter, and the reporting tools are absolutely critical to us.

example, Djangos.com has a promotional contest called "Win Free CDs For Life" available from its home page.

"WebTrends recently let us know not only how many people were going to the contest page, but that about 35% of the people going to the contest page don't sign up," said Alder. "So we're trying to correct that. Specifically, WebTrends tells us whether users went through the two pages necessary to enter the contest, or whether they visited the main contest page and then left. Because our online business is new, these promotions matter, and the reporting tools are absolutely critical to us."

Alder also uses the WebTrends software to identify exactly how users find Djangos.com in the first place, so more can be encouraged to do so. "The reporting tool has told us that the precise statement of the most commonly used search phrase people use at portals to find our site is 'Used Hard To Find Records.'"

Office Depot is an example of a more established retail business that uses the WebTrends reporting tools with its Web site. Accrue Software sells several product suites, such as Insight and Hit List, that offer functionality similar to WebTrends' products, in addition to facilitating online marketing campaigns. Accrue, NetPerceptions, and Siebel Systems are among companies that specialize in products that can help coordinate and track co-marketing campaigns originating on the Web and tying into product offerings in place at brick-and-mortar stores.

The Customers Are Always Right

No one subscribes to the combination of old wisdom and new technology more stringently than drugstore.com, the Bellevue, Washington-based start-up launched in January of 1999 and a leader in the online drugstore market. Following a solid year of blanketing the airwaves, the portals, and the morning talk shows with the virtues of buying vitamins and toiletries online, the company had a watershed month in early 2000 when it hit the million-customer mark, handily beating out competitors like PlanetRx. Though the occasion was heralded with the usual hoopla, it was only the beginning of the struggle for this young company.

The folks at drugstore.com must engage the individual customers in what they hope will be a lifelong relationship. To accomplish that, this e-tailer is using every technological and strategic arrow in its quiver to understand what its customers buy and why—and to make sure that drugstore.com is the only place they purchase any one of the 15,000 products available through the site.

On the technology front, the company uses an array of sophisticated data-analysis tools, many of which are homegrown, to gain a complete picture of its customers and their behaviors. Every time a visitor logs on to drugstore.com, the path that individual takes, or the click stream, is logged to a massive data warehouse running on Oracle8i. Transaction and order data are simultaneously pumped into the data warehouse. In the background, proprietary software is correlating that data with existing customer and marketing data.

Then comes the real work of slicing and dicing, often referred to as *business intelligence*. Using custom-made analytical software, drugstore.com's marketers look at that customer data in, well, about a million different ways. For example, reports are generated to reveal which customers buy which brands, how many customers purchased a particular sale item and whether they clicked through from an ad, and how customers are responding to direct-marketing campaigns, as well as which customers use online shopping lists. This analysis is fed back into the company's overall marketing strategy, helping to determine everything from where the next ads should be placed to what kind of email newsletters should be created and to whom they should be sent.

"You have to understand how to segment all the customer-related data available so that you can figure out how your customers want you to interact with them," said Judith McGarry, vice president of strategic partnerships. "Those interactions are crucial, because they are the way you retain your customers. Trust and loyalty aren't built on one incident but rather on thousands of little interactions."

McGarry and company's efforts are paying off. In the first quarter of this year, 50% of the orders logged on the site were from repeat customers, and that number jumped to 59% in the second quarter. In addition, customers are spending more when they come back. The average order size hovers around $43, up from $17 in Q2 1999. And with many orders coming from folks replenishing their rations of shampoo, razors, and deodorant, much of that is money in drugstore.com's pockets.

In addition, the company is brokering partnerships that will bring even more shoppers into its fold. This past summer, agreements with national health insurance companies Wellpoint and CIGNA Healthcare were announced. Under these agreements, drugstore.com will be the exclusive provider of online prescriptions for Wellpoint's 22 million members and CIGNA's 25 million members, and it will market special promotions and sales to those individuals.

> *Companies have to take advantage of decidedly unsexy technology—things like serious data mining and business intelligence—and they have to do a better job of making a commitment to being customer-focused.*

Use the Right Tool

Many online retailers, especially in the pure-play Internet space, are only now waking up to the heavy data-lifting and hardcore marketing strategies required to entice customers into staying for the long haul.

"Customer retention is part of a bigger challenge that comes under the heading of customer relationship management and companies are struggling with this online," says Eric Schmitt, an analyst with Forrester Research in Cambridge, Massachusetts. "Companies have to take advantage of decidedly unsexy technology—things like serious data mining and business intelligence—and they have to do a better job of making a commitment to being customer-focused."

To be fair, commercial high-octane tools designed from the ground up to root around in Web data are only now emerging. The first generation of Web site analysis tools, from stalwarts like WebTrends, was geared mostly toward counting page views and unique visitors. More traditional business-intelligence packages from the likes of Business Objects and Cognos weren't built to understand click streams or online advertising campaigns. The next versions of online-intelligence tools, however, should provide a deeper, richer understanding of customer behavior.

Accrue Software, Coremetrics, NetGenesis, and Personify are all bulking up their product lines to help companies gain insights into how effective their online marketing and customer-service efforts are. Other players in this space include Quadstone, which recently released CustomerConversion, a product geared exclusively toward this online customer conundrum. Ithena, a spin-off of Business Objects, is proffering so-called e-customer intelligence applications; and SAP offspring TeaLeaf Technology has an analytics solution that reconstructs session data piece by piece.

The next, most obvious hurdle for many of these vendors is to tie the data generated by Web sites into the other customer and order data that businesses have lying around their networks. All these product vendors, however, are working to address this challenge by one-off integration efforts, by creating adapters for off-line data stores, or by as-yet-unannounced techniques.

Alongside the analysis tools are e-marketing products, which are also getting progressively more sophisticated. Responsys.com, a player in the direct e-marketing space, is offering services that let its customers send personalized, targeted e-mail campaigns based on consumer profiles and shopping habits. PrimeResponse, a marketing software company, delivers both data analysis and online campaign management through its Prime@Vantage line. Another company, Xchange, offers a three-pronged product line for synchronizing customer data across channels, conducting marketing campaigns, and measuring their effectiveness.

In addition, E.piphany is hawking its E.5 platform, which is a smorgasbord of electronic CRM, data analysis, and marketing tools. And newcomer Revenio officially unveiled Revenio Dialogue in September, which allows companies to conduct the equivalent of electronic conversations with individual customers and convert those into sophisticated marketing campaigns.

These technological developments and others are certain to help companies down the path of better customer relations. But as Joel Book, director of e-marketing strategy for Prime Response, points out, all the technology in the world can't replace solid business practices. "We talk about understanding what's working and why, and you need data and analysis for that," says Book. "But you must have a solid marketing strategy before you can get to that point."

Legendary Legacy

Nordstrom is a company that knows about following the game plan, no matter what. This 100-year-old retailer waited what seemed like forever, at least in the fast-paced Internet environment, to launch its Web site: It went live at the end of 1999. But with a sterling reputation for customer service in the retail and catalog worlds, the company wanted to make sure its Internet channel wouldn't let its core customers down or turn off potential converts.

"We have to be able to treat customers the same no matter how they're coming to us, because to them, it's all Nordstrom," says Kathryn Olson, Nordstrom.com's executive vice president of marketing. "We're very conscious of our responsibility to our customers and to the Nordstrom brand."

Toward that end, Nordstrom has deployed an online marketing strategy that is all about integration. For starters, the store's URL is plastered on every catalog and piece of marketing collateral, and online shoppers get an early crack at retail-store sales. The bargain bell gongs at midnight on the Web. But perhaps most important, the company is committed to offering the same breadth of selection on its site that is available through its other channels. Just consider footwear alone: Some 30 million pairs of shoes are up for grabs online. And as is always the case with Nordstrom, customer convenience is paramount. That means online shoppers can return or exchange any wrong-footed shoe purchase at the closest retail store or through the mail.

The same tie-it-all-together approach applies to the company's technology choices. Though Nordstrom.com has a relatively conservative set of features compared with some sites, chief technology officer Paul Onnen says a solid, reliable site is more important than flash that crashes. As a result, heavy-duty personalization won't surface until next year, and the site will be in lockdown by early October for the holiday season.

And as with the marketing side of the business, customer-centricity is a driver here as well. All customer and order data captured by the Web site, which is running entirely on a Microsoft platform and Microsoft products, is delivered each day to the company's internal network. It is then cleaned up and correlated with existing customer records.

Like drugstore.com, Nordstrom has designed its own set of tools to assist with segmenting and analyzing the customer data. In addition, shoppers who order on the site can opt to receive email updates, which are created from scratch by the internal marketing team and passed off to a series of list servers. Though Olson and Onnen were coy when it came to doling out specific numbers regarding Nordstrom.com, they did say the average online order is $150, which is high for the industry.

Thanks to its long history, Nordstrom is all too familiar with the behind-the-scenes work necessary to keep customers fat and happy. But even companies that have been focused almost exclusively on the buzz are getting back to the basics of analysis and strategic marketing—with an Internet twist.

In the early days of e-commerce, all of a company's up-front efforts were focused on driving as many people as possible to the Web site. Now the emphasis is on keeping those people coming back. Jill Frankle, director of retail e-commerce for Gomez Advisors, says, "That's going to be very good for the customer and for the retailers themselves."

Catch a Customer

Though it sounds like a public health alert, viral marketing might be one of the next big things when it comes to reeling in customers. As consumers get increasingly overloaded with email, companies are doing everything in their power to make their messages stand out, and a handful of start-ups are standing by to help them.

More are rapidly moving into the space, but three of the most prominent players to date are FireDrop, Gizmoz, and RadicalMail. All three offer network-based services through which companies can create targeted and interactive direct-marketing campaigns that individuals can easily zip off to friends and co-workers. For example, both Gizmoz and RadicalMail allow businesses to stream interactive, multimedia messages directly to an individual's inbox—or desktop in the case of Gizmoz. And to make e-commerce even more convenient, Buy buttons can be embedded right into those messages, so users don't have to launch another browser to purchase a sale item.

FireDrop's claim to fame is its Zaplets, which cofounder David Roberts likens to a combination of email and instant messaging. So far, Zaplets have been used largely for interactive surveys and discussions, but the company plans to combine them with commerce.

Getting people to make that first purchase online can be the biggest hurdle to converting them into repeat customers. Kestral Communications (`www.kestralcom.com`) offers specialized premium marketing programs that use software and the Internet itself as tools in helping Web sites acquire and retain customers. Kestral's Digital Premium Programs have resulted in some relatively high response rates for client companies—in the upper-20%–30% range—which is "spectacular," says Kestral's executive vice president of marketing Kerry S. Leppo.

Kestral programs are quick-click arrangements whereby e-customers can buy full-version, retail consumer software titles for under $5 (barely enough to cover shipping and handling). In many cases, buyers can even pay by check instead of credit card, if that's a hindrance. Kestral helps the companies use the programs to gather data on shoppers and turn it into valuable marketing information. In some cases, Kestral even covers the fulfillment end of the deal.

Customers For Keeps

Stickiness. For any Web site, stickiness means giving the customers a reason to visit your site, providing them with the promised experience, and making them always want to come back for more. For GoodHome.com, stickiness requires finding customers who are ready to decorate, giving them the merchandise and the tools they need to "get the look" now, and compelling them to click on an impulse decorating project.

Doug Mach, CEO of GoodHome.com, told us about his company's approach to being sticky. "Stickiness is a concept that is often put to use but is seldom supported by a strategic combination of targeted marketing and useful technology to create a customized user experience. Too frequently, companies plow the bulk of their Internet expenditures into broad-based marketing efforts that simply find consumers to try their sites for the first time."

Mach continues, "These customer-acquisition efforts are just half—the less important half—of building a loyal base of users for a Web site. The more important part is visitor retention and repeat visits, and this is where creating a great consumer experience—stickiness—comes into play. At GoodHome.com, we have focused on building a superior front-end user experience, supported by robust back-end management tools that allow us to provide a compelling user experience.

"The front end: Give them an experience that keeps them coming back. From the first click on a home page to the final click in a shopping cart, what meets the eye of a customer must be both satisfying and compelling and, even more important, must give the customer a reason to come back. At GoodHome.com, one way in which we've enhanced our front-end experience is with our proprietary iDecorate technology. Housed in our Decorating Studio, iDecorate is a tool that lets consumers mix and match different products and "try on" different fabrics, paints, and wallpaper in room scenes, ultimately allowing them to create and visualize their dream room.

"This tool has engendered great consumer loyalty. It is consistently one of the two most popular areas at our site and extends the average user's time at the site to more than 20 minutes. This technology has encouraged people to visit the site and return with regularity. It has proved to be an asset to the consumer and a long-term selling tool for GoodHome.com.

"The back end: What customers don't see is just as important.

Creating a good user experience goes well beyond what meets the eye. Behind the scenes, for example, GoodHome.com has developed and deployed two key management tools that let the business team systematically enhance the user experience on an ongoing basis.

"First, our internally developed Content Management System enables our nontechnical team, including merchandisers and copywriters, to manipulate content and products on the site, easily keeping it fresh for consumers. Second, our internally developed Decision Support System (DSS) analyzes online traffic and measures revenue coming from each location, so we can maximize and target our online advertising dollars.

"DSS also tracks consumer-shopping behavior on the site and provides data on the content and products that are most (and least) liked by consumers. For example, we see the items that are most (and least) frequently clicked on throughout the site each day, providing a clear indication of what is popular and what is not. The business team can use such tools to optimize the consumer experience quickly, continually tweaking the site to elevate the most successful elements and to demote less successful items. This fact-based approach of using actual consumer interest data, combined with tools to make changes quickly based on such learning, ultimately results in the attention to detail that keeps visitors coming back again and again.

"From our experience, we believe that most companies would be well served by allocating a much larger portion of their spending and mind share to stickiness—using both front-end and back-end tools—and reducing the proportion spent for securing the initial visit. Over time, marketing expenditures are ephemeral, and the value fades if the spending slows. By contrast, hard investments in the user experience and management tools will last over time—and ensure that your visitors continue to stick around."

Keep Them Coming Back

We know your name. We know what you like. We have what you like. We make it easy to find what you like. Those are familiar rules of retailing. They're easy things to say, but they're difficult things to do—particularly as your base of customers expands and grows in every direction. Fortunately, the modern tools of e-business can make many of these tasks almost as easy to carry out as they are to say.

CHAPTER 10

Crashproof Your Web Site

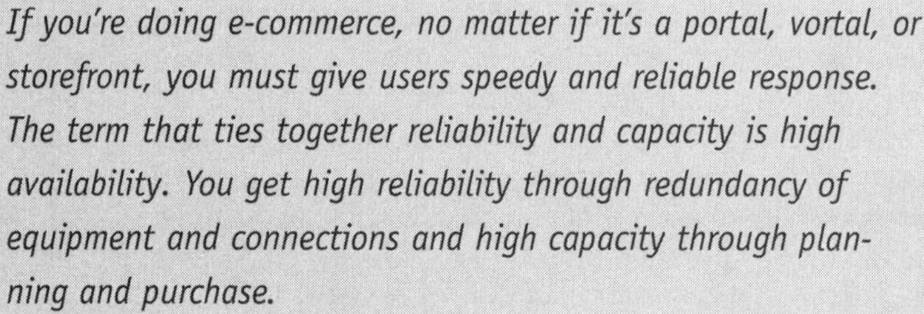

If you're doing e-commerce, no matter if it's a portal, vortal, or storefront, you must give users speedy and reliable response. The term that ties together reliability and capacity is high availability. You get high reliability through redundancy of equipment and connections and high capacity through planning and purchase.

Specific techniques, such as load-balancing and clustering, make it easier to apply the rule of redundancy. Specific approaches, such as using multiple disk drives in arrays, can also add reliability through redundancy.

Outsourcing or outhosting some or all of your Web site operation makes a lot of sense. You can elect to outsource specific functions such as content caching or you can outhost the entire operation.

In one respect, the new economy is just like the old one: Customer service can make or break a business. Faulty products, late deliveries, or inadequate sales staff still send people scurrying to the competition. But the Internet also raises expectations of snappy screens in consumers' minds. Whether your business sells goods or services, it's likely that your customers have alternatives only a click away. And users are not willing to wait more than a few seconds for pages to come when they're clicking around your site. More customers have fast connections from cable and DSL modems and they expect screens to pop onto their monitors. How do you make sure your Web site delivers top performance during peak demand periods? How do you build in the flexibility to deal with a sudden spike in traffic when you launch a new product, or a surge of complaints if you make a mistake? How do you handle an attack from vandals intent on flooding out the legitimate traffic? How do you avoid even a moment of downtime?

Infrastructure as a Strategic Imperative

"Companies with a superior network infrastructure will have a distinct competitive advantage: The ability not to just survive the shift, but to flourish. A superior infrastructure for e-business is a critical leveraging factor." Jamie Lewis, The Burton Group.

The answer is in the term *high availability*: building your Web site infrastructure so no single part can ever get overloaded enough that it slows to a crawl or fails, regardless of the assault. High availability is the combination of reliability and capacity, and availability bottlenecks can appear at any point from your site's connections through to the servers and out to the storage systems. Your need for high availability will depend on whether your site offers mainly content, like NASA, or mainly merchandise, like Amazon.com. But no matter what your business, the basic elements of a high-availability Web site involve equipment, connections, and skills. Even if a bottleneck isn't directly your fault, it's still clearly your problem.

Buzzwords

High availability—Availability is the sum of reliability and capacity. The capacity must include connections, processing power, and data storage. If any one of these areas becomes a bottleneck, then total availability suffers.

Today, many companies elect to keep their Web server equipment and connections in a commercial hosting center. Practically every national ISP has one or more of these centers and companies such as Verio specialize in hosting. These hosting facilities typically can use all the techniques such as load balancing and clustering that

Buzzwords

Load balancing—A technique that routes IP service requests to a specific server within a group of servers with similar functionality. The action can be based on the server's workload, on timing, or on a need for specific services.

we will describe, but it's up to you to find out whether they do. Today, there can be some fantastic bargains in hosting. You can set up a commercial storefront for a little more than $100 per month. But what level of availability (reliability plus capacity) do you get for that? How much more do you get for $500 or $1000 a month? Follow along with our discussion and you'll be able to judge the quality and options offered by hosting centers or apply the techniques of high availability to your own facilities.

It's Harder Than You Think!

The glitter of some of the dot.com companies faded in 2000 because it's harder than most people think to build a strong e-business infrastructure. Network planning should take plenty of the management time of every would-be or actual e-business executive. You can't direct, wish, or contract it away.

Redundant Redundancy

Buzzwords

Clustering—An interaction between practically identical servers to ensure reliability. Clustered servers monitor each other's operation and pick up the workload of one server or process when a server fails.

Redundancy is a primary technique for building reliability. Redundant network connections, server CPUs, server power supplies, and clusters of servers keep things running despite component failures and malicious attempts at overloading the system. Redundant sources of AC power, including uninterruptible power supplies (UPSs) and generator systems designed for server rooms, are also fundamental. But software glitches and legitimate system overloads caused by an overabundance of success—the real nightmare of every manager of a successful, growing Web site—are more common than component failures or outside attacks, so it's smart to have completely redundant appearances of the application on separate servers. Server redundancy improves reliability and provides a performance cushion that can soak up unanticipated surges.

Who Needs It?

If you put a Web site up for public use, you need some measure of high availability. If you measure downtime in terms of dollars or tens of thousands of dollars per minute, then you need a lot of it. The keys are reliability and capacity. How much of each is it worth paying for? You have to balance reliability and capacity and evenly raise them both to build high availability.

Redundant Web servers process requests under the control of devices called *load balancers*, which distribute incoming requests among a bank of Web servers according to a variety of methods. Balancing the processor load is a practical, inexpensive way to rev up the performance of your site. These devices let you add new Web servers on-the-fly when loads increase. If one Web server fails or is taken offline, the load balancer cuts it out and shares the load among the survivors.

Buzzwords

UPS—Uninterruptible power supply. A device that can deliver AC power from batteries, typically for a period of a few minutes.

The database and application servers that sit behind the Web servers do more internal processing and don't communicate with the same intensity. They typically use a technique called *server clustering* to keep operations reliable. Typically, one server in a cluster takes over full operation from a server that falters.

Mix 'em Up!

Keep in mind that the servers running behind the load balancers don't have to have identical hardware or even run the same operating system. The load balancer looks at service, not hardware. Some schemes for clustering servers aren't as eclectic. They want very similar hardware.

Load Balancers

A high-availability Web server system combines redundant Web servers with load balancers that control the workload going to each server. Figure 10.1 shows an extended configuration. Companies such as Alteon WebSystems, Cisco Systems, Coyote Point Systems, F5 Networks, Foundry Networks, RADWARE, Inc., and Resonate offer products in this area.

At first glance, all load balancers look alike. Most have two or more Fast Ethernet connections, and connect into the IP data stream between two or more servers on one side of the box and the Internet or intranet connection on the other. The load balancer distributes connection requests to specific servers based on the nature of the request and the availability and capability of the server.

Three basic classes of load balancers are *switching balancers*, a technique found in products from Alteon and Foundry; *software balancers*, represented by Resonate; and *appliance balancers*—the most common type. Appliance load balancers are essentially single-purpose servers running an optimized balancing program on a built-in CPU. They're convenient pieces of hardware that blend into the server rooms of middle-size companies. Software-based balancers operate much like appliance balancers, but they run as an application program on top of an operating system such as Windows NT, Linux, or Unix. If you have existing PC hardware and a tight budget, these are the best way to balance the incoming load. Switching balancers combine the features of an appliance server with an Ethernet switch, allowing for faster throughput and simplified management. Theoretically, they're the most robust, although the communications channel will clog before you'll stress the capacity of practically any load balancer.

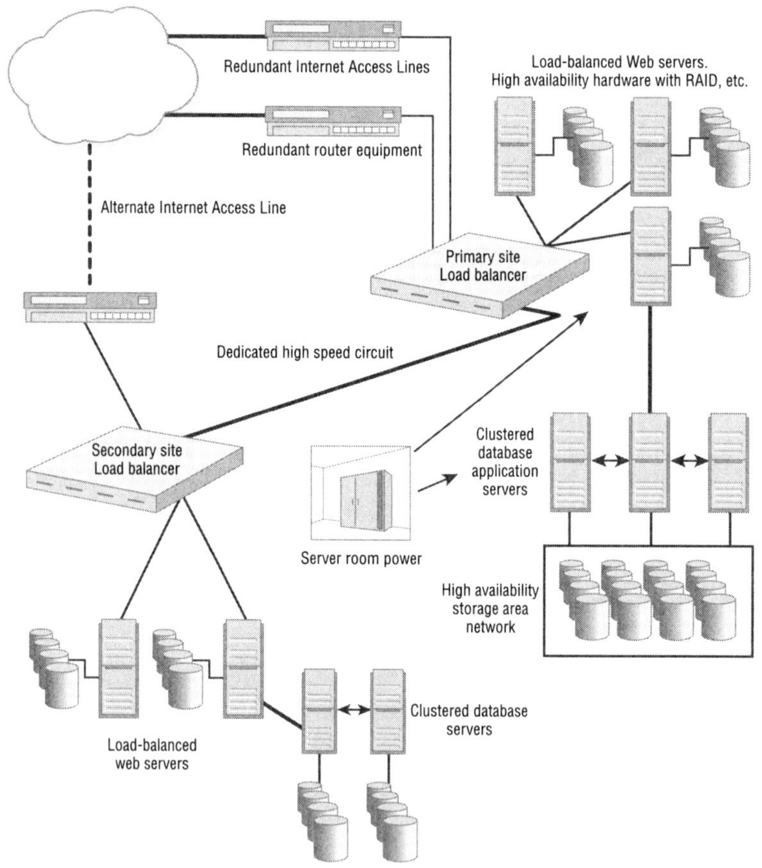

Figure 10.1

Redundant Web servers with load balancers that control the workload going to each server contribute to a high-availability Web server system.

Balancing Firewall?

In the next chapter, we'll discuss security devices called *firewalls*. Some companies now combine firewall and load balancing devices at a lower price than two separate units. However, many network designers choose to keep the firewall a single-purpose device. If the combined device fails, you have fewer recovery options.

Load balancers use fairly straightforward techniques to check the health of each server in the farm. The simplest method is to simply ping the server or test for a response on a specific TCP port (for example, port 80 for http) before sending a connection on to the server. After the load balancer has determined that a given server is alive and well, the load balancer can use other criteria. If the server responds, the load balancer assumes that the server is alive and available to handle connections. But this method doesn't tell the load balancer whether the server's application is actually alive and running, so all the products include the capability to query the server for a specific piece of information—a piece of a specific Web page, for example—before sending traffic to the server. If the server doesn't respond to the request, or if it responds with an error message, the load balancer stops sending requests to that server until the error condition is corrected.

After determining the health of the servers, load-balancing products can use a variety of methods to determine where to send traffic. These include measuring server CPU load, response time, the number of current server connections, and the type of content requested. Content-type balancing provides an extra level of flexibility because it allows the load balancer to send requests for a specific file type to a specific server.

For example, you can configure the load balancer to send all requests for bandwidth-hungry `.wav` and `.avi` files to one high-performance server while sending normal `.html` requests to the rest of the servers in the group. Load balancers can distribute service requests on a round-robin basis as they come in, but you'll probably use one of the more sophisticated techniques that weight the workload or assign jobs based on the addressed URL. Devices can also establish relationships between requestor and server, termed *persistent sessions*, based on factors such as source IP address and special information contained in the VIP request protocol or in returned cookies.

Controlling Clusters

Load balancing and clustering are closely linked: Load balancers provide Web servers with fail-over and smooth response times, and server clusters tackle fail-over chores for back-end file and database servers' software.

Clustering is a function that keeps the contents and operation of the servers synchronized, and, in the event of a primary server failure, automatically calls on another appropriate server in the cluster to pick up the load. Clusters are by no means plug-and-go operations; in most cases, they require cluster-aware services or applications. A sample of cluster-aware Windows NT applications includes Exchange Server, IBM DB2, Lotus Domino, SQL Server, and common ERP packages. Clustering solutions are also offered in today's network operating systems.

Windows 2000 Advanced Server supports two-node clusters and Windows 2000 Datacenter Server supports four nodes. Microsoft has streamlined cluster creation and administration in Windows 2000 with a revamped MMC (Microsoft Management Console) snap-in. Through what Microsoft calls Network Load Balancing (NLB), Windows 2000 also performs load balancing in a farm of up to 32 Windows NT-based Web servers.

For NetWare 5.x shops, Novell's Cluster Services add-on (`www.novell.com`) creates distributed clusters that have from two to eight NetWare 5.x servers, starting at $9,990 list price for the NetWare 5 Starter Kit for two server clusters and ten connections. Novell's Cluster Services enables fail-over for NetWare services and applications. A Java-based tool is used for remote cluster administration and management chores.

"Sun likes to consider itself the company that put the dot in dot-com."

Sun likes to consider itself the company that put the dot in dot-com, but it's known in its circles for shining in the clustered-solutions department. Sun Cluster provides fail-over support for a four-node cluster of Sun systems. Sun's forte is a wide range of Solstice cluster agents that cluster-enable DBD, Informix, Oracle, and Sybase databases.

Legato is neutral when it comes to operating systems and specializes in high-availability solutions for Windows NT, NetWare, and OS/2. Its StandbyServer product creates mirrored servers in an active/active or active/passive configuration, whereas Co-StandbyServer for NT defines one server to be a hot spare for another and fully slips itself into the failed server's place, right down to the IP addresses.

What Do You Need?

Do you need a load balancer, a certificate server, a proxy server, or dual-homed access? How much security is enough? Here are our recommendations for optimal Web site configurations based on the type of site you're running.

- Development Web Site

  You need a development Web server to try your software combinations before you put them on a live site. The development Web server must run the same software combination as your primary site. It's on a local network with no outside connections and so it doesn't need security or high-availability features.

- Intranet

  An intranet server holds the company together, so it needs the high availability, but reliability is probably more important than capacity. Reliability can be provided by redundant server hardware. If appropriate, the servers can be in different locations. The intranet server is behind the corporate firewall, so it doesn't need special security features.

- Marketing

  A marketing server is on the Web to tell your corporate story, so this server needs snappy response. Traffic loads and security threats are low. Consider a hosting facility with fast Internet access and intrusion safeguards. Regularly change all internal passwords and apply the latest software patches.

- Vertical Portal

  A portal craves high availability in terms of both reliability and (hopefully) capacity. Traffic levels and security threats are moderate, so you can keep this site in-house. Serious B2B portals use load balanced Web servers with clustered application and database servers. B2B requires strong user authentication, perhaps using smart cards, and a certificate server for intrusion protection.

- Store Front

  Store fronts must be fast and reliable. This is where both reliability and capacity come into play. Consider Web hosting facilities with multiple server locations and connections to credit card services. Sites often split the delivery of different portions of the Web page elements and SSL transactions between servers. Hardware and connection redundancy protect against denial of service attacks.

- Content Delivery

  Searching for content requires fast and reliable database servers. The front-end Web servers aren't stressed, but clustered database servers and redundant storage work hard. Large content delivery systems have multiple sites around the country and around the world. Redundancy protects against denial of service attacks and legitimate traffic surges.

Server Reliability Through Redundancy

Redundancy is important throughout your Web site system, but it's easiest to see inside your server. Even small-scale server packages have high availability options such as multiple CPUs, redundant power supplies, disk drives arranged in fault tolerant RAID configurations, and error-control memory modules. One valuable technique, server monitoring, is under-utilized. Practically all server-class computers can report internal cabinet temperature, drive status, intrusion into the cabinet, and other factors affecting reliability to network management consoles.

Buzzwords

RAID—The term originally meant *redundant array of inexpensive disks*, but with the drop in the price of storage, it's now often described as an array of *independent* disks. In either case, the idea is to run multiple drives for greater reliability. A number of different ways exist to relate multiple drives and so there are levels of RAID from 0 to 6, but for most high availability servers today, RIAD 5 is what you want.

Our advice is to use redundancy inside servers, particularly in hard disk drives, and redundancy in the design of server systems. Adding redundant CPUs, power supplies, and special error-control memory are less popular reliability options, but power supply and memory failures do happen and a little up-front investment can prevent an expensive outage.

RAID storage is the most commonly used high availability option. With RAID, you gain all the disk drive reliability you choose to buy because there are several types. You can create RAID level 1 by mirroring two drives through the capabilities built in to popular operating systems like Windows 2000, NetWare, or various flavors of Unix. The mirrored drive takes over if the active drive fails, but mirroring imposes a performance penalty because it doubles the write actions. RAID level 5 uses a different technique to copy data across multiple disk drives for very high reliability and high-speed data access. RAID level 6 adds redundant disk controllers, connections, and other elements to RAID level 5. Selecting a RAID 5 option typically adds about 20% to the price of a mid-range server. We think that RAID level 5 is a good investment in the reliability of practically any Web site.

Other high-availability techniques make sense in specific situations. If you're primarily delivering content, such as NASA or Victoria's Secret, then caching can help. If your Web pages are taking orders and credit card numbers, you can still use caching to deliver logos, menus, ads, and other page elements that aren't interactive, but you have to add more Web servers and more application servers to process transactions. If your site handles a lot of e-commerce transactions involving SSL encryption, consider encryption acceleration products, such as Intel's NetStructure. These products improve performance by speeding up CPU-intensive SSL decryption and certificate transactions.

To achieve the highest possible reliability, consider placing your Web servers and other servers in two or more locations served by different ISPs. Practically all load balancers include or have options for balancing traffic among two or more sites, so a network outage, natural disaster, or sabotage striking one location won't take your site off the Web.

Stash a Cache Around the Web

Server farms, load balancers, and multiple redundant Internet connections require a large outlay in equipment, personnel, and connection service contracts. Here are some cost-effective ways to increase your site's capacity and reliability without spending a fortune.

If your site uses mostly static data and you're not ready to put together a large server farm, you can set up a cache server in front of your Web servers. Even e-commerce sites can use cache servers to store logos, menus, and other static pages. The cache server stores the most frequently hit pages in memory or on a very high-performance disk drive. When a person requests a page or a page element that is stored in the cache, the server delivers the cached copy to the client rather than requesting a new copy of the page from the Web server.

Several vendors make high-end, high-reliability cache servers, including Network Appliance (`www.netapp.com`), InfoLibria, and CacheFlow. Inktomi's Traffic Server is a sophisticated caching software product that runs on Solaris, FreeBSD, Windows NT, and several other operating systems. Traffic Server includes a real-time content management system that provides—among many other features—the capability to dynamically refresh the contents of one or more cache servers on an ad-hoc basis. This technique maximizes the effectiveness of the cache while maintaining the freshest possible content on the cache servers.

If you like the idea of having redundant servers in multiple locations that are closer to your users, but you don't want to invest in the equipment and resources they require, consider using a content distribution service. Akamai and Digital Island are two companies that specialize in providing high-availability content hosting for e-business and e-commerce. Akamai and Digital Island host some of the busiest sites on the Web, and each has the infrastructure to handle even the highest-volume site.

Both maintain extensive, high-performance server farms, linked by high-speed backbone connections that let them bypass congested Internet routes when necessary. Akamai, for example, maintains over 2,000 servers in 40 countries and plans to add an additional 1,500 servers this year. Both companies use a combination of load-balancing and content-caching technologies to route client requests to the closest content-serving server.

Akamai's business is centered on the company's FreeFlow content-delivery system. FreeFlow uses sophisticated, proprietary traffic-handling algorithms that let Akamai's network make intelligent content delivery decisions, even in the event of a major communications failure. According to the company, FreeFlow can deliver content to browsers two to ten times faster than conventional load-balancing technologies.

Digital Island—thanks to its recent acquisition of Sandpiper Networks—offers a complete suite of services that includes content delivery as well as e-business transaction hosting. Digital Island's FootPrint service is similar to Akamai's FreeFlow, but Digital Island claims to host more content types—including more streaming-media types—than Akamai does.

Build or Buy?

By now you should agree that you need an e-business infrastructure. Your alternatives are to build it from scratch, to assemble some component modules from disparate vendors, or to buy and implement the complete solution from some outsourced service. Your decision factors revolve around time, cost, and risk. The new economy complicates the relationship of the decision factors because time and risk multiply each other. The longer you take to establish your presence in the new economy, the larger the risk that your competition will occupy the space before you. But outsourcing comes with its own risks, typically in the form of a non-customized solution and a non-responsive service provider. The development of the e-business infrastructure is a strategic corporate decision that involves corporate culture as much as it involves corporate balance sheets.

Content hosting is most effective for delivering critical, high-volume traffic such as ad banners, graphic and multimedia files, and downloadable software. Typically, content-hosting services host the high-volume portion of a client's site, with the bulk of the site remaining on the client's own Web server. To use either of these services, clients upload a copy of the material to be hosted onto the content host's servers. If the content changes, it is the client's responsibility to re-upload a fresh copy to the content host. Making some minor changes to your site's Web pages is also necessary to redirect specific portions of your site to the content-hosting service. Both companies provide easy-to-use content management tools that make this process relatively painless. Content hosts generally charge by the hit, so there are no expensive start-up costs or monthly fees.

Both Akamai and Digital Island offer service guarantees, and both can provide clients with extensive traffic monitoring and activity logs.

Outsource the Web Site

The jury is in. The verdict is clear. You will probably host your e-business Web site in a data center owned and operated by somebody else. Unless you already have an experienced staff of Web warriors and an existing data center, it makes economic sense to host your e-business Web site with an outside service.

Outside hosting services offer fast deployment, strong resources, and low cost. Paying an affordable and predictable monthly fee to a Web hosting service buys high reliability, 24/7 expertise, and fast connections. The site can be active with your content minutes after you type in a credit card number. You can outhost a high-traffic, high-content Web site for several hundred dollars a month, which is a small percentage of what it would cost to hire a single employee to run it in-house. You can host a very capable retail site for under $100 a month.

Outsource What You Know

"Outsource What You Know" is the advice of Mark Buchstaber, director of the Internet Technology Center at the UnitedHealth Group. Mark explains that your team can manage the outsourced service better if they understand the work involved in providing the technology. It's a good and proven philosophy, but you have to weigh it against the time needed to deploy new e-business services as you learn the ropes. Other experienced managers agree with Mark, but also say that companies often initially outsource the expensive infrastructure and then gradually bring it in-house if the project proves itself.

If the desirability of outsourcing Web site hosting isn't in doubt, the problem comes in selecting between the thousands of hosting services that want your business. They range from neighborhood ISPs, which offer basic Web site hosting as part of a connectivity package, through specialized hosting companies, and on to the multinational carriers that see hosting as part of a bundle of a much bigger bundle of connection services. Re-selling services provided by a mega-hosting company is a common practice. Buying through a re-seller is a good way to get the benefits of a big facility.

Generally, the hosting services divide themselves into those aimed at Webmasters with some knowledge and those aimed at novices. Services such as AT&T, Interland, Verio, Web2010, and Cable and Wireless are comfortable for any administrator who understands something about file structures and HTML. That's not to say that they don't have plenty of wizards and help, but they also offer flexibility and they don't cramp knowledgeable users. Web2010 is particularly well suited to knowledgeable Unix administrators.

Services such as IBM and Microsoft bCentral services are probably the best for a total novice. Microsoft's bCentral is tightly integrated with Microsoft's development software. If Microsoft FrontPage is all you know then bCentral is fine for you. The IBM service is good if you have no other experience, but experienced administrators will have to re-learn to do things the IBM way.

DellHost offers a complete list of e-business add-on features and a comprehensive site toolbox for management. The company also offers direct mail campaigns, banner ads, PR services, and direct e-mail services, at extra cost. None of this is unique, but altogether it's a nice all-in-one service for a small business.

The Fortress Factor

Resources make up the biggest differentiator between the bigger hosting companies and the smaller ISPs that also do hosting. The bigger companies operate within fortress-like data centers with strong physical security, internal fire protection, redundant and filtered power sources, and highly qualified staff on duty 24/7. They offer multiple high-capacity data connections to high-level Internet peering points and most of them have connections to several backbone carriers. They typically have several data centers around the country or world that can act as cache sites for very heavy traffic loads. In short, they offer the power to support you in all circumstances and room to grow. If the going gets tough, whether it's the pleasant problem of too much holiday traffic or an unpleasant hacker attack, they have the resources to keep you going.

If you evaluate the services of local ISPs, you should ask about and even visit their facilities. If they can't show you a good home for your valuable data, then don't trust it to them.

Services and Consulting

It's one thing to provide a reliable server and connections, but hosting companies add value by making it easy for you to create your site and by providing add-on services like a shopping cart, a commercial bank to handle credit cards, and services to register your site with search engines. They also provide site design and e-business consulting services. General service carriers such as AT&T and Cable and Wireless will design and manage your entire IS infrastructure if you want that level of service.

How much you value online Web site creation tools depends on your skill and your desire for a unique look. If you want to differentiate your site, you'll have it created by a professional designer and upload it to the hosting facility.

Virtual? Dedicated? Co-Hosted?

Do you want virtual hosting and do you want fries with that? One of the first things you'll decide is whether you want your own dedicated server hardware in the hosting facility, or whether you'll share a server, or want your own leased space to segregate equipment you own. Although sharing a server might initially seem undesirable, it's actually a very attractive option.

Shared hosting, also called virtual server, is a service that might deposit your Web site applications in any of hundreds of identical servers within the facility. By chance the processor running your applications might also run applications for other clients, or it might not. But to you, it doesn't matter. Your transactions and data are private. Importantly, your action should also be snappy and reliable.

The shared hosting facilities get a lot of attention in the data center. These server boxes, stacked as high as 70 in a rack, are load balanced, monitored, backed up, filtered, virus checked, and highly redundant. The hosting sites typically guarantee that the entire connection and hardware system will work 99.9% of the time. There is no reason why you shouldn't trust your retail storefront to a shared facility.

However, a 99.9% reliability rate still allows for almost nine hours of downtime a year. A co-hosted facility is the solution for those needing higher reliability. You can create your own nest of redundant, clustered, and load-balanced servers in the hosting company's facility. The hardware belongs to you and typically resides within a segregated cage, but the hosting facility maintains the hardware and connectivity for you. This is the most expensive option and the costs depend completely on the service and space contract you negotiate with the hosting company. Something just under a thousand dollars a month describes the right order of magnitude.

"A 99.9% reliability rate still allows for almost nine hours of downtime a year."

You'll need a dedicated server if your special applications demand a unique operating environment or place special demands on the server. A custom database application is the most typical example. The cost is negotiated based on the hardware, software, and level of reliability you need, but you should expect to pay several hundred dollars a month.

Go with the Biggest?

The Web hosting facilities maintained by the biggest ISPs can impress you with their statistics. They have many hundreds of megabytes of connectivity to multiple points in the Web, high security, and impressive staffing. Smaller ISPs can compete on the numbers. The key difference is often in responsiveness. The smaller companies, where everybody knows your name, might respond more quickly to serious problems, or they might not.

Nothing is wrong with using either a large or a small hosting facility, but make sure you tie a service of any size to specific promises about responsiveness in terms of answering queries and restoring services.

You can combine outsourcing with your own operation and keep physical control of your hardware while outsourcing network monitoring, management, and security. All major Web-hosting companies offer remote monitoring and management services. They can report problems and control network devices such as your routers. Most importantly, they have plans and resources to meet emergencies. The expertise and big picture viewpoint they can provide can speed the resolution of problems. You can also contract out for the on-call surge capacity you might need to meet a welcome rush of legitimate traffic or an unwelcome flood attack.

There's no single secret to high availability—except perhaps overbuilding everything. All the things you ever heard about Mr. Murphy's Law are living in Internet Web sites. Double up on everything.

CHAPTER 11

e-Business Network Security

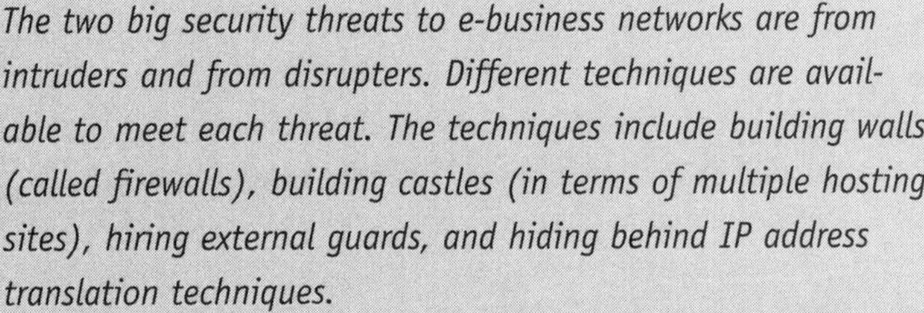

The two big security threats to e-business networks are from intruders and from disrupters. Different techniques are available to meet each threat. The techniques include building walls (called firewalls), building castles (in terms of multiple hosting sites), hiring external guards, and hiding behind IP address translation techniques.

But other aspects of security are also evident. Fighting viruses on your e-business network is part of security. Protecting employees from harassment of any kind through your network is security too. This can involve limiting and monitoring what kinds of information employees gather from the Internet and what kinds of words they put into email.

Like all forms of physical protection, from insurance and fences to television cameras and security guards, the effort you put into network protection depends on the threat and on what you have to lose. Some security techniques can limit employee privacy and flexibility, but if the threat and value are high enough, that might be a part of doing e-business.

Okay, we'll admit that not all Web site intruders and disrupters are sociopaths. Some do it for money. The most costly intruder is the one who leaves nothing behind, but who copies corporate files and walks away with customer lists and business plans. Similarly, some disruptions of service could have monetary or even strategic economic motivation. So, whether the source is a sociopath, an entrepreneur, or the arm of some government, the threat can come from many directions.

When threatened, animals know to run away, duck in a hole, or climb a tree. Maneuvering, concealment, and fortification have been the three elements of defense since big fish started eating little fish. It's no different on your network. The Internet has plenty of vicious fish, so you should take steps to build walls, hide, and get out of the way.

Flexible Access

The traditional security models, such as providing a password for each application, assume a reasonably static set of authorized users. But the new economy is about building relationships that change quickly. The use of directory services allows business partners to enter the network with specific and limited rights.

The kind of security threat you face depends on how you use your Web site or network. Practically all Web sites and networks attached to the Internet face intrusion attempts. Organizations with a high public profile have a greater risk of also suffering denial of service (DoS) attacks, but even desktop computers in innocuous organizations can be co-opted as instruments to create distributed DoS attacks from unexpected sources. You should plan your investment in network security like you plan your investment in building security. If there's a big threat, build a big wall and hire guards.

Buzzwords

Denial of service (DoS) attack—An attempt to overload the capacity of a site or network by generating bogus requests for service.

Security Policies

Security begins with a policy and ends with an audit. If you get the order backward, you have a big problem.

Buzzwords

Distributed Denial of Service (DDoS) attack—A DoS attack that uses hijacked computers anywhere on the Internet to generate service requests aimed at a specific site.

Rent-A-Cop Security

Corporate security challenges are huge, and the number of people qualified to deal with them is tiny. Hence the tremendous surge in security outsourcing, a market that Infonetics Research (www.infonetics.com) predicts will nearly triple within the next year—from $229 million to $716 million. A number of players are currently jockeying for dominance, from behemoths like IBM to independent agents like NetSolve.

With hundreds of employees devoted exclusively to security, IBM Global Services is a force to be reckoned with. In addition to a wide range of consulting, assessment, and ethical-hacking services (ethical hacking implies that you hire hackers to find vulnerabilities in your network), IBM offers managed firewall and intrusion detection packages.

Another component of its service portfolio is the Internet Emergency Response Service. Though the price tag looks steep at $37,000 per year, this service provides on-the-spot protection and recovery during and after a hack, alleviating your need for having someone on call in the middle of the night, when most hacks occur.

GTE Internetworking specifically targets the country's 3.2 million small to midsize businesses with its Security Advantage package. Starting at $795 per month, this turnkey service includes firewalling courtesy of the WatchGuard product line, 24-hour monitoring and response, product management and maintenance, and monthly reports.

You don't have to go with a major telecommunications company to get security outsourcing. A startup, NetSolve is also gunning for midsize businesses. Its ProWatch Secure Services use Cisco's PIX firewall and NetRanger intrusion detection products, which the customer has to buy; the services include both managed firewall and intrusion detection and response services. These run $1,295 and $1,495 per month; a combo package costs $1,995 a month.

Pilot Network Services (www.pilot.net) takes a different approach by constructing its own security infrastructure, through which it hosts and monitors its clients' networks. The company's Secure Access and Gateways service, which provides fortified email, secure Web services, and secure FTP/telnet gateways, starts at $5,000 a month.

When any network picks up an assigned block of permanent Internet addresses, it's like plopping a fresh kill in front of Internet sharks. They bite on a permanent address because it's an easy target. This is true of multinational corporations and true of a small office with a cable or DSL modem. Hiding is the easiest and least expensive defense against intrusion attacks and it's probably the easiest technique for small offices and homes.

Hide Out

You hide yourself on the Internet through a technique called *Network Address Translation* or *NAT*. NAT, available on every firewall and even less sophisticated gateways aimed at homes and small offices, camouflages your networked computers with IP addresses that the bad guys can't see from the Internet. A NAT device translates between safe addresses on the LAN and its own permanent address. Figure 11.1 shows how NAT works. As an added benefit, NAT eliminates IP address hassles that many businesses suffer when they try to use a block of routable IP addresses assigned by an ISP. NAT is simple to use and it's effective against most intrusion threats. However, it doesn't help you against denial of service or sophisticated intrusion attacks.

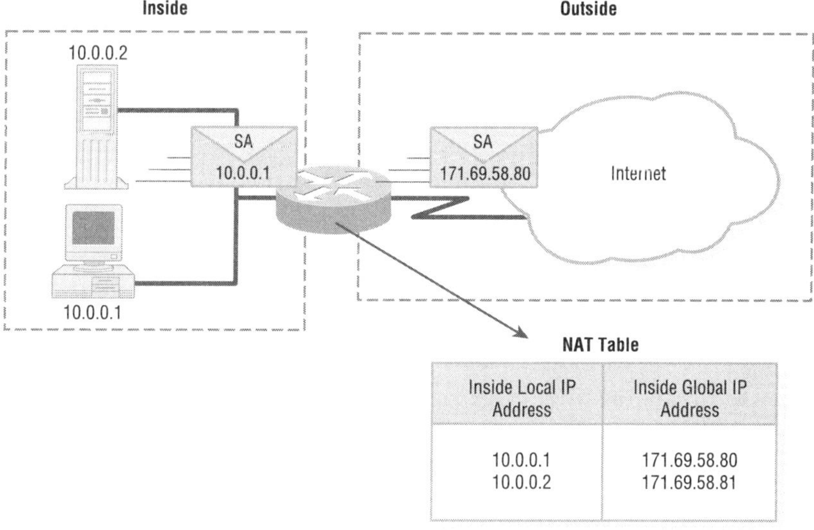

Figure 11.1
A NAT device camouflages your Internet address so hackers can't see it.

Not NAT, but PAT

We don't want to appear technically arcane, so we have given you the common definition of network address translation. But, for the purists, we should mention that NAT is often implemented as *port address translation (PAT)*. The device does more than simply translate from one IP address to another. PAT enables the network manager to conserve IP addresses by allowing source ports in TCP connections or UDP conversations to be translated. Different local addresses then

Buzzwords

Firewall—A device that examines each inbound packet to ensure that it has a legitimate reason for entering the local network. Firewalls use several different techniques to determine legitimacy.

will map to the same global address, with port translation providing the needed unique routing. When translation is required, the new port number is picked out of the same range as the original, following the convention of Berkeley Standard Distribution (BSD). The difference doesn't matter to any user, but we know our NAT from our PAT.

Buzzwords

Network Address Translation—A service that presents one valid routable IP address to the Internet and then translates and distributes traffic to non-routable IP addresses inside the local area network. This hides the addresses inside the network and conserves routable addresses.

Move Out of the Way

Maneuvering and evasion make up another classic form of defense. When you hire someone else to protect you, they clear a safe space for you. Outside services will filter your email, check your packets, provide a hot backup for your entire facility, and send in expert teams at the first sign of attack.

Many factors, including the shortage of IS staff and the scarcity of security expertise, make outsourcing appealing. Outsourced companies can bring expertise that isn't available in the typical IS staff. Their remote management services have particular value if you have several operating locations with Internet connections. Later in this chapter we'll talk about outsourcing email virus protection.

The Final Defense

The Japanese have a saying that "the tall grass gets cut first." You can try hiding from and evading trouble, but if your resources are too big or too inviting, trouble is going to find you. The final defensive alternative is to build a wall to protect your network. Devices called *firewalls* use several techniques to identify, check, and filter packets going into and out of a network. Establishing and maintaining a firewall takes some expertise, so you might look for help from a value-added reseller.

The most popular turnkey firewall products include those from Cisco, Checkpoint, eSoft, SonicWALL, and WatchGuard. Checkpoint's popular VPN-1 software is bundled in systems sold by other vendors, such as Nokia and Nortel. Many IS departments and VARs buy the VPN-1 software separately and use it with their own hardware. Firewall products for corporate networks can range in cost from a little over $2000 to over $10,000. Many products settle in just under $5000, but you'll also have an annual cost, perhaps as much as 20% of the original product cost, for support and upgrade services.

Firewall security often starts with NAT, but then it adds other techniques. Packet address filtering, also done by routers, checks for legitimate inbound and outbound IP addresses. A more sophisticated application proxy firewall inserts itself in the transaction between a client and server program and watches for inappropriate requests. A process called stateful inspection, pioneered and patented by Checkpoint, but available in practically all products today, dynamically tracks and validates client/server interactions. Theoretically, stateful inspection creates less overhead and delay than the proxy firewall process, but in typical installations the communications circuits cause so much more delay than the firewall that you don't see a difference.

Buzzwords

DMZ—Demilitarized zone. A segregated network, behind the firewall yet separate from the local area network. Devices requiring some public access go into the DMZ.

You can use these products as a single combined router and firewall and the VPN-1 offers the most flexible router in this review. But if the single system is penetrated, you're wide open to intrusion. Conservative administrators use a router for packet filtering and use a firewall to place Web servers and other Internet servers on a separate peripheral network—often called the *demilitarized zone* or *DMZ*. The large firewalls offer a special port for that peripheral network, while some of the small office gateways can create a subnetwork through packet filtering. Figure 10.2 shows a firewall with a peripheral network that constitutes the DMZ.

The important things to look for in firewall systems include effectiveness, affordability, and the availability of other features such as a virtual private network. Practically all modern firewall products can create encrypted virtual private network (VPN) connections for remote access, but not all VPNs are the same. The most secure VPNs use the IPSec standard for encryption and data handling. IPSec is the wave of the future; however, unless you're facing a highly sophisticated threat, PPTP security is adequate and less difficult to set up in smaller networks.

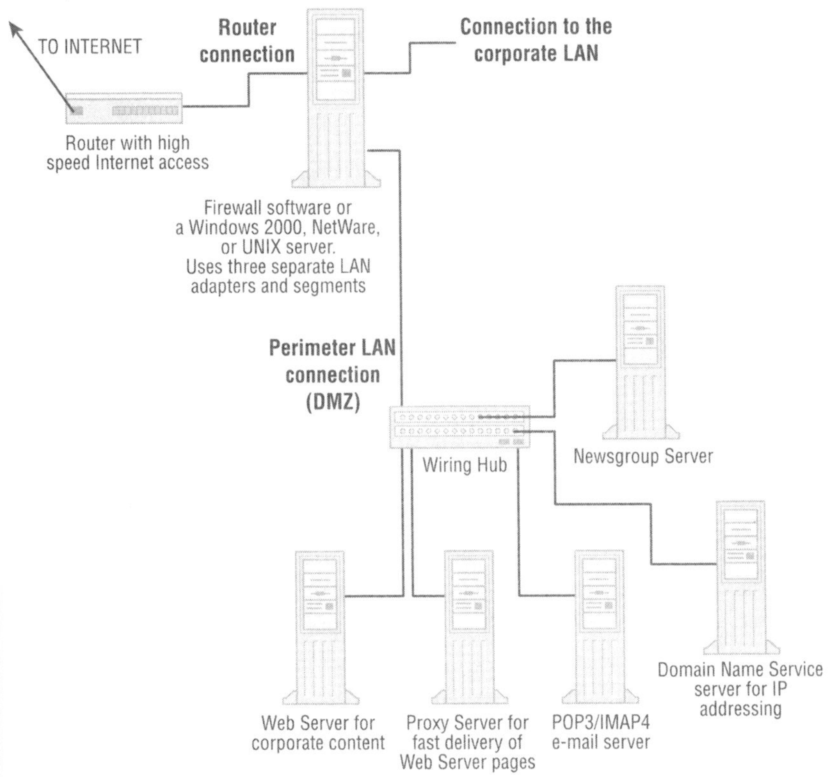

Figure 11.2

By isolating your Internet server in a peripheral network behind a firewall, you create a DMZ.

VPN Client Hassles

Many of our *PC Magazine* editors use VPN connections from our homes and from hotels and remote locations across the country. But the move to Windows 2000 has turned the desire to use a VPN into a major challenge.

We've been using third-party VPN products for Windows 95, 98, and NT from companies such as Intel (Shiva) and Cisco (Altiga) with generally good results for a long time. But these clients typically work by using the IPSec protocol and their own propriety VPN clients, which often replace or modify the Winsock file on earlier versions of Windows. But with Windows 2000, we have a new TCP/IP stack and Winsock that are protected by Microsoft's new system file protection. So the proprietary clients don't work.

Windows 2000 comes with a native VPN client, but it only communicates through PPTP (Point-to-Point Tunneling Protocol) or over the

L2TP (Layer 2 Tunnelling Protocol) version of IPSec. The L2TP method requires setting up an external certificate authority and that's a hassle. We were eventually able to get the native client working with PPTP on a Cisco VPN, but are still having problems when multiple clients try to connect from a single IP address, as you would if you had a simple DSL router in a remote office. Meanwhile, most VPN vendors are working on new versions of their clients, but it's a big process.

In short, it has been a real pain.

Windows Millennium incorporates many of the changes to TCP/IP that are in Windows 2000, but it implements them in a way that offers more backward compatibility. It supports IPSec, but with enough slight changes that new versions of some of the clients will be necessary. Still, we have run into a number of problems with firewalls and VPN clients—Microsoft says most of the vendors will have new versions around the time that the operating system is actually on shelves. I hope so.

But this points out two essential lessons. The first is that every OS—even those aimed at home users—can cause problems for IT and network managers who might have to support the remote access aspects of employees' home PCs. Even if your company doesn't change OSs, some of your home users will. The second lesson is one we've seen before—that every upgrade has its issues.

On the DMZ

A truly secure firewall would deny all access to any PCs or services running on the LAN. But that is not always possible if you want to set up an email, Web, or FTP server for outside access. There are basically two ways to open up your network and still keep it secure: You can set up a demilitarized zone (DMZ), or you can use filtering.

A demilitarized zone is a segment between the Internet connection and your LAN where you would put your firewall or other servers that you want to publish to users on the Internet. Yes, you could say that the DMZ contains the sacrificial servers. They have the lowest level of protection because they are open to the public. Most DMZs require a separate LAN connection for attaching the servers.

If a firewall device doesn't offer a third DMZ port, it will typically provide port filters. A port filter lets you open specific addresses and ports that you want to have open access.

Content Filters

Most people think of a firewall as a tool for preventing outside access to your LAN, but it can also serve to control what your internal users access on the Internet. Most firewall products contain what are called URL filtering or content filtering features. These features provide another aspect of security: freedom from harassment and distraction.

The Web contains a lot more information than is relevant to our jobs. Corporations, as well as libraries, schools, and any Web kiosk operator, are grappling with how to provide Internet access while avoiding the potential legal and productivity pitfalls that come with it. Regardless of the type of organization, networked Internet content-filtering and monitoring software, such as the five packages we review here, is the primary tool used to walk this precarious line.

"For businesses, the decision of whether to block is a sticky one."

For businesses, the decision of whether to block is a sticky one. Although prohibiting pornography and hate speech is a no-brainer (not doing so can leave corporations vulnerable to possible sexual harassment and discrimination suits), companies are also concerned with the effect of unlimited surfing on productivity.

For those companies that think they should restrain employees from vacation planning or portfolio checking, URL filtering products include features to block those types of activities. These so-called productivity filters can weed out, say, sports and travel sites, to let companies decide for themselves what surfing is useful and what isn't.

To help companies define their filters, these products list sites that the vendors deem inappropriate because of pornographic images or hate speech, or because they aren't job-related. These lists are divided into categories; corporations can choose which types of content employees will not be allowed to access.

Because the crown jewel of each product is the list of URLs it has amassed, corporations that purchase the monitoring tool cannot view it directly. Rather, if a company finds a site that it doesn't want to block, it can override the product's list. Similarly, companies running any of these products can add a site to the list if the site is accessible but the company wants it blocked. Each purchase price includes a one-year subscription to the vendor's list updates, which can be downloaded manually and sometimes automatically.

The Future of Filtering

Today's corporate filtering and monitoring solutions rely on huge databases chock-full of naughty and unproductive sites. To compile these databases and keep them current, companies such as NetPartners Internet Solutions and SurfWatch have relied on a combination of automated and manual processes, including teams of what wiseacres refer to as smut surfers.

RuleSpace appears poised to render manual site gathering a thing of the past with its RuleSpace Enterprise Suite, a blocking/filtering product that relies on artificial intelligence.

Based on the findings of its in-house neural networks, which use a combination of proprietary fuzzy-logic and artificial-intelligence problem-solving methodologies, the RuleSpace Enterprise Suite can determine what is pornographic and what is not without the overhead and inherent limitations of a finite database. So when a user requests `Playboy.com` or even a freshly minted adult site, the product can block it simply by consulting the finely honed patterns—and not any site list.

At the simplest level, neural networks attempt to emulate the functions of the human brain in that they learn based on experience. In the case of RuleSpace, its neural networks are trained to understand the difference between a pornographic site and a health site, for instance, or between a site with an article about online gambling versus one that lets you gamble. These distinctions are made based on previous encounters with such material.

These products also let companies set different types of access based on time of day and day of the week. Products like CyberPatrol, Little Brother, and SurfWatch go a step farther, letting companies set different levels of access for different user groups; this way, R & D can be given freer rein than the sales department.

In a logical extension, many corporations are developing acceptable-usage policies to clarify their positions on Internet access with a written document that each employee signs acknowledging that such access is being closely monitored and that certain sites will be blocked. The document also usually details the disciplinary action that will accompany violations. Products like LittleBrother and WebSense include sample acceptable-usage policies to help you craft your own.

Flood Protection

The same high-availability techniques that we described in the last chapter to protect against outages and traffic surges also help mitigate the memorable distributed denial-of-service (DDoS) attacks that plagued eBay, Yahoo!, and other large Web sites in February of 2000.

In a DDoS attack, the hacker breaks into insecure networks across the Internet, hijacks their systems, and uses them to flood the target site's communications bandwidth with bogus packets, overloading the target's servers, connections, and routers. This is easier than it seems; hacker utilities with names like Tribe Flood Network and Trin00 are freely available on the Web and easy to use.

If your site is the target, the first line of defense against such attacks is having the surge capability available in redundant connections, routers, and servers as well as multiple geographic locations to handle the onslaught. At the same time, you can work with your service provider to identify originating IP addresses and block the attacks. A technique called ingress and egress filtering lets ISPs control traffic flow at their networks' points of entry and exit and lets them eliminate packets with forged IP addresses, which are frequently used in these attacks. IT managers can also use the anti-spoofing capabilities of their routers to block forged IP addresses. Getting in-depth defense through an on-call contract for services with a major ISP is essential.

Prevention is another story. Most of the victim sites already had tight security infrastructures. The hijacked sites did not. These events are a wakeup call; the security of the Web depends on every site having a secure infrastructure in place. Intrusion detection tools, including tools from commercial vendors such as Internet Security Systems (`www.iss.net`), can detect today's DDoS attacks for both the targeted and the hijacked site.

Another subtle attack, the TCP-SYN attack shown in Figure 10.3, starts TCP synchronization sessions, but then abandons them. The target servers and firewalls keep the sessions open and search for incoming acknowledgements, which ties up their internal resources so they can't respond to legitimate TCP requests. A variation called the UDP attack tries to tie up servers using the UDP protocol. Administrators can defeat nuisance-level TCP and UDP attacks by adjusting server parameters. But massive attacks can have a big initial effect when they overrun capacity.

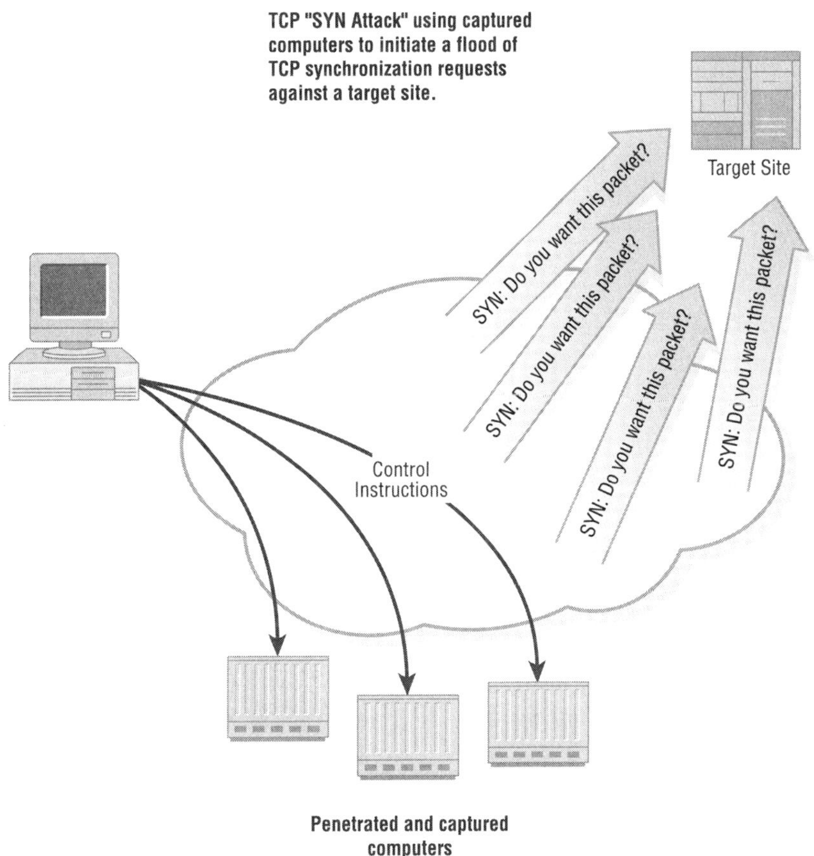

TCP "SYN Attack" using captured computers to initiate a flood of TCP synchronization requests against a target site.
Target Site
SYN: Do you want this packet?
SYN: Do you want this packet?
SYN: Do you want this packet?
SYN: Do you want this packet?
Control Instructions
Penetrated and captured computers

Figure 11.3
The TCP-SYN attack is one of the more subtle weapons in a hacker's arsenal.

Firewall companies upgraded their systems after the denial-of-service attacks in early 2000 and many firewalls can now recognize DDoS attacks and drop packets. But the best way to meet a big DoS attack is to have the surge capacity available in connections, routers, and servers to contain the attack until an emergency response team can backtrack to its sources and coordinate blockade actions among carriers.

Generally, managers of all sites should make sure that every piece of software on every server, whether in-house or outsourced, has the latest security software patches. All operating systems have updates and so do most applications. Sophisticated intruders can find arcane holes in ports and buffers to gain entry into the server, so those holes must be plugged with the latest patches.

Virus Protection

Firewalls and NAT can protect you against bold intruders. But viruses sneak into networks as illegitimate payloads inside of legitimate packets. Viruses are yet another threat to your e-business network.

The Internet is to computer viruses what the airplane is to human viruses. Today, a new virus of either kind can spread worldwide in a matter of hours. Furthermore, things that used to be safe, like email and handshakes, aren't positively safe anymore. Human problems aside, companies of all sizes need computer antivirus systems able to detect and destroy even the newest threat. Ideally, the corporate system should monitor all files moving on the network. This kind of protection initially costs from $25-$50 per client computer, but automated features keep down the long-term management overhead. Testing in *PC Magazine* Labs shows that virus testing imposes almost no penalty on network performance.

The leading antivirus products include F-Secure's F-Secure Anti-Virus, Panda Software's Global Virus Insurance, Symantec's Norton Antivirus Enterprise Solution, and Trend Micro's NeaTSuite. Each of these products uses the Internet to provide up-to-the-minute protection against new outbreaks and each product can ease the burden of installing and maintaining a cohesive network antivirus policy. Any of them is an improvement over standalone, unmanaged virus protection on an e-business network.

Safe Email

It used to be that email was safe as long as you didn't run any files attached to email messages. The majority of today's infections are macro viruses that arrive as email attachments. But the Bubbleboy virus, first discovered in late 1999, made headlines because it was the first virus able to infect victim's computers through email—*without* requiring the recipient to open an attachment. The growing use of JavaScript, ActiveX, and Visual Basic on the Web and in email clients such as Outlook Express provides another opportunity for virus writers.

All of the antivirus vendors typically offer email and Internet gateway products that sniff out viruses embedded in email and file transfer traffic to and from the Internet. Some vendors provide the Internet and mail server products as part of their standard package, and others offer them as add-on products. These products augment the protection provided by conventional antivirus software. Putting antivirus protection on the email server also protects off-site users who send and receive email from home offices or portable PCs, even if those users don't have conventional antivirus software installed.

You can outsource the protection of your email either on its own or in conjunction with these antivirus suites. Outsourcing can give the job of integrating virus protection with email service to the professionals for as little as $1 per account per month.

Internet Updates

Most antivirus vendors work around the clock developing updates to their software to battle each new virus variant. But any given PC's virus protection is only as good as its last update, so it's important to deploy new virus updates as soon as possible. Unfortunately, distributing virus updates to hundreds or thousands of PCs can be a logistical nightmare. The top products include an Internet updating feature that allows system administrators to automatically receive the latest virus updates from the antivirus vendors, and they also include tools to automatically distribute the update to all the PCs on the local network.

Network antivirus suites solve the deployment and updating problems by providing network administrators with a suite of management tools to help deploy, monitor, and update antivirus software running on client PCs on the LAN.

Networked Antivirus

You'll pay dearly if your e-business network becomes clogged or disrupted by a virus. The continued growth of client/server computing, wider availability of Internet access, and increasing numbers of mobile workers all pose new computer virus threats. To cope with these risks, you need a three-tiered strategy to guard not only desktops, but also network messaging servers and Internet gateways. Figure 10.4 shows the three layers that need virus protection.

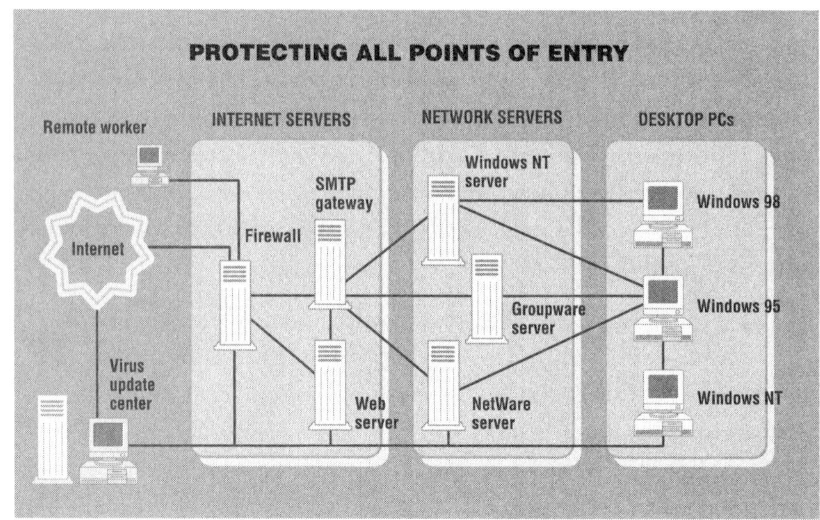

Figure 11.4
You need virus protection on three distinct tiers of your network.

Different servers require different types of protection. For example, HTTP is the carrier for ActiveX controls and Java applets, which could contain viruses that must be removed before they reach the browser. To protect email (SMTP), the products must open up each database and look for any hidden viruses attached to the message before the recipient reads it or forwards it to others. Finally, FTP is a perfect way to download applications that could be laced with a virus.

Products such as Trend Micro's InterScan VirusWall, Symantec Corp.'s Norton AntiVirus for Firewalls, and Networks Associates' WebShield address all these threats by scanning all packets coming in from the Internet, including HTTP (Web), SMTP (email), and FTP (file transfer). Most of these products run on Windows NT, but some are also available for Sun Solaris. Norton AntiVirus for Firewalls and WebShield come free with the standard network suites. InterScan VirusWall costs $21 per node.

These Internet antivirus products are fairly easy to set up, but they require knowledge of IP addressing and the configuration of your particular network. For example, the administrator must configure the IP address and TCP port number for each service running on the different servers. After setup, these products provide the same detection, disinfection, and notification options as desktop and network server solutions. In addition, they can be administered from the centralized tools bundled with the suites.

The major networked virus control products all operate somewhat differently, but they all use a three-part client-server-console architecture. The antivirus server is the centerpiece of the system; it provides client software and updates to the client PCs on the LAN. The server also collects virus alerts from the client software, and it is typically connected to the Internet so it can download the latest virus updates from the antivirus vendor.

Clients are most often desktop PCs, but servers running Windows NT/2000 and NetWare can also be antivirus clients. All the antivirus products we tested provide protection for NT/2000 and NetWare servers, either as part of the standard package or as an extra-cost product.

The management console is usually installed on the same PC as the antivirus server, but it can be installed on a separate machine to enhance security or to reduce CPU demand on a busy server. Management consoles are the command center in the battle against viruses. They provide the interface that the administrator uses to manage clients on the network.

Network antivirus clients differ from standalone antivirus programs in three important ways. First, the clients are configured from the management console, not from the client PC itself. Products typically provide a lockdown mode that allows the system administrator to lock down the client PC's configuration. This prevents users from modifying or interrupting the antivirus client software, and it enables the system administrator to create and enforce a consistent antivirus policy across the entire enterprise. Second, networked clients report all virus incidents back to the LAN antivirus server. This allows the server to monitor the LAN for new virus outbreaks, and it provides the administrator with an accurate, up-to-date picture of virus activity.

Typically the client products can respond to commands from the management console and to database updates from the antivirus server. This feature lets system administrators initiate a scan of client PCs, perhaps in response to a suspected virus breakout, or set up scans on a schedule as a preventive maintenance tool. It also provides a mechanism to ensure that all client PCs are using the latest virus database.

Checking Email Content

"Email content-filtering is more about internal security than protection from external threats."

Like URL content filtering, email content-filtering is more about internal security than protection from external threats. Special email products can help you get a handle on a wide range of messaging woes, from inappropriate content to confidential company information, spam, and large attachments.

Companies are more dependent on email than ever before, but email can be abused. Consider the implications of a user knowingly or unknowingly disseminating your company's top-secret product launch date to the wrong outside people through email. Even internal email has its risks; the competitive zeal that was demonstrated in Microsoft's own internal email was key evidence in the Justice Department's case against the software giant. Recent firings at Solomon Smith Barney and *The New York Times* involved internally generated email messages containing offensive language.

There is a way, however, to get all of the considerable advantages email has to offer while protecting your company's liability, confidentiality, and productivity: email-filtering tools. If you decide to implement an email filtering solution, you won't be alone. International Data Corp. estimates that by 2003, some 3.9 million businesses will have implemented email-filtering tools either solo or in combination with a Web-filtering product.

Although it might seems like a nascent market, at least four strong entries—Elron Software's CommandView Message Inspector, Symantec's Mail-Gear, Content Technologies' Mail Sweeper, and Tumbleweed Communications WordSecure/Mail—let you set up customized rules and use content-filtering engines based on statistical processing or natural-language algorithms. You can use these to catch messages with confidential company information, inappropriate language, or annoyingly large attachments that eat up network bandwidth. The most important feature of these products is their capability to scan emails and attachments for sensitive information on upcoming or current projects, legal information, and the like. You configure them to scan email messages for key words and phrases and the products will find a message that contains those items. They will then either discard the message and notify the user, send the message back to the user, or, in the case of MailSweeper and Word- Secure/Mail, send it to a quarantine location for further evaluation by an administrator. These solutions also let you set up user exceptions so that you can keep trusted parties outside your organization in the email loop on pertinent projects.

Although scanning for sensitive information is a very valuable feature, it is also the most difficult part of these packages to configure and maintain. Each new project contains its own set of phrases and players, which means creating new rules and new exceptions. Make no mistake: Learning the rule-writing nuances of these products takes practice, though we found that WordSecure/Mail was the easiest to use in this regard.

Using these products to prevent libel is easier, especially if you use an email-filtering package in conjunction with a Web-filtering solution. Web-filtering products let you set up and enforce policies that either monitor use of the Web or prevent users from accessing inappropriate Web sites. Content Technologies, Elron Software, Tumbleweed Communications, and vendors such as Surf Watch offer separate Web-filtering packages. By creating email policies that block or alert managers and human resources departments to racist, sexist, or other blatantly libelous correspondence, you can protect your company from inadvertently creating a hostile work environment.

Finally, email-filtering can help your network and your employees operate more efficiently. All four products we reviewed can block attachments based on file type, so you can keep executables and MP3 files, for example, off the network. MailSweeper and WorldSecure/Mail can even block messages based on attachment file size, a feature available in many email systems as well. If you don't want to deprive employees of these, MailSweeper and WorldSecure/Mail let you defer delivery of certain file types or sizes until the end of the day. This can cut down considerably on network traffic during business hours. The ability to block spam or email from troublesome domains can keep unnecessary emails to a minimum.

Keep in mind that a determined user can get around any of these products. None of them can scan HTTP-based emails sent from free Internet accounts such as Yahoo! Mail or Hotmail, though Elron and WorldTalk take care of this little problem through their Web-filtering products. And unless you have desktop PCs completely locked down, any file can be copied onto a disk or printed.

An email-filtering system lets you control those things that are within your control, such as the type and size of files users are sending through corporate email accounts and their contents. It is still up to you to decide how rejected messages are handled, but these packages can protect someone from the consequences of doing something he or she didn't mean to do—like hitting the send button a moment too soon.

Security Holes

In most cases, simply deploying technology isn't enough to ensure secure systems properly. Security holes can develop despite well-intentioned attempts to utilize security technologies.

Let's consider a fictitious discount computer reseller called MicroEmporium. This company has a Web site hosted on an outsourced service. The IT team has done a good job of securing its Web server by installing security patches and enforcing the use of good passwords for system access.

But one day at the height of a much-advertised spring sale, customers go to the site yet don't see computers for sale. Instead, they find a completely different set of pages mocking MicroEmporium's business practices. After some hours of testing and analysis, the IT team realizes that MicroEmporium's customers are being redirected to a totally different site owned by a malevolent attacker. The tool in this attack is a corrupted Domain Name System (DNS) entry at MicroEmporium's authoritative DNS server.

In this scenario, the attack can take place because the DNS implementation has not been secured against caching a fraudulent entry. When a requester (such as a Web browser) needs a DNS name to be resolved to an IP address, a local DNS server scans the Internet to locate the authoritative DNS server for that domain. It then asks that server to resolve the name. The authoritative server replies to the local DNS server, which then forwards the answer to the requester.

The answer is also cached at the requesting server for future reference.

A skilled attacker can exploit this process by corrupting the cache of an authoritative DNS server. First, he modifies the record of a domain that he owns (such as `attacker.com`) to add an additional entry mapping the MicroEmporium site to an IP address the attacker owns.

Second, the attacker queries MicroEmporium's DNS server to resolve `www.attacker.com`. To service the request, that server will query the attacker's DNS server and receive a record containing not only `www.attacker.com`'s IP address but also the IP address the attacker chose for MicroEmporium.

If the DNS server was properly configured to reject secondhand information, it will simply disregard all server entries that aren't part of the `attacker.com` domain. But in this case, it stores the corrupted entry in its DNS cache. As a result, subsequent client requests to resolve the `microemporium.com` domain name will direct users to the attacker's Web site rather than the original site.

This problem is widely understood in the security community, but despite that, a significant percentage of servers are subject to this vulnerability. CERT has published an advisory describing the details of this attack at `ftp://info.cert.org/pub/cert_advisories/CA-97.22.bind`. In July 1997, Eugene Kashpureff at AlterNIC used the vulnerabilities in DNS to redirect users from `www.internic.net` to AlterNIC's site in a protest against InterNIC's claim of ownership over the Internet's high-level domains.

Despite the IT team's attempts to secure Web server software, the site was still compromised through infrastructure not managed by the MicroEmporium team.

No comprehensive fix is available to address all the DNS servers on the Internet, but the team can take steps to reduce risk of attack. The team could also use Secure Sockets Layer (SSL) and digital certificates for sensitive portions of the site. If they did so, careful users going to the redirected site would find that the server's digital certificate doesn't match the intended destination. Unfortunately, this isn't a foolproof solution because many users pay little attention to certificates they receive while surfing.

The simplest solution would be to bring security expertise in-house and review security procedures at the provider. A more stable solution would be to bring its systems and DNS services in-house and have its dedicated security team keep them up-to-date with security patches. The team must consider the system as a whole from the start before actually designing and implementing security features. Technology fixes, such as securing Web servers and configuring firewalls, are one part of the answer, but building effective security mechanisms requires a top-down approach.

GLOSSARY

ACD—Automatic call distribution. Equipment that routes incoming calls to appropriate agents.

Affinity Group—People who have demonstrated similar behavior.

Authentication—In this sense, proving a person's identity. The simplest authentication is a username and password. But this authentication requires strong administrative practices including secrecy and frequent changes, to be more than marginally effective. More convenient and effective authentication schemes include biometrics and smart cards.

B2B—Business-to-business. The greatest dollar volume in e-commerce.

B2C—Business-to-customer. Includes storefront e-retailing and customer relationship management.

B2E—Business-to-employee. This means of internal communications can include email, collaboration software, video conferencing, and corporate portals.

Biometrics—The use of images of the eye, the face, fingerprints, voice prints, and other physical inputs to authenticate the identity of a person.

CA—Certificate authority. An organization that people agree to trust. The CA issues certificates of authenticity for identities, software, and transactions.

Call Center—A place where agents use automated tools to interact with customers. When integrated with a full CRM solution, contacts are logged, categorized, and tracked as customer histories.

Clustering—An interaction between practically identical servers to ensure reliability. Clustered servers monitor each other's operation and pick up the workload of one server or process when a server fails.

Contact Management Center—The traditional call center expanded to handle email, online chat, and other forms of customer contact.

CORBA—Common Object Request Broker Architecture. A program that helps transfer messages to and from objects between various platforms in a distributed environment.

Corporate Portal—A Web site containing information specific to the company and typically providing browser-based access to corporate applications such as ordering and inventory databases. Corporate portals now must also respond to demands for wireless entry.

CRM—Customer relationship management. Automation of all of the best customer relationship practices. This isn't a new idea. Business has always been about relationships with customers. But when you try to prioritize and control the important actions, then it becomes a management science. Most CRM software packages are front-office products that sit on top of databases to track all forms of customer contact.

DCOM—Distributed Component Object Model. A Microsoft programming architecture for communications between applications across a network.

Denial of Service (DoS) Attack—An attempt to overload the capacity of a site or network by generating bogus requests for service.

Digital Signatures—The U.S. Electronic Signatures in Global and National Commerce Act of 2000 paved the way for the use of digital signatures. This act gives the force of law to digital signatures affixed to broad categories of documents. But digital signatures depend on strong authentication services.

Direct Costs—The costs paid for materials that go directly into the production of the product. They don't include the indirect costs of advertising, personnel, building space, and so forth.

Directory Service—A service, often contained in the operating system, that keeps track of the rights assigned to each user, the requirements of all applications and devices, and coordinates between authenticated users and the resources they have the rights to use.

Distributed Denial of Service Attack—A DoS attack that uses hijacked computers anywhere on the Internet to generate service requests aimed at a specific site.

DMZ—Demilitarized zone. A segregated network, behind the firewall yet separate from the local area network. Devices requiring some public access go into the DMZ.

Document Management—This function, performed by special monitoring software, identifies and catalogs documents by keywords, titles, or even word-by-word.

EAI—Enterprise application integration. Providing a way for applications to exchange information and to use common stores of information.

e-Commerce—A broad category encompassing all business done using Internet technologies.

e-CRM—Automating CRM.

Enterprise Application Integration (EAI)—Linking all business applications to provide a single sign-on for users, transfer of information between applications, and a common user interface. Today's business applications are often vertical stovepipes with no link between them. Enterprise application integration aims at linking existing applications to new Web-based applications such as corporate portals and customer relationship management activities.

EPBB—Electronic bill presentment and payment. Electronic billing and collection also facilitates collection of marketing information. You get your money faster and potentially learn something about your customer.

e-Procurement—Buying specialized goods, materials, services, raw materials, and tools needed to produce manufactured goods or to provide specialized services. Typically done by procurement professionals. This usually involves browser-based purchase orders sent from behind a corporate firewall to electronic catalogs on the Internet. The orders are often logged and payment made through integration with other corporate programs.

e-Purchasing—Buying online common products and services that the company needs to do business. Examples are light bulbs, computers, coffee service, and travel tickets. Many employees often do this with different job titles placed throughout the organization. See MRO.

ERP—Enterprise Resource Planning. Large software systems that encompass accounting, human relations (HR), and perhaps functions such as shipping, inventory, ordering, and receiving. The system includes many reports.

e-Tailing—Selling online through a Web site or storefront.

Firewall—A device that examines each inbound packet to ensure that it has a legitimate reason for entering the local network. Firewalls use several different techniques to determine legitimacy.

Groupware—A term that includes many types of collaboration, conferencing, and discussion software packages.

High Availability—*Availability* is the sum of reliability and capacity. The capacity must include connections, processing power, and data storage. If any one of these areas becomes a bottleneck, then total availability suffers. Systems designed for high availability often include a great deal of redundancy in equipment and connections.

Just-in-Time Delivery—Refers to the ability to deliver raw materials to the loading dock just before they're needed for production. This ability reduces the cost of inventory, warehouse space, and handling, so it significantly reduces production costs.

Knowledge Management—This function, performed by special monitoring software, links document management, email management, and other similar functions to tell you who was or is working with similar information and how it's linked to other information.

LDAP—Lightweight directory access protocol. An agreement describing how applications and directories will exchange and access information about users, devices, and applications.

Load Balancing—A technique that routes IP service requests to a specific server within a group of servers with similar functionality. The action can be based on the server's workload, on timing, or on a need for specific services.

Marketplace—In e-commerce, a specialized Web site containing catalogs, order forms, and other useful information provided by product suppliers. Sellers can post catalogs, price sheets, and other information. Like a real market, it's a place where buyers and sellers of specialized products meet to buy, haggle over, and exchange goods and services.

Metadirectory—A metadirectory is a process that translates between various types of directory entries. Because we don't have agreement on entry formats, a metadirectory provides the Rosetta stone.

MRO—Maintenance, repair, and operation. The basic products needed to keep the doors open. Examples include floor wax, desks, office equipment and supplies, light bulbs, and services such as cleaning, snack bars, and travel. e-Purchasing is typically about buying MRO products. MRO costs are indirect costs. Typically, many employees can purchase MRO products.

Network Address Translation—A service that presents one valid routable IP address to the Internet and then translates and distributes traffic to non-routable IP addresses inside the local area network. This hides the addresses inside the network and conserves routable addresses.

Portal—A Web site that provides a variety of information presented the way you want it. Portals often function as a directory for more specialized paths of interest.

RAID—The term originally meant *redundant array of inexpensive disks,* but with the drop in the price of storage, it's now often described as an array of "independent" disks. In either case, the idea is to run multiple drives for greater reliability. There are a number of different ways to relate multiple drives and so there are levels of RAID from 0–6, but for most high availability servers today, RIAD 5 is what you want.

Screen Pop—Displays forced to agents in association with an incoming call.

Secure Sockets Layer (SSL)—The term describes a method of encrypting the data stream between a browser and a Web server. People use SSL every day to retrieve financial information and to order through Web sites.

Single Sign-On—The ability for an authorized person to sign on to the network from anywhere using only one form of authentication and have access to all resources without any further authentication.

Sticky—The attribute of having interesting content able to bring back customers.

Supply Chain Management—Controlling the procurement of high-cost raw materials, tools, and services that go directly into product cost. e-Procurement is an important part of supply chain management. The supply chain feeds raw material into the manufacturing process. It's concerned with quality, quantity, delivery, timing, and payment of goods and services that go directly into the finished product.

Syndication—A way to get news stories, photos, and other specialized content from general purpose sources.

UPS—Uninterruptible power supply. A device that can deliver AC power from batteries, typically for a period of a few minutes.

Vertical Portal—A Web site where people with common business interests meet.

Vortal—A vertical portal. The available information is specific to an industry, trade, technology, or special interest.

VPN—Virtual private network. A way to create a secure link across a private network or the Internet so that authorized users can reach the corporation's assets from anywhere.

WYSIWYG—What you see is what you get, pronounced "wissy-wig." Indicates that the finished document or Web page looks like what you see on the editing screen.

XML—Extensible markup language. XML is the most popular and practical language for e-business, although it now has many extensions and special libraries. XML is the new generation of markup language for Web content designed to make it easier to efficiently search and to automatically exchange data on the Web.

C

D

E

F

G

H

I

J - K

L

M

N

R

S

T

U - V

W

X - Y - Z